Southern Biography Series
Bertram Wyatt-Brown, Editor

Lucy Somerville Howorth

NEW DEAL LAWYER, POLITICIAN, *and*
FEMINIST *from the* SOUTH

Dorothy S. Shawhan *and* Martha H. Swain
With a Foreword by Anne Firor Scott

LOUISIANA STATE UNIVERSITY PRESS
BATON ROUGE

Published by Louisiana State University Press
Copyright © 2006 by Louisiana State University Press
All rights reserved
Manufactured in the United States of America
Louisiana Paperback Edition, 2011

Designer: Michelle Garrod
Typeface: ITC Century
Typesetter: The Composing Room of Michigan

Library of Congress Cataloging-in-Publication Data

Shawhan, Dorothy.
   Lucy Somerville Howorth : New Deal lawyer, politician, and feminist from the South / Dorothy S. Shawhan and Martha H. Swain ; with a Foreword by Anne Firor Scott.
     p. cm.
   Includes bibliographical references and index.
   ISBN 978-0-8071-3133-6 (cloth : alk. paper)
    1. Howorth, Lucy Somerville, 1895–1997. 2. Women legislators—Mississippi—Biography. 3. Legislators—Mississippi—Biography. 4. Mississippi. Legislature. House of Representatives—Biography. 5. Women lawyers—Mississippi—Biography. 6. Women lawyers—United States—Biography. 7. New Deal, 1933–1939. 8. American Association of University Women—Biography. 9. Feminists—Mississippi—Biography. I. Swain, Martha H., 1929– II. Title.
F341.H698S53 2006
976.2'063'092—dc22

                                                2005018599

ISBN 978-0-8071-3875-5 (paper : alk. paper)

The paper in this book meets the guidelines for permanence and durability of the Committee on Production Guidelines for Book Longevity of the Council on Library Resources. ∞

With Our Love to the Two Margarets
Margaret Anne Mitchell and Margo Swain

Contents

Foreword: Memories of Lucy Somerville Howorth, by Anne Firor Scott	ix
Preface	xv
1. Girlhood in Greenville	1
2. "A whole human being," 1912–1922	13
3. "Hustling in the law," 1922–1927	35
4. Howorth and Howorth, Attorneys-at-Law, 1928–1931	56
5. "I have a few things to say": The Mississippi Legislature, 1932–1934	67
6. A Watchdog for Women, 1935–1946	84
7. "I glory in being a feminist," 1947–1954	108
8. "Just being Cleveland folks": Retirement after 1957	134
9. "Nothing like living a long time": The Last Years	154
Appendix: Recorded Speeches of Lucy Somerville Howorth	167
Notes	173
Select Bibliography	211
Index	221

Illustrations follow page 66

Foreword
Memories of Lucy Somerville Howorth

OURS WAS AN extraordinary friendship of nearly forty years, conducted mostly via the U.S. mail. Nellie Nugent Somerville's papers, somewhat improbably housed at what is now the Schlesinger Library at Radcliffe College, led me in 1958 to seek an interview with her daughter Lucy. I had become convinced that the Progressive movement in the South, at least its social-justice component, was largely a woman's movement and that Somerville was an archetypal southern Progressive. When I came across a reference to her daughter, an administrative judge in the federal government, in the *AAUW Journal,* I wrote asking whether she would be willing to talk to me. She must have said she would, for I took the train from Philadelphia in the midst of a major snowstorm that almost upset the whole plan. However, I finally made it to Washington, and I find in my journal the following record of that visit: "Tremendously stimulating two and a half hours with Lucy Somerville Howorth whose mother's activities I hope to examine soon. Quite a gal herself." My memory is that she confirmed many of my notions about southern women of her mother's generation and that we found ourselves responding to each other with enthusiasm.

So the friendship began. It is documented in my files and no doubt in Lucy's papers (neither of us was conscientious about carbon copies in those days), which continued until her death. As I began to write about southern women I sent her drafts, and she commented at length. In October 1968 she sent four single-spaced pages of detailed comments on the manuscript of what would be published two years later as *The Southern Lady.*

Ten days later Lucy replied in similar detail about another Mississippi woman, Belle Kearney, about whom I had agreed to write for the biographical dictionary *Notable American Women.* She shared all her memories of "Miss Belle," but she also warned me that Kearney and her mother, though sharing causes, had not, as she put it, "been on the same wave length."

As time went by we exchanged ideas about books, each recommending what the other should read. Occasionally the books themselves went back and forth in the mail. In most of her letters Lucy included something about her own life experience, so that bit by bit I began to develop a picture of her extraordinary career as woman lawyer and feminist activist. In one interview late in her life she said that her early exposure to her mother's activism should have turned her into either an adult recluse or the opposite: "What I did . . . started joining, started maneuvering, started leading and started having fun all along the way." The description would remain appropriate until she was in her late nineties.

In 1977 Lucy sent me a copy of *My Dear Nellie: The Civil War Letters of William L. Nugent to Eleanor Smith Nugent*, a volume of correspondence between her maternal grandparents. She took care to tell me that Bell Wiley, a noted historian of the South, had assured her that the book was "a real contribution to Civil War history."

That was the year that I signed on to write the essay about Nellie Nugent Somerville for the first supplement to *Notable American Women*. The pace of our correspondence quickened; sometimes there were four or five letters in quick succession. I wanted to get the story right; Lucy of course shared that desire. She answered my questions at length and then edited the essay when it was finally written. We both fretted about the constricting word limit.

In 1982, concerned as always that the South was not much understood in other parts of the country, I suggested to someone at the Schlesinger Library that Lucy might be an appropriate recipient of one of the lifetime achievement awards being planned as part of an anniversary celebration. The idea caught on. Her speech on that occasion upset many Yankee preconceptions. Here was a southern woman, from Mississippi no less, who had taken the lead in ending segregation in the American Association of University Women, a woman who had worked in many venues to improve opportunities for women, had served in the state legislature, and then had had a distinguished career in Washington. Her speech was a huge success, and since another Mississippi woman, Eudora Welty, was honored in Cambridge that year, Mississippi began to look quite different in northeastern latitudes.

Thereafter our correspondence escalated. Letters in my file are dated sometimes in successive weeks, often in successive months. Lucy's handwritten notes simply instructed me to go at once to read such and such a book. Others commented at length on books I had suggested to her.

Twenty-four years after our "tremendously stimulating" conversations in Washington, we met in person for the second time when I visited her, then in retirement, in Cleveland, Mississippi. The visit was vintage Lucy. She had planned each day to be as educational as possible. I visited Delta State University, where interest in Nellie was high, and met various members of Lucy's circle and her family. Then there was an extraordinary dinner party designed like a seminar. College professors, leaders of voluntary associations, and political friends gathered around a big square table in the dining room of the country club, and it was made clear to me that the dining was only incidental: the real purpose was to discuss Mississippi politics, women's activities, and Life. It was quite an evening.

In the interstices of the visit Lucy reminisced at length about her family history, about Mississippi history, and especially about her work for women. I sensed that she was saying all this in hopes that it would be recorded somewhere for posterity. That night in her guest room I felt impelled to write notes before I went to sleep. She must have enjoyed the visit almost as much as I did, for a few weeks later, when the Southern Historical Association met in Memphis, she and two friends drove the 115 miles to have lunch with me and talk more about her life.

In a letter thanking me for the plant I had ordered as a hostess gift Lucy wrote, "I subjected you to a deluge of words about my family and myself . . . I hope you were not overcome." She enclosed photographs of Nellie Nugent as a child and as an adult. Whereas before the visit she had signed her letters "Sincerely yours, Lucy Somerville Howorth," now she wrote "Affectionately, Lucy SH." And by 1986 the signature had become "Love, LSH."

Every subsequent letter added bits and pieces about Lucy's life as she looked back and remembered one thing after another. I had said that I would write at more length about Nellie Somerville, but life's inevitable busyness interfered. She continued to send me ideas in case I should ever undertake the task, though she never exerted pressure.

When Lucy was ninety-two and I was in the midst of a book about women's voluntary associations, she sent me two single-spaced pages describing, among other things, the failed effort of women's organizations to put Judge Florence Allen, of Ohio, on the U.S. Supreme Court:

> I think every established woman's organization, large or small, [had] joined to secure the appointment for her to the Circuit Court of Appeals which came through. . . . It was generally understood that the men on the Ohio Supreme Court were persecuting her and trying to make her life unbearable. . . . After FDR took over it was natural for me to be asked to do what I could to secure a federal judgeship for her. . . . I suppose that you have heard that Judge Allen would have been appointed to the Supreme Court . . . but someone around the President asked the views of the [members of] the Supreme Court and the word came back that the presence of a woman would make the judges "uncomfortable."

She went on to describe the political work of a number of women's organizations and to caution me not to be too selective in the ones I dealt with since although not all followed the same pattern, all were to some degree trying to improve the position of women. She reinforced my view that women in religious organizations had played a vital role in the civil rights movement.

Not long after that, Lucy thanked me for suggesting that she read Christine Stancell's *City of Women*, of which she provided a detailed analysis based partly on her own observations of New York's Lower East Side in the 1920s. Later she had read that the Mississippi Department of Archives had, improbably enough, acquired some of Judith Sergeant Murray's papers, and she hastened to let me know that this source for Colonial women's history existed in her state. In yet another she urged me to read Lelia Rupp's new book, *Survival in the Doldrums*, which she had found enlightening, though of course she had a few astute comments from the vantage point of one who had lived through the period. In a letter written earlier that spring she spoke of flying to Europe on the Concorde just for a little break. I think she was in her mid-nineties when she experimented with sending tapes rather than letters; talking was by then easier than writing. But occasionally letters still came.

Lucy had turned one hundred when we had our last reunion, on the deck of the *Delta Queen*, which was on its way to New Orleans (my husband and I were the so-called experts for an alumni excursion). Lucy's niece and her ever-helpful friend LePoint Smith had brought her to Greenville, and the bemused young men who made up the crew of the *Queen* lifted her to the deck, where she finally met my husband and talked to him about his work. He took a picture as she talked. Time had caught up with her, as it does when one lives long enough, but she was still capable of lively talk.

In almost forty years we probably spent the equivalent of four days physically in the same place, yet there are few people with whom I have had such a vigorous intellectual-cum-personal relationship or who contributed more to my thinking about southern women. I wish for words to properly convey the spirit of this extremely intelligent, effective, straight-talking lawyer. Study the pictures in this biography, and then read what its authors can tell you about one of the truly impressive women of the twentieth century. I told her many times that she was my model for aging, and when I wake with creaky joints or an unwillingness to start the day, I think of her and get to work. A wonderful legacy.

Anne Firor Scott
Chapel Hill

Preface

LUCY SOMERVILLE HOWORTH (1895–1997) always had a sense of history. As a lineal descendant of a family of strong "foremothers" and the daughter of a noted national suffrage leader, she grew up in the presence of remarkable women who were making and writing history long before her birth. When her indomitable mother, Nellie Nugent Somerville, pondered the disposal of the hefty manuscripts she had accumulated, Lucy was quick to say that they must be preserved. That corpus became the nucleus of the expansive Nellie Nugent Somerville—Lucy Somerville Howorth Collection in the Arthur and Elizabeth Schlesinger Library at the Radcliffe Institute for Advanced Study.

Anne Firor Scott, in her afterword to the twenty-fifth-anniversary edition of her book *The Southern Lady: From Pedestal to Politics, 1830–1930* (1995), describes her early discovery at Radcliffe of the papers of Nellie Nugent Somerville and a "pivotal" interview with Lucy Howorth, who "had a good historian's instinct for what was important." Lucy Somerville grew up fascinated by the South's rich, seductive history, but she was never victimized by it. The future, with its possibilities for positive change, engaged both her imagination and her energy. Any historian of the modern women's movement owes Howorth a large debt of gratitude for her augmentation of the papers that Scott describes as those of "four generations of southern women whose collective biography encapsulated the history of southern female activism over a century."[1] The already inestimable worth of the original donation of the manuscripts of her foremothers grew over the years as Lucy added her own papers.

Through her mother's leadership for suffrage and temperance Lucy Somerville developed a great admiration for leaders of the women's movement and social reform. Her early skill in parliamentary procedure, her acumen, and her quick appraisal of problems won for her leadership positions. Her good humor, southern charm, and femininity offset her candid and sometimes blunt demeanor, and thus she was nonthreatening as she pursued her agenda in politics or reform. Howorth found her short stature and unimposing appearance to be a certain surprise factor that disarmed those potentially opposed to her ideas.

Howorth's own public career was long and distinguished. One of the pioneer women lawyers in Mississippi after her graduation from the University of Mississippi Law School in 1922, she established a successful office and trial-law practice. She never held the position of judge in a court of law, but her appointment in 1927 as a commissioner, or magistrate, of a federal district court gave her the honorary title "judge," and after that she was known affectionately more than legally as Judge Lucy even after she moved to Washington. With the Depression and the New Deal, she turned to administrative law when President Franklin D. Roosevelt appointed her to a job in Washington. Service on the Board of Appeals of the Veterans Administration led her in 1949 to the War Claims Commission, where she became the first woman to be named general counsel for an executive commission. A brief stint as a private citizen practicing law in Washington ended when she became a member of the Legal Research Department for President Dwight Eisenhower's Commission on Government Security (1956–57). In 1962 and 1963 she returned to Washington from her home in Cleveland, Mississippi, for meetings of a task force of President John F. Kennedy's Commission on the Status of Women. Blessed after 1957 with a forty-year retirement in her hometown, she remained active in civic and women's organizations. She had a deep conviction that professional women who succeeded did so because of the support they received from others and that they in turn were obligated to help others advance. That was a credo by which she lived, and her advocacy of women's rights, particularly through her strong leadership in the American Association of University Women, is telling of just how she brought her strong personality to bear on major issues of her day.

Howorth was unabashedly a feminist. "I just decided to proceed like a human being. The idea that women can't do something just because we're women . . . phooey," she said.[2] She exhibited a wonderful sense of humor, admitting to a certain degree of braggadocio but always exhibiting a compelling candor about herself and others. She retained many, many friends until their death and finally hers. Her loyalty was exemplary. Her words to individuals she knew personally and to those audiences she knew impersonally were full of wit, intelligence, and optimism. In a modest moment Howorth said, "I never thought I was different from anyone else. I think a lot of people could do as much if they had the initiative."[3] In an age cynical about politics and government and beset with social ills, her life and advice remind us of our basic values as citizens and of our responsibility for the future.

Lucy Howorth's major contributions in public life were not made in the context of her government jobs. There are few resources in federal archives for a biography, for the records of the offices she held were either destroyed or are closed for reasons of confidentiality. This biography deals largely with Howorth's more than sixty years of work toward the advancement of women, singly and collectively, primarily through the women's organizations that attracted her. "What is accomplished in the United States today is largely accomplished through organizations, and it's important to support those that will speak up for women," she wrote in 1984.[4] Her "life and times" history is that of a twentieth-century professional woman's experience and advancement to success and eminence.

From the time of her graduation from Randolph-Macon Woman's College in 1916, Howorth knew she would be more than a bystander in the women's movement. Her Cleveland friend LePoint Smith has said that she was like the fictional Forrest Gump, always present when important events were happening. She was diligent in preserving her own papers and documents of the organizations to which she belonged, adding notes to accompany her correspondence and news articles. She once told us what all historians know, that is, that official documents do not tell the whole story, and she did what she could to fill in what really happened. She had infinite patience with the many writers and historians who came to see her, and we appreciate the long hours she spent with us and the diligence with which she answered our queries.

We have had the generous assistance of a number of people who have granted interviews, particularly LePoint Smith, Keith Somerville McLean, Couprey Shands, Arch Dalrymple, Eleanor Shands, and James Eaton. The support through grants made to Dorothy Shawhan—grants from the Research Committee of Delta State University in 1984–86, from the Mary Lizzie Sanders Clapp Fund at Radcliffe College in 1985, and from the American Association of University Women in 1986—has been very helpful. Most recently the generosity of the Mississippi Arts Commission has enabled us to return to archival sources to complete our research.

A number of archivists graciously aided us when we sought material from their depositories. We wish to thank Sarah Hutcheon and student assistant Melissa Hackman at the Schlesinger Library; Kate Weigand at the Sophia Smith Collection, Smith College; Lynne Mueller, Mattie Sink, and Sara Morris at the Mitchell Memorial Library, Mississippi State University; Tara Zachary and Meredith Johnston at the Capps Archives, Delta State University; and Dawn Letson at Texas Woman's University. We express our special gratitude to Dennis E. Bilger at the Harry S. Truman Presidential Library for locating material for us. Linda Morrison, of Newton, Massachusetts, assisted in compiling the appendix. Interviews with Judge Lucy conducted by the historians Allen Dennis, Jane Whiteside Elliott, Chester (Bo) Morgan, Constance Myers, and Marjorie Spruill Wheeler have been of immeasurable value. We wish to express our deep gratitude to Judy Barrett Litoff, Cora Norman, and Anne Firor Scott, who read our manuscript and offered cogent suggestions and deserving criticism that we hope we have addressed. An anonymous reader alerted us to places where we could sharpen our analysis, broaden the context of our narrative, and reword certain areas for greater clarity. Professor Scott, one of Lucy Howorth's many longtime friends, has added immensely to our story by agreeing to write of that friendship, a recollection that Professor Scott obviously enjoyed.

Tove Peacock, at Delta State University, performed miracles at the computer in preparing the manuscript. We wish to extend our gratitude to Joanne Allen, our copyeditor, for her astuteness and diligence. Finally, we wish to acknowledge the devotion and patience throughout this project of our sisters, Margaret Anne Mitchell and Margaret "Margo" Swain.

Lucy Somerville Howorth

1

Girlhood in Greenville

LUCY HOWORTH'S husband once said that he knew she had enjoyed any meeting when she had made a speech. By his reckoning the highlight of her career occurred in June 1944, when she made the keynote speech at the White House Conference on Women in Post-War Policy Making just after First Lady Eleanor Roosevelt gave her a reassuring smile. In her speech, now recorded in a growing number of primary-source documents on twentieth-century feminist thought, Howorth called for the appointment of women to positions of authority in the federal government, a cause to which she devoted much of her energy during a twenty-year career in Washington that followed a distinguished tenure in Mississippi as a young lawyer of great promise and a state legislator.[1] Above all, she believed in the power of organized women to bring about social reform once they achieved office, whether at the state or national level or in the private sector.

"Judge Lucy," as she was known by then, summoned to action the notable clubwomen and women appointees in the administration of President Franklin D. Roosevelt who were assembled in the East Room of the White House. Her fact-laced rally was convincing. "Never get up until the moment of decision is at hand and then blast them with your knowledge" was the credo by which she swayed many an audience.[2] Her own knowledge was extensive, made so by the advantages of a fine education, expertise gained through a variety of legal work, her forays into practical politics, and her leadership of national women's organizations. Above all, she had been influenced throughout her life by a mother who possessed enormous political acumen as well as common sense and savvy.

Lucy Robinson Somerville was born on 1 July 1895. She often told people that she had been born just as the whistle blew on the train from Memphis. She admitted that the tale could be apocryphal, a matter of "her imagination trotting along,"[3] but she knew why she liked it: the whistle signaled her love of travel on trains and all other modes of transportation, one major facet of her life. She was the last of four children and second daughter of Robert and Nellie Nugent Somerville. She was named Lucy Robinson at the request of a friend of her mother's who bore that name but could bear no children.[4] The older children in the family were Robert, Abram, and Eleanor; Lucy remained close to them throughout her life.

Both parents descended from men and women of sober and substantial character and unquestioned community standing. Her Somerville grandmother was Laura Anna Gray (1818–90), a pious Virginia Presbyterian whom Lucy never knew. She married Robert Briggs Somerville, the first of three Robert Somervilles, and bore ten children, the last in 1858, among them Robert, who was Lucy's father.[5] Less is recorded of Lucy's father's lineage than of her mother's. More than one person observed that Lucy had come from a long line of strong women. As she herself once wrote, "There may have been some weak women in my mother's inheritance, but there are no stories about them. All that we ever heard of were extraordinarily strong."[6] She revered accounts of her mother's ancestors, particularly the women, and took pains to record their achievements. She saw in the lives of her foremothers responsibilities for children and slaves on farms and plantations, the hardship of frequent moves due to wars and natural disaster, officeholding in churches and women's clubs, activism in temperance and suffrage crusades, and for some untimely and painful deaths. When Lucy herself assumed leadership of yet another organization in 1951, a friend wrote, "Women in your family have never yet failed in taking responsibility."[7] From her mother's side of the family Lucy received her political bent, her gift of public speaking, her penchant for the law, her ambition, and her love of music and literature.

Lucy's maternal great-great-grandmother, Nancy Hardeman (1774–1832), a Virginian once described as a "belle and a beauty," moved by flatboat down the Mississippi River after her marriage to Seth Lewis, who became chief justice of the Mississippi Territory in 1800.[8] Their daughter Anne (1807–73), the eighth of twelve children, was born in Natchez and educated at Elizabeth Female Academy at nearby Washington, Mississippi, the first college in America to confer degrees upon women and an institution whose history Lucy sought to perpetuate. Anne married John Pratt Nugent, a merchant, and they were the parents of William Lewis Nugent, Lucy's grandfather, born in 1832.[9] His influence would loom large in her life. The Civil War and a levee break on a Louisiana river drove the family to nearby Woodville, Mississippi. It was uncanny that wars and rivers would play so great a role in the lives of Lucy's foremothers, as they did in her own. Anne bore up under all the distress and was reportedly the only human being of whom her granddaughter, Nellie Nugent, was afraid. Of Anne a son-in-law said, "She could have ruled Great Britain."[10]

John and Anne's son William was twenty years old and a recent graduate of Centenary College, in Jackson, Louisiana, when he arrived in Greenville in 1852 to tutor the children of Myra Cox Smith.[11] Among them was eight-year-old Eleanor Fulkerson Smith, whom William married in 1860, when she was sixteen and he was twenty-eight.[12] Nugent's letters to her began then and continued through the Civil War. More than a century later their granddaughter Lucy, along with William M. Cash, edited the letters for publication under the title *My Dear Nellie*.[13]

Eleanor Smith Nugent lost a baby daughter, her home in Greenville, and her father, Abram Fulkerson Smith, in a period of less than six months. A second daughter, born on 25 September 1863, was named Eleanor Fulkerson Nugent, or Nellie; she was a fragile infant born with a deformed right hand on which the fingers were fused together. This was Lucy's mother.[14] Eleanor Smith died in 1866, most likely of consumption, although Lucy later added to that "privation, malnutrition, and grief."[15] Little Nellie was reared by her maternal grandmother, Myra Cox Smith, and learned to compensate for her deformity and to mask it from view, often by concealing it in a handkerchief held closely to her side.

Other than reverence for her mother, Lucy reserved her greatest admiration for her indomitable great-grandmother Myra. Myra, who also descended from a Virginia family that migrated to a site near Natchez, was sent to Nazareth Academy in Bardstown, Kentucky. Through her brother, a state legislator, she met and married Abram Fulkerson Smith. The couple had eight children, half of whom died young. Myra's life was full of tragedy, yet she rose above her difficulties, especially incalculable losses suffered during the Civil War: a son disabled during the conflict, her Greenville home burned by fire from a federal gunboat, her husband killed by a shot from another, and a second home sold for debts. But Myra gathered her meager resources, began life anew in Greenville through a profitable catering business and investments, and at her death in 1887 left young Nellie a sizable estate, built up through thrift and industry. It is not surprising, in view of the war-related deaths and devastation her ancestors endured, that Lucy never held any romantic illusions about the Civil War and its aftermath as Lost Cause.[16]

Lucy never knew Myra, who died in 1887, but her grandmother's never-say-die ways would be reflected in her own life. No doubt there are other bases for Lucy's viewpoints. It could be that she developed an antipathy to the misguided glorification of the war and its aftermath that she saw in her mother's unreasoned viewpoint. Lucy, who read voraciously, was much more accepting of historical revision on the subject of Reconstruction than Nellie, who evinced pride in her father's role in the campaign to free Mississippi from the debauchery of reconstruction politics. But it is clear that contacts in the classroom and in the workplace during her years in New York shaped Lucy's thought on a number of matters in social relations that would become evident once she returned home.

If the women among her ancestors were strong, the men also were noteworthy and admired by Lucy. Many of her forefathers were venerable men—lawyers, legislators, judges. She was proud of the accomplishments of Seth Lewis, the territorial chief justice. Then there were her great-grandfather Abram Fulkerson Smith, Myra's husband, who was a member of the Mississippi House of Representatives (1846, 1857–58), and her grandfather William Lewis Nugent, one of the best-known lawyers in the state. It is no wonder that Lucy Somerville eventually was drawn to the practice of law and took her own place in the Mississippi legislature.

Nellie Nugent, although more thoroughly written about than any of Lucy's other foremothers, remains a paradox. Despite her very public persona, she was an extremely private person. "Nobody gets to who she really was," Lucy once said.[17] Those who knew her describe her variably in terms ranging from "gentle" and "lovely" to "fierce" and "formidable," and she is even referred to as a "she-bear." In whatever she undertook she was, in Lucy's words, "a fighter to the last ditch."[18] There is no doubt, however, that Lucy drew from her mother a strong sense of commitment to social reforms, particularly those that advanced women's rights.

Nellie had been a precocious child, and that would be true of Lucy. At the age of twelve Nellie was enrolled in Whitworth College, a Methodist boarding school in Brookhaven, Mississippi, where the serious young girl appreciated the spartan life that knocked "any foolishness out of [her] head."[19] In 1880 she earned a bachelor's degree at Martha Washington College in Abingdon, Virginia, where she was valedictorian of her graduating class. Declining to study law in her father's office, she became a tutor for a banker's children in Greenville, where she met Robert Somerville, a University of Virginia–trained civil engineer who in 1883 had come to Mississippi, where he worked as the assistant chief engineer of the Mississippi Board of Levee Commissioners. Nellie and Robert married in 1885.

Nellie Somerville ran her household in a conventional, orderly manner. She was adept at delegating household chores to servants, which allowed her time for her increasing civic activity.[20] Lucy would follow Nellie's advice to "never let your husband think he fares better when you're in the kitchen instead of a paid cook."[21] The home atmosphere was serious and intellectual. Years later Nellie's daughter-in-law said that her husband, Bob, "had to learn Mother Goose and Fairy Tales with his children, and experience the joy of Christmas festivities never having had them in his own youth."[22] Nellie was also pious, a trait that Lucy did *not* inherit. Lucy inherited the Wesleyan call to social action without the personal piety or need to be a part of an organized church that were strong motivations of her mother's work.

Nellie first emerged as an advocate of women's rights in the Hypatia Club, ostensibly a literary society but one in which she tackled issues of women's rights.[23] Like many other southern women, she first experienced organizing and leadership through her church's mission work.[24] Thus, as was true of many women, the deep religious conviction and sense of injustice in church governance that were catalysts for Nellie's suffrage activity combined with a religious impulse to lead her into decades of activity in the Women's Christian Temperance Union (WCTU). She became convinced that women should have the vote both because it was their right and because they could use the ballot to bring about positive change.[25]

In 1897, when Lucy was two years old, Nellie was elected president of the Mississippi Woman Suffrage Association. From then until the ratification of the Nineteenth Amendment in 1920, Nellie used her considerable talents as an organizer, a writer, and a speaker toward achieving women's suffrage.[26] Under Nellie's leadership, the Greenville suffragists took the name Civic Improvement Club, and by petitioning the city council they brought about substantial improvements in the quality of town life.[27] An illness that has never been explained caused Nellie to give up her suffrage work between 1899 and 1906; Lucy believed that the illness was not Nellie's but her own because of her frailty. Lucy was a slight child, small in frame, who did not walk until she was two years old. Her parents took her to doctors in Cincinnati and North Carolina and worried that she would not live, and that may account for Nellie's hiatus from suffrage activity. Nellie kept Lucy's hair cut short like a boy's because of a theory that hair sapped a body's strength.[28] If Lucy was sick in her early years, there was no evidence of any lingering illness as she grew.

Lucy was certain that she grew up in a "real" Delta family, one unlike the fictionalized Delta families of William Faulkner or Tennessee Williams, whose first generations are marked by avarice, ruthlessness, and dreams too ambitious to hold and whose second generations sink into alcoholism, insanity, or passive decadence. The Somervilles were hardworking, God-fearing, and public spirited, staunch Methodists and community leaders. They belonged to that element of the community that David L. Cohn described as "a meaningful group of mellowed, informed, perceptive men and women." Although Nellie would always consider Greenville her true home, life there must have been a challenge given her ideas of child-rearing. Both parents were horrified by the mores of the "fast crowd" that dominated Greenville society. James C. Cobb has described the "moral laxity and social pretensions" of the Delta's social pacesetters, and Bertram Wyatt-Brown has written of the "high flying and dance-crazy aristocrats of the Delta." William Alexander Percy, whose family were Greenville's undisputed social arbiters, wrote, "No doubt about it, our town was plumb social," with the high life centered on the downtown Elysian Club's frequent dances. "Delta girls were born dancing and never stop," he added. But his description stands in sharp contrast to the preachings of the temperance women whom Nellie led and the restricted life that Lucy led prior to her leaving home. She never evidenced any longing for social contact with the Percy crowd and once described a party she attended at the Percy home as stiff and boring.[29]

Robert Somerville, the engineer, was on constant alert for breaks in the river levee. He kept meticulous journals of all the work of the Levee Board and left the Mississippi Levee District "the most complete records of any levee district," two admirers wrote. To him Lucy attributed her sense of duty, her willingness to work quietly behind the scenes, her mind for detail, and her "literal mindedness."[30] He had a reputation for being scrupulously honest and avoided involvement in levee politics. Lucy's older sister Eleanor remembered a dinner party given by her ambitious mother for Levee Board members with the hope that her husband would be named head of the board, but he demurred, "That's politics," and he wanted no part of it. The Levee Board held enormous power and political influence because it granted lucrative construction and repair contracts, and it was one of the sources of power and patronage that LeRoy Percy's Levee Board "cronies" could often control in "managing Delta affairs." The board proved to be only one bone in the growing contention between Nellie and LeRoy Percy, scion of Greenville's most powerful and deeply rooted political family, whose hold on Washington County was formidable.[31]

Quiet and mild-mannered, Robert was called "sweet" by his children.[32] Even if he lacked a sense of humor, he was attentive to them. Lucy recalled that in 1910, when she was fifteen, he smoked a piece of glass so she could safely observe Halley's comet.[33] Of his wife's campaign for women's rights he had no understanding, although he offered no resistance. Robert's mild, retiring manner and Nellie's assertive bearing may explain why some remember him as a very small man and Nellie as a very big woman, an assessment photographs do not bear out.

Nellie kept Lucy at home with her until she entered the sixth grade. Lucy's childhood sickliness may have been a factor, but her mother also may have wanted more direct supervision of her instruction. Uninterested in domestic science herself, Nellie deemed housekeeping and cooking unimportant skills for her daughter to learn. She saw to it that instruction in French by a Greenville woman began for Lucy at age five, and Lucy continued to study the language until she entered the University of Mississippi in 1922. She regretted that she never learned conversational French to her satisfaction because she was too engaged in speaking English. Nellie tried to interest Lucy in piano lessons, but the child balked, preferring the violin, which she studied until she entered law school in 1922. She had no interest in dolls and once dashed one against the wall; she also kicked a doll cradle that Lucy Robinson brought for her to play with.[34] Thus, from an early age Lucy gave no evidence of an interest in things domestic. Nor did Nellie even encourage needlework. At her mother's knee the child learned her colors by sorting suffrage pamphlets according to their hue.[35]

In 1886 Myra Smith visited the Monteagle Sunday School Assembly, near Sewanee, Tennessee, and returned to tell Nellie, "I have found the place for you."[36] In 1893 Nellie purchased a cottage at the storied southern Chautauqua, and for generations Katydid Cottage was an escape for Somervilles from the humidity, malaria, and mosquitoes of Delta summers. In child-rearing Nellie thought she had to battle the world, the flesh, and the devil, but at least at Monteagle the world was not a combatant.[37] The Somerville children reveled in summer pastimes at Monteagle, where Victorian cottages were scattered around the ninety-six-acre grounds and wooden fences spanned the ravines throughout the rugged landscape. In the mall area were a chapel, an auditorium, and a hotel for summer visitors, who came for recreation and the educational courses that were the hallmark of this "Chautauqua atop the Cumberlands." At age five Lucy was sent to the Monteagle kindergarten, but her objections to the "foolish" routine and games led her mother to withdraw her.[38]

Later the annual lecture series became an important element in Lucy's education. Professor Henry L. Southwick, of the Emerson School of Oratory, in Boston, excited her with his talks about Shakespearean drama and his dramatized excerpts of well-known orations. From an early age she was familiar with most of Shakespeare's plays. Professor F. F. Frantz, of the University of Tennessee, lectured so well on French drama that Lucy, his front-row admirer, never felt the need to pursue the subject in the classroom. Edwin Mims, of Vanderbilt University's English department, provided a fascinating series on English poets. Lucy observed, in particular, techniques by which the lecturers held or lost their audiences. And if a lecturer, such as the one who spoke on "Fletcherizing," the theory of chewing each bite seventy times for good health, failed to hold her attention, she left. Lucy greatly enjoyed the annual oratorical contest that engaged contestants from all the states represented by Monteagle residents.[39]

Lucy made lasting friends at Monteagle. She and Kate Savage (later Zerfoss), who later entered medical school at the same time that Lucy began her law course, were only a day apart in age. Upon emerging from the hack that served train passengers who arrived for the summer at Monteagle, Lucy would race down the alley to see whether Kate's family had arrived from Nashville. The playmates were never at a loss for something to do, romping on stick horses, inducing the uninitiated to chew a bit of a peppery leaf of the elephant ear plant, running until they collapsed in breathless laughter, or riding the "elephant tree," an oak that had been bent as a sapling by Choctaw Indian scouts and had grown into a seat that spurred children to "gallop on."[40] Lucy and Kate remained close until the latter's death.

At home in Greenville Lucy's favorite pastime was reading, and she would often cite the moment when she realized that she could read as the most memorable in her life.[41] Afraid she would ruin her eyes and desirous that she play outside in fresh air, her parents too often required her to lay aside her book. She merely moved quietly to another room and began to read a book stashed there; she had books hidden all over the house. She may have been a frail child, but from early on she was imbued with a sense of her innate value as an individual, and a female individual at that. Her brother Abe, with whom she had more than one conflict through the years, found her reading a book and began to grumble that he could not see "what good she was." Sister Eleanor "did some things around the house," but he did not believe that Lucy served any useful purpose at all. Nellie overheard the exchange and rebuked him. "Some people are born with attitudes," Lucy said later, "and Abe was born a male chauvinist."[42]

Although an avid reader who was kept close to home, Lucy had a great awareness of Greenville, a town she described as "an oddly metropolitan community with an extraordinary interest in ideas." She spent much time with the family of Judge and Mrs. W. R. Trigg and their three daughters, one of whom was Lucy's sixth-grade teacher. The bonneted Mrs. Trigg had infinite patience with Lucy, who visited often. On Christmas mornings the Somerville children romped next-door to the Triggs' for a "haul." Another family to whom the Somervilles were close was that of Kate Kretschmar, Nellie's cousin and also Myra Smith's niece, whom Smith reared.[43] Kate was a widow with a son, Wils. It was Wils who helped Lucy coax her mother to relent in her ban on live theater, which Nellie condemned as a bad influence. Wils persuaded Nellie to permit Lucy to see *Buster Brown,* a play based on the comic strip; the performance piqued Lucy's lifelong love of the theater.[44] Wils became a confidant of the adult Lucy and a financial adviser to Nellie. If Nellie kept the world at bay at Monteagle, the task was not so easy in Greenville, at least as far as Lucy's inquiring mind was concerned. The child found another lifelong interest through circumvention of yet another of Nellie's strict rules. While a visitor from Clarksdale engaged Nellie in suffrage promotion, her husband took Lucy to the horse races at the Greenville fair.[45] Eighty-five years later she watched on television the Kentucky Derby and the Belmont.

The Herman Cohns, an Orthodox Jewish family, lived next-door to the Somervilles. As a child Lucy preferred the scholarly sermons of the Cohns' rabbi to the "Bible thumping" exhortations of the Methodist minister, and on Saturdays she often attended Jewish services. One of the Cohn boys, David, was only a year older than Lucy. Later a widely read author, he wrote a nonfictional account of the Delta, *God Shakes Creation* (1935), that Lucy later described as "the best depiction of the community in the period of our youth."[46] In a Methodist Sunday school orchestra Lucy played in the violin section with Ben Wasson, another future writer four years her junior, who would surface at interesting junctures in her life.[47]

Like many other southern children, young Greenvillians grew up among storytellers. Three aged Confederate veterans who lived down the street often came for the refreshments Nellie served and told war tales. Such stories, along with what she knew of her own family's experiences, repelled any romantic notions Lucy may have had about the Civil War and were probably another reason that she did not cling to Old South myths.[48] Mealtime conversations at the Somerville home were generally about affairs of the day or some esoteric topic, such as the strong chins of ancient achievers, among them Aristotle. Lucy was so impressed that she stood before a mirror to practice thrusting her chin forward, which later resulted in orthodontic problems.[49]

Lucy's closest friend in Greenville was Augusta Stacy, a year younger. The two met at an Episcopal church egg hunt soon after the Stacys moved from a plantation to town so that Augusta could attend school. Lucy thought Augusta was a "perfect comedienne" and asked Nellie to call on her mother so that she and Augusta could become friends. Their friendship was to be the most enduring of all the many friendships that Lucy enjoyed in her life.[50] Together in both school and college, they were devoted to one another.

Both girls enrolled at Delta Preparatory College, a private school started by a wealthy Greenvillian for his children but attended by others. Lucy's public-school education, not begun until the sixth grade, ended when school officials later refused Nellie's request that Lucy skip a grade. It was then that Nellie sent Lucy to Delta Preparatory on the condition that she be prepared for college in three years. The headmistress, Dr. Lili von Loewenstein, who held a doctorate from the University of Lausanne, taught English, Latin, German, and French, as well as other subjects.[51] Despite their modest means, the Somervilles were determined that their children attend fine colleges. Robert graduated in law from the University of Mississippi; the less serious but still bright Abram was removed from the university for lassitude and sent to Washington and Lee in Virginia. He graduated a year before Eleanor entered Randolph-Macon Woman's College in Lynchburg, Virginia.[52]

Lucy described her social life during her adolescence as "a simple life in a small town at that period." There were teas and parties, but apparently she was not interested in the "boys making glances in my direction." She began to sense a difference in her own aspirations and those of most of the other girls she knew. When she and her friends visited the gypsy tent at a school-sponsored bazaar, the fortuneteller spoke to Lucy's friends of the "dark stranger" they would meet and the children they would have, but she foretold no such future for Lucy. When Lucy asked her mother why her destiny should differ from that of her friends, Nellie dismissed the subject and merely explained that the woman had seized the opportunity to vary her spiel. The distinct treatment puzzled Lucy, however, and led her to think that perhaps her future would be apart from that of her Greenville origins.[53]

Her mother's work for suffrage and other causes and her own studies absorbed Lucy's interest during her school years. Nellie had taken her to a district suffrage meeting when she was only six months old. As a young girl, Lucy served as a page at suffrage conventions and met and heard prominent leaders of the day. At age fifteen she marveled at the enormous energy of her mother. In 1910 Nellie Somerville was president of both the Mississippi Woman Suffrage Association and the Greenville Civic Improvement Club. In a February blizzard Nellie went to Jackson to petition the House Eleemosynary Committee to place female physicians in the state's insane asylum. She chaired an intense antituberculosis campaign, with public meetings, press releases, and speaking appearances throughout the state. She wrote a series of articles on suffrage for the *New Orleans Star*, and in 1912 she invited Dr. Anna Howard Shaw, an ordained minister and medical doctor and a spellbinding orator, to Greenville and managed her appearance there.[54] Dr. Shaw made a profound impression upon Lucy. She concluded early that suffrage leaders were not "battle axes . . . warhorses . . . unattractive women. . . . They were stylish . . . full of wit and full of fun." Decades later Lucy wrote, "I can still hear the wholesome laugh of Dr. Anna Howard Shaw when she was in Greenville as she relaxed between speeches."[55]

After graduation from law school, Lucy's brother Robert, or Bob, began a practice at nearby Cleveland, thirty-five miles north of Greenville. This big brother, Lucy's favorite of her siblings, had taught her how to shoot guns on the river levee, and they shared many interests. On an April day in 1911 she boarded a train for Cleveland, traversing via rail-and-crosstie ribbon the virgin forests of a swamp, for a weekend visit. Founded only ten years before her birth, Cleveland was "a little old country town" clustered around the rail artery from which it drew its life. There were small shops, several department stores, a square brick courthouse, the ubiquitous monument to the Confederate dead, and the usual scattering of saloons and roaming dogs. It was a town Lucy thought was going to "spark" and one that eventually held great promise for her.[56]

By 1912 Nellie and Dr. von Loewenstein concurred with Lucy that she was ready for college. Randolph-Macon Woman's College was a natural choice. It was Methodist with a sound academic reputation, and Lynchburg was the home of her father's sister Laura. Moreover, Eleanor had graduated there in the spring of 1912. Eleanor was noted for her beauty, her ability in mathematics and science (she was the first student to graduate in physics), and her aptitude for sports, especially basketball. She had learned the game in Greenville from Emma Ody Pohl, one of the premier physical-education teachers in the South, who gained a national reputation in her field after she joined the faculty of the Industrial Institute and College at Columbus, Mississippi, the first public college for women in the nation.[57] The trail that Eleanor blazed at Randolph-Macon was not the one that "Little Somerville" would follow, as the faculty soon learned. Her intellectual and extracurricular endeavors lay in another direction.

2

"A whole human being," 1912–1922

IN SEPTEMBER 1912 Lucy Somerville rode the train to Lynchburg, Virginia, and except for one year she spent almost a decade away from Mississippi, returning to study law in 1920. Graduate studies in New York City, a wartime defense job, and an entree to women's organizations would have such a profound effect upon her that she later said, "It was in New York that I learned to be a whole human being."[1]

At the one-hundred-acre, shaded campus of Randolph-Macon Woman's College (RMWC) with its tall brick buildings on the banks of the James River, Lucy felt at home at once. In 1903 it was one of only two women's colleges in the South to offer a full four-year program,[2] and RMWC had established a student government in 1899, the first southern woman's college to do so.[3] The Young Women's Christian Association (YWCA), an organization for which Howorth later worked in New York City, was active on campus, and students were encouraged to engage in voluntarism and practice the Methodist "social gospel" of helping the poor and promoting better interracial relations.[4] A founding statement of the college made clear that while its mission was an education equal to that elsewhere offered men, it should not be at the expense of the "highest ideals of womanhood": intellectual development must be "acquired by our daughters without loss to woman's crowning glory—her gentleness and grace." Lucy knew that her parents had chosen the college "because of its reputation as an outstanding educational institution" and its location in Virginia, where both had attended college. Moreover, RMWC was affiliated with the Methodist Church, of which both parents were members. The academic climate that drew Lucy to Randolph-Macon also attracted another student, Pearl Sydenstricker (later Buck), whom Lucy would know well. "My mother approved it because the education there was planned to be exactly what a man would get," Pearl Buck would recall. "We were not corrupted by home economics or dressmaking or cookery or any such substitutes for hard thinking."[5]

Lucy was not homesick for a minute; having grown up in a neighborhood of mostly boys, she found an all-girl college to be more fun than she imagined. The great excitement, she recalled, was the rivalry between the "Evens" and the "Odds," one in which she early assumed a leadership when her "Even" class of 1916 were only freshmen. She was gleeful when her class set out to disrupt the party of an upper class with noise and heckling. When her classmates refused to desist, the tormented "Odds" turned the firehose on them. Wet outside but warm inside, Lucy "climbed on a nearby stump and in Gideon Planish style exhorted one and all to stay and fight."[6]

Lucy's first roommate was an unhappy, weepy Alabama girl. Lucy was not at all sympathetic and advised her to return home because she was wasting her parents' money. The girl left. Lucy found much to do. For one thing, there were two Lynchburg theaters, one of them presenting two shows a week of standard vaudeville performers. Looking back, Howorth thought she must have seen nearly every show during her years at RMWC.[7] If her lack of athletic ability disappointed upperclasswomen who remembered Eleanor, she compensated through her participation in a range of activities. She pledged the Kappa chapter of Alpha Omicron Pi, a social sorority. Membership took on added meaning when Augusta Stacy joined after she transferred to Randolph-Macon from Washington National Cathedral School for Girls.

In 1912 Lucy set out to organize a suffrage club at Randolph-Macon, and by 1915 the Equal Suffrage League had become well established on campus.[8] The campus newspaper, the *Sun Dial*, published regular columns on the club during Lucy's junior and senior years,[9] and the yearbook, *Helianthus,* devoted a page to the organization in 1914, listing Lucy Somerville as corresponding secretary.[10] She routinely placed suffrage items on a bulletin board for club notices and through her student government involvement was able to have the suffrage club recognized as a legitimate campus organization.[11] In 1915 she was president of the League as well as of the Mississippi Club.

Howorth's first encounter with campus bureaucracy occurred in her freshman year when she learned that Anna Howard Shaw was to appear in Lynchburg, and she wanted her to speak also at Randolph-Macon. Despite Shaw's credentials as a medical doctor and ordained minister, college authorities denied her the college auditorium because suffrage was too controversial. Knowing that seniors could entertain anyone in the senior parlor, Lucy persuaded those who remembered Eleanor to invite Shaw as a guest. She was elated when Dr. Shaw remembered her Greenville visit and greeted her, "Why, child, I know you."[12] Lucy circumvented the ban against suffrage activity again when her suffrage league petitioned the administration to invite Mary Johnston, the well-known Virginia novelist, author of *To Have and To Hold* and a fervid suffragist, to speak on American literature. Before the entire student body, Johnston spoke only briefly on literature and then delivered her enthusiastic message on suffrage.[13]

In December 1915 Lucy, then a senior, and her mother were both delegates to the National American Woman Suffrage Association (NAWSA) convention at the Willard Hotel in Washington, DC. Nellie was the second vice president of NAWSA, and Lucy attended as the representative of the RMWC Equal Suffrage League.[14] The meeting was an education in itself. Lucy remembered Anna Howard Shaw's comment that she was always anxious before a public talk: "I never know if I will be able to make a sound." From Shaw she learned that a certain amount of nervous tension prompts a speaker to raise her voice to reach an audience.[15]

Three events at that convention were memorable for Lucy. She witnessed the transfer of the NAWSA leadership from Shaw to Carrie Chapman Catt in what Lucy perceived, as did others, to be a strategic political move and an example of how a leader must sometimes relinquish office for the sake of an organization's unity. Shaw, a brilliant orator and the most highly educated of NAWSA's leaders, had been president since 1907, but under her the organization was "an inactive sleepy arena." NAWSA was decentralized and had no real national strategy; it had focused upon state-by-state suffrage rather than upon achieving a federal amendment. It was Catt's "winning plan" for a federal amendment that would help bring about victory in 1920. Even though Nellie and Lucy had both had positive, personal contacts with Shaw, they acknowledged that NAWSA's achievements under her had been limited, and they respected Catt's strategy.[16]

The National Woman's Party (NWP), founded by Alice Paul and Lucy Burns, originated in 1913 as a dissident committee of NAWSA known as the Congressional Union. It concentrated upon securing an amendment to the U.S. Constitution. Animosity toward NAWSA leaders led to a breakaway suffrage organization and bitter dispute over the tactics and increasing militancy of Paul and her followers. Lucy also witnessed for the first time the methods of disruption the NWP devised to thwart the NAWSA. She called the tactics "raising cain." "I have never liked bad manners," she later explained, "although a certain amount of 'scrapping' is good." Nor did she like the NWP's personal attacks against Shaw or its accusations that southern suffragists were elitist.[17] Finally, at Nellie's insistence, Lucy represented her mother at a reception hosted by President Woodrow Wilson whose hand, she shook: "At every stage Mother was there to give me a boost," she would say later, although she believed that Nellie had wanted to avoid extending her deformed right hand to the president.[18]

Lucy's membership in the Franklin Literary Society at RMWC dovetailed with her interest in suffrage and other public affairs and provided an opportunity to hone her speaking and debating skills. She argued topics as frivolous as whether mother in the fairy tale "The Old Woman Who Lived in a Shoe" was an ideal mother and as serious as, in a verbal joust with the opposing Jefferson Literary Society, whether the United States should intervene in Latin America, probably the most popular collegiate debate topic of the day. Lucy's team won with the argument that the United States should not intrude into Latin American republics because they would not accept leadership from outside and offered no stability within.[19] During her senior year she was president for a term of the Literary Society and was chosen to represent it in the commencement debate with the Jefferson Society on the subject of immigration restriction.[20]

Lucy's extracurricular activities, including a third vice presidency of the student government organization, presidency of her class, and the treasurer's office of the Pan-Hellenic Association during her senior year, did not seriously affect her academic standing. She was so well prepared by Dr. Loewenstein that she "tested out" of medieval European history. She chose a double major in political science and psychology, consistently earning As in political-science courses, Cs in violin, and a scattering of Bs in other subjects.[21] She simply did not give grades a priority over a well-rounded campus life. Nonetheless, she graduated in 1916 with the highest regard of the faculty. Ezra B. Crooks, with whom she studied Kantian philosophy and metaphysics, wrote in a letter of recommendation that "she received high grades, but this is not her chief consideration." He added, "She has real independence in her thought. . . . In any position requiring a strong and well-balanced mind, courage, and determination of character, Miss Somerville will be sure to give a good account of herself."[22]

Just what she would do after graduation weighed upon her mind. The nature and extent of Lucy's campus involvement suggest that she was contemplating a career in politics. Ever pragmatic, she realized that her gender and short stature were not in her favor. Her physical ideal was a Randolph-Macon student who was "tall," "substantially built," with a "comfortable expression" that "reassured people," but the girl was not very intelligent. As she walked by Lucy on campus one day, Lucy remarked to a friend, "You know, if I looked like her, I would be in the United States Senate some day."[23] She recognized the advantage of height and volume in the public realm, and she consciously sought to compensate for her short stature.

Lucy Somerville shared a spirit of idealism and ambition, as well as an urge toward social action or the professions, with many of her friends. There was Virginia Allen, who went to the Congo as a Presbyterian missionary for thirty years; Virginia Howlett, who, as executive director of the Junior League in Philadelphia, directed the League into social work; Mary Stahlman, who would later edit the book page of the *Nashville Banner* and help her husband write books; and Pearl Sydenstricker. Sydenstricker, a daughter of Presbyterian missionaries in China, graduated two years after Lucy arrived on campus; they knew each other as members of the Franklin Literary Society. Pearl's main interests were China and religion, neither of which interested Lucy, but she attended Pearl's public talks because she admired her and found her sense of duty appealing. In one speech she recounted the incident, which later appeared in *The Good Earth*, of a woman who gave birth and returned at once to work in the field. That was "raw meat" at Randolph-Macon in 1913, Lucy said. Her disappointment in Sydenstricker was that she never showed a "spark of interest" in suffrage.[24] Pearl Buck, the first woman to receive a Nobel Prize for Literature, in 1938, and Howorth together were honored as outstanding RMWC alumnae in 1951, but the two never had any personal contact after leaving college, although Lucy attended Buck's public lectures while in Washington during the 1930s.[25]

Howorth's senior yearbook captioned her photograph with a quotation from the Elizabethan poet Edward Dyer: "A mind to me a kingdom is."[26] With a wide range of interests, she had not determined what she would do next. Her reaction to a comment made by her dentist her senior year suggests that she was toying with the idea of following her brother Bob into the study of law. In questioning her about talk that she would become a lawyer, the dentist remarked, "I don't think much of women being lawyers." As she left his office, she thought, "There is no reason why I can't do it like anybody else." But she feared that "there would be a lot of quarreling and fussing [at home] and I had better see if something else would appeal to me."[27] Time would prove her apprehensions unfounded.

Randolph-Macon offered the opportunity to explore another field after graduation. The psychology department invited Howorth to return as an assistant at a monthly salary of fifty dollars. She was to grade papers, direct laboratory work, and deliver a few lectures.[28] At age twenty-one she seriously considered pursuing a doctorate in psychology preparatory to college teaching. One year's experience changed her mind about an academic career. Faculty meetings, "deadly dull . . . [with] all those Ph.D.'s and what not [who] didn't have the foggiest notion about parliamentary procedure," soured her on academia. Nor did she find laboratory work appealing. In later life when asked about the worst job she ever had, she replied, "Looking after white mice in the psychology lab." Thus she declined both a promotion to return to the psychology faculty in 1917 and a position in the political science department.[29] Her mother wanted her at home, ostensibly for a rest but also because she needed assistance with new undertakings related to the world war.[30] And it is fair to presume that her mother also wanted a direct hand in shaping a career that she knew was potentially brilliant but as yet unfocused.

According to Howorth, she spent the year 1917 in Greenville "trying to be a lady." For many of her contemporary women college graduates, a year at home was the obligatory "social" year before marriage. During Lucy's years at Randolph-Macon the Somerville family had had a spate of marriages. In 1912 Bob had married Keith Frazier, of Chattanooga, the daughter of a former Tennessee governor and U.S. senator. In 1914 Eleanor had married Audley Shands, a widowed lawyer with a small son. Nellie disapproved of the match because of the groom's age and worldliness and at the wedding did not sit in the traditional place reserved for the mother of the bride. And in 1916 Abram had married Evelyn Estes, a marriage that ultimately ended in divorce. Marriage was far from Lucy's mind, and from her mother's too. Asked what she would have done if Nellie, like so many of her friends' mothers, had pushed a marriage, Howorth replied, "I would have poisoned her."[31]

Like women nationwide, Nellie put aside the suffrage campaign for war work. She chaired of the Woman's Committee of the Washington County Council of National Defense, and Lucy was secretary. Its goal was to cooperate with the male-dominated County Council of Defense to promote child welfare, health, and education and to monitor the county's moral and spiritual welfare, a task that Nellie welcomed. The work involved organizing county women into a number of activities under the direction of the state chairperson, Mrs. Edward McGehee, of Como.[32]

It was clear that the domestic front was not Lucy's forte as can after can of beans and tomatoes exploded in her work with the Food Production Section of the Woman's Committee. Her assignment was to supervise a group of girls who were to be taught vegetable canning by the home-demonstration agent. Throughout the state some ten thousand women and girls participated in canning clubs, but Lucy's assistance in the Washington County war effort was short lived.[33] Her friend Augusta "Gus" Stacy's invitation to accompany her to the 1918 summer session of Columbia University was appealing and provided a convenient escape. In August the two girls, accompanied by Stacy's mother and sister, left for New York, where Lucy decided to enter the Columbia University graduate school.

In New York City Howorth broke what she has called "the spell of the South." Within a week she knew that New York was her "dish," although the impersonality and "factory-like atmosphere" of the university shocked her. However, she was encouraged that Randolph-Macon had a good reputation at Columbia and her credentials were unquestioned. Only the year before, in 1917, RMWC had been one of only five southern women's colleges to meet the criteria for accreditation by the Association of Colleges and Preparatory Schools of the Southern States, formed in 1895.[34] Flirting with the idea of becoming a psychiatrist, Howorth enrolled in two courses, Abnormal Psychology and Psychology and War Problems. The class in abnormal psychology made field trips to institutions in the area, which prepared her for the some fifty thousand clinical records she would examine in her work at the Veterans Administration in the 1930s and

1940s.[35] By summer's end she knew that she wanted to remain in school and moved from the dormitory into an affordable but "very staid and dignified" boardinghouse two blocks west of Central Park.[36]

Knowing that her parents could not afford to support an extended stay, Howorth began to look for a job. A Randolph-Macon friend had transferred to Smith College, from which the Allied Bureau of Aircraft Production was recruiting young women. The friend found a job for Howorth, who was hired in August 1918 as a gauge inspector to measure the angles of screws and bolts to ten thousandths of an inch. The Allied Bureau was a British-owned, U.S.-financed war industry that first placed Lucy in a loft near Wall Street, but she was later moved to a floor in the Abercrombie and Fitch building.[37]

In what Lucy described as "shop work" the workers were all women, the supervisors all men. The floor supervisors were "rough and tumble industrial types," and she learned firsthand the labor problems that female workers experienced. Limited restroom facilities led some women to leave early for lunch, a practice that caused one supervisor to engage in abusive talk that infuriated Howorth. She reported the matter to an Allied Bureau assistant chief and tendered her resignation, but when he required the supervisor to apologize to the women, she decided to remain at work through a sense of duty and a determination not to be harassed.[38]

Because the job did not require, as she said, "one ten-thousandth of a brain cell," Howorth continued her studies at Columbia University in the fall of 1918, earning an A in both business law and international law.[39] Evidently, she had abandoned psychiatry as a career field. In one classroom she was startled to see a black student enter, the first time she had seen a black man enter a room in any capacity other than as a servant. She decided that she could return home to accustomed social conventions or she could remain in New York and see how people behaved differently. In staying she took a major step toward freeing herself from racial prejudice. Her first encounter with a black student and her decision to make a social adjustment was very much like the experience of Alabamian Virginia Foster (Durr) at Wellesley College in 1922.[40]

At the war's end Lucy joined the jubilant throng that poured into the streets to celebrate the armistice. There she heard Madame Ernestine Schumann-Heink, barred as a German from American opera during the war, sing "The Star-Spangled Banner." The Allied Bureau closed at the end of 1918, and with a supervisor's certificate in hand stating that she had "fulfilled her duties in a most patriotic and conscientious manner," Howorth set out to search for another job.[41]

This time it was Howorth's mother who offered help. Nellie Somerville had astounded New York administrators of the YWCA by raising ten thousand dollars in Mississippi for war work. While at a YWCA reception in St. Louis, she learned that there was an opening in the New York office and recommended Lucy for the job. Invited for an interview, Lucy was not certain the YWCA appealed to her. She had not been active in it at college because she had not considered herself "a missionary type."[42]

Howorth soon learned that the opening was for a research clerk in the Industrial Department of the National Board. Established in 1906 with Florence Simms as executive secretary,[43] the department identified the increasing numbers and needs of young women industrial workers.[44] Simms moved the department from one that provided minimal social services to one that analyzed the effects of industrial capitalism and demanded far-reaching economic and social reforms.[45] She created a talented staff to organize working girls' clubs and to study work conditions in industrial cities; she was able to enlist upper-class women, often married to rich industrialists, to support her labor agenda. By 1918 the Industrial Department that attracted Howorth had grown from 375 clubs in 1915 to more than 800 clubs and more than thirty thousand members and was making inroads among southern workers.[46]

Howorth had no idea what a job with the department entailed, but her political-science background was an advantage. The final decision on her employment lay with Eliza Butler, a sister of Columbia University's president, Nicholas Murray Butler. "Like a steamship under full steam," Miss Butler entered the room to interview Howorth, whose limited analysis of her own aptitude was that she had always been asked to write the by-laws of any organization to which she belonged. That made no impression upon Butler; nonetheless, she hired Howorth at a monthly salary of $150.[47]

As the YWCA responded to the dramatic increase to four hundred thousand women in the wartime work force, many in industrial jobs previously closed to them, it intensified its focus upon women's labor issues.[48] Howorth took steps to remedy her deficient knowledge of the Industrial Revolution by reading stacks of books from the New York Public Library recommended by a coworker from Massachusetts. She kept it to herself that her scant understanding of the era was limited to what she had learned through the novels of Charles Dickens and Charles Reade. Many years later she explained her deficiency in economics. "We had a very simple style down there in the Mississippi cotton-growing country. We didn't discuss at the dinner table wages, hours, and a fair labor standard."[49]

Howorth's unforgettable first glimpse of Florence Simms was that of a tall woman standing in a doorway on a Christmas Eve when Howorth had volunteered to keep the office open. Other staff had family with whom they could spend the evening, but Lucy had no close relatives in the city. And so she sat alone in an office darkened because of the need to conserve energy. Simms, who had been in the field when Lucy was hired, suddenly appeared on Christmas Eve with roses for the staff. Howorth described her as a "large fine-looking woman, not pretty," but completely natural and at ease, one who "pulled people in." The close association between the two women began when Howorth wrote one-page reviews of the many books on industrial problems that Simms was expected to know about, but her assignments eventually extended far beyond that.[50] The image of Simms framed by a lighted doorway on that Christmas Eve would remain in Howorth's mind long after her mentor's untimely death in 1923 at age forty-five. In subsequent years Howorth spoke many times of Simms's influence on her developing social consciousness. Not even her mother's influence, for all that she did for her daughter, could equal that of Florence Simms in directing Lucy toward a commitment to social reform.

It was under Simms's magnetic leadership that the YWCA made its sustained commitment to the welfare of "industrial girls": their safety, health, and moral welfare, an eight-hour day, the minimum wage, equal pay for equal work, collective bargaining demanded by trade unions, and the abolition of night work for women. Howorth accepted the YWCA's social program as her own; through her work as a research and information secretary she helped promote the study and discussion of issues through Industrial War Service Centers, developed for working girls. Not only did Howorth adopt the social ideals proposed by Simms but she learned from her mentor how to deal with challenges to the YWCA's social program from husbands of the benevolent women who served on the YWCA board. Simms sometimes had Howorth accompany her into homes where she conducted what Howorth called "programmed conversations." Asked in

1975 by Constance Myers if she had been "programmed to say anything," Howorth retorted, "I was programmed to keep my mouth shut." Often silent in Simms's presence, Howorth learned personal skills useful in advocating unpopular ideas. Of Simms she said, "She's the one that shifted me politically, decidedly to the left and gave me this basic interest in industrial and social welfare." Simms had a similar effect upon others. Years later, when Lucy Randolph Mason sought Howorth's membership in the National Consumers' League, she evoked the memory of Florence Simms, whom she described as "a vital force in my life."[51]

Olive Van Horn, another officer in the YWCA central office, had what Howorth admired as the "quickest mind" she knew, and the two became close friends. Howorth believed that Van Horn "tended to flirt with the extreme left" and was concerned about her friend's political tendencies, although Van Horn denied that she ever joined the socialist movement. They remained friends long after their affiliation with the YWCA ended. During the Senate investigations of subversives by Joseph McCarthy in the 1950s, in order to protect Howorth's reputation for loyalty, Van Horn requested that she meet with her in an open park where there were no microphones. It was their last visit together. Howorth concluded that Van Horn was not a Communist but "very much a civil libertarian."[52]

Howorth met other prominent YWCA figures, including Margaret Wells Wood, a Mt. Holyoke graduate who was later the public health chair of the General Federation of Women's Clubs. Through YWCA conferences Howorth came into brief contact with Frances Perkins, then a member of the New York State Industrial Commission and later the first woman to serve as secretary of labor. She first met Mary W. "Molly" Dewson when Dewson was Florence Kelley's chief assistant in the National Consumers' League drive for state minimum-wage laws for women and children. At a conference in upstate New York, Lucy spoke following Raymond Robins, who, along with his wife, Margaret Drier Robins, president of the National Women's Trade Union League, was an advocate of industrial programs designed to develop leadership among working women similar to those of the YWCA's Industrial Department. And it is highly possible that through her work with the Industrial Department Howorth met Lucy Randolph Mason, who in 1917–18 was director of YWCA programs for working girls in Richmond.[53]

Howorth's YMCA work from December 1919 to August 1920 involved conducting industrial surveys in eastern cities, preparing pamphlets on state labor legislation, writing magazine articles, public speaking, and adult teaching. She was sent to report on meetings of the American Academy of Political and Social Science, the American Federation of Labor, and the American Association for Labor Legislation. Investigations took her into factories on New York's East Side and in northern New Jersey and to textile mills in North Carolina. She was "horrified [and] in constant shock." The Industrial Department's commitment to the particular needs of women in industry who lived "close to margins and realities of life" had a deep influence upon Howorth, who later said that the experience had "changed her whole attitude toward life," for it was the first time she had seen the problems of the poor and immigrants. The exposure was crucial in her emerging social conscience and her attitude toward protective legislation for women. On the one hand, she saw that maximum hours and minimum-wage laws provided relief from the abominable working conditions she observed; on the other hand, she did not support the premise of such laws that as mothers women were important to the well-being of the state. "I gagged at the 'wards of the state' phrase in the Supreme Court opinion that granted protective legislation to women only."[54] She remained ambivalent on the matter until the debate on the Equal Rights Amendment (ERA) first proposed in 1923 intensified a decade later.

As the plight of working women in industry raised Howorth's consciousness, her interest in the labor movement grew, and she attended three conferences for working women. For the October 1919 National Industrial Conference, called by the Industrial Committee of the YWCA in Washington, DC, Howorth and Ruth Chivvis prepared a seventy-page *Handbook for Delegates.* The handbook cataloged lists of attendees, including ten from South Atlantic and South Central girls' industrial clubs. The handbook also served the first International Congress of Working Women, which followed later that month under the auspices of the National Women's Trade Union League of America (WTUL). For both conferences the handbook analyzed subjects such as state-by-state legal restraints for women before and after childbirth, the employment of children, safety and sanitary strictures, the eight-hour day, and the means of preventing women's unemployment and facilitating reemployment.[55] The War Work Council also assigned Howorth to assist the WTUL in on-site preparations for the International Congress.

Also in 1919, while attending a Socialist Party convention in Syracuse, New York, she sent a postcard to Augusta Stacy, who wrote back of her surprise: "Not that I haven't been noticing your socialistic tendencies for a long time, young lady, what are you doing at a convention?" It was Howorth's first contact with "hard bitten, real women of the labor movement," and for a few years she maintained a personal contact with a few European delegates. Her eagerness before and after the end of World War II to have American women attend international conferences undoubtedly had its origin in her earlier commitment to the cause of working women everywhere. She heard dynamic speakers at the International Congress, and she thought of herself as "prolabor" or even "radical." She thought that at one time she had "tinkered" with socialism, but she never joined the socialist cause because she ultimately preferred to work for change within the Democratic Party. She joined the Democratic ward club, and in 1918 she cast her first vote, for Alfred E. Smith, the Democratic candidate for New York governor.[56]

YWCA work also liberalized Howorth's thinking on race. At the time of her employment with the Industrial Department there were more than fifty industrial clubs for black women throughout the country. YWCA leaders sent Howorth to a camp on Martha's Vineyard because through an accident in scheduling, black members from several chapters had arrived at the same time as a white group from Boston. Administrators thought that Howorth, as a southerner, could handle the problem, and she had no difficulty in integrating the two groups, except for a few dissidents whom she "set straight."[57]

Outside the YWCA job, Howorth sought involvement with organizations that offered a chance to meet new people, a practice she never abandoned. "You get ahead with acquaintants," she said, "somebody knowing about you." She joined a Red Cross group, and the skills she learned and the personal contacts she made in that group would prove useful in future crises arising from a Mississippi River flood and a war during which she would become a volunteer. She helped organize a Randolph-Macon alumnae chapter, and she joined the Alpha Omicron Pi alumnae chapter, through which she met women lawyers who were graduates of the New York University Law School. Cecile Iselin, a young practicing lawyer, became one of her permanent friends. And it was in New York that Howorth first joined the American Association of University Women (AAUW).[58]

Howorth initially became interested in what would become the National Federation of Business and Professional Women's Clubs (BPW) when she met Lena Madesin Phillips in New York. "Meeting someone [like her] was right down my alley," Lucy wrote in a long memorandum on her years with the BPW. Phillips, who had just returned from YWCA overseas relief work, set about to organize clubs for the growing number of business and professional women not heretofore encompassed by YWCA programs. Howorth helped organize a club in midtown New York and remained a member of that group until she left the city. Shortly afterward, in 1919, Phillips separated her white-collar club members from the YWCA to form the national BPW to encourage a union of business and professional women among lawyers, teachers, and entrepreneurs whose interests were beyond the YWCA emphases. Howorth joined the new club in the 1920s once she was an established professional woman herself.[59]

Howorth was not, as she put it, one to stay in her room at night and wash her underwear. "I figured as long as I could earn more than the washer woman, I would pay her . . . and be out doing something better." She embraced as much of the city's culture as she could. She developed a lifelong addiction to the *New York Times,* and when the editor of Randolph-Macon's alumnae magazine wrote to her asking for a photograph illustrating a hobby, Howorth had one taken of herself in Central Park reading the *Times.* In two years she saw almost every play that ran as long as a week, held season tickets to the New York Philharmonic, heard other orchestras and concert artists, attended lectures by writers, politicians, and public figures, read most of the new books, and "sharpened my wits" with talk from Greenwich Village to Morningside Heights. Like Gertrude Stein, she believed that "when one is young, much can be done in a year."[60] Her third cousin, James Somerville, a Washington and Lee graduate whom she did not know until he paid her a visit at Randolph-Macon, was a favorite companion. He had served with the Young Men's Christian Association in Russia during the war and had returned to New York City.[61]

Friends led Howorth to believe that James loved her, but she had no romantic thoughts about him. After he returned to Russia with the Hoover Relief Commission he urged Howorth to apply for a job there when the YWCA Overseas Committee began making plans to enter Russia.[62] The YWCA speculated that a postrevolution Russia would be more open to its work. To be in Russia with the YWCA became Howorth's ambition, but meanwhile she began to give serious thought to the study of law. Stimulated by a convergence of her experimentation with difficult kinds of work, the law courses at Columbia, and the strong family tradition in law, she was more and more drawn to the field. She wanted to attend Columbia University Law School, but it did not admit women. She recalled, "I was just irritated beyond words that I could study international law in a room and then when I left, they took up a course in evidence, and I was not permitted to stay." Harlan Fiske Stone, dean of the law school, boasted that women would be admitted over his dead body, and he often turned women away, in the words of one historian, "with a remarkable lack of civility." When Frances Marlett, a 1922 Barnard graduate, questioned his decision, he simply replied, "We don't because we don't." When women finally were admitted in 1927, Howorth and other women who were denied entrance telegraphed United States Supreme Court Justice Stone to ask whether he were "lying prone on the steps of the Court today."[63]

The University of Mississippi Law School had accepted women since 1882,[64] but Howorth did not apply, still waiting for the opportunity to enter Russia. The YWCA offered her a job as research secretary that she declined because Mildred Corbett, acting executive of the YWCA Overseas Committee, in June 1920 wrote saying that she expected the post in Russia to materialize.[65] But as the summer wore on, chances dimmed for a Russian clearance for the YWCA, and thus Howorth set 1 September as the deadline by which she must know whether the Russian assignment would come through.[66]

During the wait, Howorth joined her mother at the Monteagle retreat, which presented an opportunity for her to witness a landmark event. On 18 August 1920 she was in the gallery of the Tennessee legislative chamber to see young Harry Burn cast the deciding vote by which Tennessee became the thirty-sixth state to ratify the Nineteenth Amendment. Howorth was in the company of suffrage leaders from all over the country and had watched them lobby for the final outcome. For an inexplicable reason Nellie was not there, although Howorth thought it was because she did not want "to be so public." That hardly seems plausible in view of Nellie's earlier activities. It is more likely that she was disappointed and chagrined that Mississippi suffragists had failed to win over her own state legislature.[67]

Still, Howorth waited to hear something decisive about Russia. Finally in September she wrote Olive Van Horn that she could only presume that nothing had transpired. Thus, she would leave for Oxford, Mississippi, and the university the next week. Concurrently Mildred Corbett wrote that there was still no affirmation from Russia. "What will you do?" she asked, then added, "Go on and take your beloved law course." To Van Horn, Howorth expressed regret that in leaving the YWCA she would be breaking off "all official connections."[68] The two, however, remained infrequently in touch for many years.

In four years at Randolph-Macon and two years in New York City Howorth made lifelong friends and discovered women's organizations that would be central to her later career. Urban life in a center of social ferment and contacts with internationally minded people opened new worlds for her and stretched her notions of what women committed to reform could achieve. She left behind New York City and her dreams of a role on the international scene. James Somerville married "a talented and attractive" Russian woman while in Russia and became a career officer in the foreign service. He and Howorth remained friends for life, and his letters gave her "a sense of having a front seat on world events" and kept alive her interest in international affairs.[69] Her path, however, was leading to a small provincial town in northern Mississippi.

Despite her earlier indecision concerning a career, Howorth now felt certain that hers should be in law. Twenty years later she advised a young woman, "You know I am a great believer in a girl's sitting down and figuring out what she wants to be, and then going ahead and doing it, regardless of how much work it may take." Howorth's family supported her decision to enter law school in Mississippi, and her parents were willing to support her financially. In 1920, when she entered the University of Mississippi Law School, the larger community still thought a law practice was inappropriate for a "lady," and few women had dared to break the barriers. Only 1.1 percent of the nation's lawyers were women. Adverse remarks to her by Greenvillians about women in the law profession made her all the more determined to attend law school. She intended to become so successful that she would reverse not only the negative views the general public held about women lawyers but also those reservations of law-school administrators, such as those at Columbia, that women were too emotional and lacking in objectivity to be lawyers.[70]

Howorth's decision to enter the University of Mississippi rather than another law school that accepted women, perhaps one in Washington, DC, was probably based upon several factors. Her brother Bob had attended the University of Mississippi Law School, Nellie wanted her nearer home, and a distant cousin, Thomas H. Somerville, was dean of the law school. She would not admit to harboring political ambition at that time, but she surely knew the truth in David Cohn's statement that "young Deltans, then, aspirant to careers in their native state—especially to political or legal careers—feel they must attend a Mississippi college." It was necessary to "master" the "different art" of contacting others, "an act overwhelmingly attractive because it 'pays.'" Howorth was not the first woman to attend "Ole Miss" in law; Bessie Young, of Grenada, Mississippi, had finished in 1915, and Linda Reeves Brown had graduated with honors in 1916.[71] Nor was she the only woman enrolled in 1920. Howorth was friendly with her classmate Vivian Cook, a bright, ambitious woman who graduated to a successful career, but Howorth took pains not to isolate herself from the male law students. She made it a practice to drop in on the "Bull Room," a place in the law school where, so she said, the men gathered between classes to "chew tobacco, spit, and tell dirty stories." She did not intend to be a "nuisance," but she thought the "hangout" should be open to any student. Learning that one student had placed a five-dollar wager that she would achieve higher grades than the male generally recognized as the brightest in the class crystallized her goal to maintain the highest class average.[72]

Howorth wanted not only to have a superior grade record but also to deliver the class oration at commencement, an honor, she discovered, that required contributions to campus life. She found student activities to be "unimaginative and few." "Dullness was in the air," and the event of the day was to go to the depot and watch the train, "Bilbo," arrive and leave. It was an event of such anticipation that the dean of women waved her edict that women students could not leave campus after sundown. "So," Howorth related, "we'd go down to an old ramshackledly near the tracks at eight o'clock, have a nickel cup of coffee, and see Bilbo run."[73] The only student ferment seemed to stem from previous Governor Lee Russell's success in banning secret Greek societies and his attempt in 1920 to outlaw subsequent secret organizations. After the faculty expelled students who burned Russell in effigy, the student body met and proposed a resolution sanctioning the burning. Howorth argued that the resolution would jeopardize the university since it was a state-supported institution. Some students present claimed that they had never before heard a woman student speak in a large meeting.[74]

When Howorth ran into her Greenville friend Ben Wasson, a law-school senior, on campus, she learned of his idea of forming a drama club. He enlisted Howorth's assistance, and the Marionettes came into existence, organized, Howorth said later, "sort of like protoplasm does in the biology class." One of Ben's friends, also a Marionette, was an artist-writer, William Falkner (he later changed the spelling to "Faulkner"). In 1920 Faulkner wrote a one-act play entitled *The Marionettes*, which was never performed, but he directed the first play the group produced, a farce called *The Arrival of Kitty*.[75] Howorth recruited for the club a cousin, Ella Somerville, the daughter of the dean of the law school, who had created a literary salon around her sandwich shop, the Tea Hound, and who was something of a local institution. Years later the Mississippi-born novelist Elizabeth Spencer said of her, "Ella was the Oxford lady to reckon with, known everywhere. . . . She held the social reins of Oxford." Howorth remained close to her cousin until Ella's death in 1990.[76] After Ben Wasson graduated in June 1920, Howorth became president of the Marionettes in the fall and directed two plays.

Faulkner, his lawyer friend Phil Stone, Ben, Ella, and Howorth formed a reading circle. Although Faulkner left the university in November 1920, he and Howorth remained casual friends and conversed about literature. She said that on a personal level "he never showed the slightest interest in what made me tick." And she never saw him again after her Ole Miss days.[77] A closer friend than Faulkner, Ben shared books and ideas with Howorth in long talks in the Grove, the shaded entry to the campus. They both wrote "bad verse" but "better prose" and criticized each other's efforts.[78]

Desiring access to new books, an advantage of New York that Howorth sorely missed, led her to the idea of circulating the gleanings of her reading group through a book-review column in the campus newspaper, the *Mississippian*. Howorth named her column "Books and Things," taking the title from a similar column in the *New Republic*. She intended to publish not only book reviews but also submissions she judged to have literary quality. Faulkner, who was the first contributor, usually left his pieces in a drop box, which led Howorth to surmise that he was sensitive about his work.[79]

Howorth discovered a history of the Crusades that recounted the fact that women assumed the jobs that crusaders vacated, including that of high sheriff. The book reinforced her conviction that women had been omitted from history except as "victims of pillage and rape." Thereafter in the study and writing of women's history she always concentrated on women as achievers and not as victims. The latter view, among others, had been one reason that she abandoned the study of psychology: she had become "thoroughly fed up with Freud and all of that ilk."[80]

If she discerned a blank in history where women were concerned, she filled her space on campus and determined that other women should do the same. She organized a group of women writers, the Ravens, as well as a women's basketball team, for which she served as referee.[81] She attended a Methodist women's Sunday school class taught by Kate Smallwood Guyton, a former missionary to China, who kept soliciting monetary donations for flood victims in China. Howorth, who had long made offerings for such a cause, suggested that it would be better to send funds for engineers to control flood ravages. Admonished that such could not be defined as "Christian good works," Howorth quit attending Sunday school; the episode furthered her skepticism about organized religion.[82]

A new friend with a passion for literature and the arts appeared at the law school in the fall of 1921. A handsome, square-jawed young man with wire-rim glasses and a cheerful open face, Joseph Marion Howorth was "not a simple country lad as were so many of the students." Like Lucy, he had a wider experience than most students. Born in Trenton, Mississippi, in 1896 to Emma Beauchamp and Joseph Robert Howorth, a Lutheran minister, he had worked for railroad companies in Arkansas and Colorado after graduating from high school in Forest, Mississippi. He had enlisted in the Marine Corps and served in France during the war, developing a passion for France and anything French. At the war's end he had enrolled at Millsaps College in Jackson and two years later transferred to the University of Mississippi to study law and literature. He attracted Howorth's attention when he submitted an article on Anatole France for her column. Joe was an interesting addition to Lucy's circle. Although he was engaged to marry a girl in Jackson, he and Lucy became close friends and were among the members of the Blackstone Club who began the law school publication the *Mississippi Law Review,* a journal that ceased publication after 1924 because of financial difficulties.[83]

After Lucy sprained her ankle playing tennis, she and Joe began to play golf, sometimes meeting William Faulkner on the university's rough, nine-hole cow-pasture course. Joe wrote an essay critiquing Faulkner's sketch "The Hill" that appeared in the *Mississippian* in March 1922. When an anonymous rebuttal appeared in the Books and Things deposit drop, Lucy declined to publish it because of a ruling against anonymous submissions. Subsequently, she received a furious letter, presumably from Faulkner, accusing her of "protecting her pet" and advising her to content herself with her own "small affairs." "I am not protective. I expect people to look after themselves. I probably was—and am—rather sticky about rules and maybe a prig," she said in later years.[84]

In the spring before her graduation in 1922 Howorth and Florence Simms were reunited. Eva Horner, secretary of the Mississippi YWCA, invited Howorth to become chair of the YWCA board in Mississippi at a time when the national office was turning over administration of its auxiliary, the Girl Reserves, to state units. Howorth was unwilling to make a commitment then, but she attended a biennial YWCA convention in Hot Springs, Arkansas, where Simms was present. Simms arranged for Howorth to introduce the featured speaker, Florence Allen, a lawyer and former suffragist who was the first woman appointed to the Ohio Supreme Court, in 1922, and, in the same year, a national spokesperson for the postwar peace movement.[85] Howorth had an opportunity to spend time with Simms when the two tested Howorth's voice projection in the convention hall and again when an automobile Howorth rented for a mountain drive broke down and they had to wait an hour for help. After the Hot Springs meeting, Howorth never again saw her beloved Miss Simms, who died a year later from meningitis. "Tell them the spirit of Florence Simms will never die," Howorth telegraphed the YWCA board. For Howorth, it truly never did. In 1923, after reading an article on Simms in the *Woman's Press* written by Mary van Kleeck, director of the Russell Sage Foundation's Department of Industrial Studies, Howorth wrote to initiate the writing of a biography of Simms. Van Kleeck agreed, and the two made the first overtures to those persons who joined in sponsoring the biography that appeared in 1926.[86]

At a later time the University of Mississippi law program would require three years of coursework, but in 1922 students received a degree after a two-year program of study. In the college yearbook beneath Howorth's picture appeared the words: "Sincere and true to her own beliefs / With a brilliant original mind / A leader who's fearless and strong and just / A girl of the highest kind." Even after taking extra courses, including practical courses in typing and shorthand, Howorth had a straight-A record; with top honors and after a faculty vote, she achieved her goal of making the commencement address.[87] Her subject came to her quickly. Nationwide public and private school and college officials had banned the teaching of Darwinian evolution. University of Mississippi Chancellor Joseph Neely Powers, a strong opponent of Darwin's theory, had told students at a chapel assembly that their parents need not fear that their religious faith would be shaken at the University of Mississippi.[88] Consulting no one, Howorth prepared a memorable address, titled "Intellectual Integrity and College Education," in which she responded to the university ban on evolution and the chancellor's boast.

Declining to speak "saccharine platitudes," she decried "the foolish twaddle" that promoted economic production as the panacea for America's social problems. A great imperative was that of "intellectual integrity ... which will not lie to itself." Therefore, colleges should teach students to think. She deplored the fact that a university chancellor would request that students apologize to parents for an instructor who taught "science according to the best of his knowledge." She asked, "Were students to be fed bits of information as a baby is given its milk ... [and] always be taught that life and its problems are absolute and not relative?" It should not be surprising that instructed thus, "college students ... fall for the first smooth talking demagogue that appears" and "Americans are becoming the most bigoted and intolerant people on the globe."[89]

Her stinging rebuke continued. "The sum total of human knowledge has never been increased by papal encyclicals and it will not be by protestant resolutions." She called into question America's labor policy, mobs, lynchings, the Ku Klux Klan, and the fact that America "is stifling any breath of intellectual life within itself." Its colleges and universities "actively assist in the smothering of such faint breaths as stir within their walls." She quoted Mark Twain's admonition that a "citizen's first duty is to the honor of his mind."[90]

The speech brought a standing ovation, flowers from friends, congratulations from well-wishers, and the wrath of Chancellor Powers. Reportedly, it triggered a faculty committee meeting to discuss withholding her degree. A woman who emerged from the shadows and introduced herself as the aunt of a graduate whose parents were dead diminished the exhilaration of the moment for Howorth. She was from one of the poorest counties in the state, a schoolteacher, Howorth thought. "I've heard you say tonight what I wanted to hear someone say all of my life," the woman told her. That encounter was the most remarkable of the evening for Howorth. It reminded her that thinking people are everywhere, even in statistically unlikely places, and that public speaking could be a powerful gift. She decided never to speak for money or for any cause in which she did not truly believe.[91] It disappointed Howorth that her mother was not present, but according to Eleanor, she had made it a practice never to hear her children's speeches ever since Abram had once forgotten his lines. Lucy's own explanation was that her mother disliked to display her emotions in public.[92]

Howorth lingered for a long time after her coup, politically astute enough even then to think that the last hand to shake could be the one that casts the deciding vote.[93] Hers was a rich experience to contemplate as she left the old Fulton Chapel, steeped in tradition; it had been a hospital during the Civil War and remained a haunting reminder of the past when two-thirds of the senior class had died in the conflict. For Howorth reward enough came when Florence Simms, to whom she had sent a copy of her address, wrote in August, "I am tremendously proud of your courage, also of your ability, and I am satisfied that if the younger generation has much of this stuff in it, it will carry us far beyond any attainment which we have yet reached."[94]

3

"Hustling in the law," 1922–1927

LUCY SOMERVILLE left the University of Mississippi Law School for Greenville on a high note, armed with good credentials to take her place in the Mississippi legal fraternity but among people not yet accustomed to women lawyers. A transfer to Cleveland and employment for four years by her brother-in-law provided valuable experience for an apprentice lawyer. She returned to Greenville in 1926 ready to open a solo practice, but the destructive Mississippi River flood in 1927 interrupted that. Nonetheless, she was beginning to gain recognition through appointments to two influential positions, one professional and the other judicial. She formed a close friendship with a freelance editor of a political newspaper for women and developed her personal credo for advancement. Both her practicality and her confidence are striking. The precepts she enunciated soon after leaving the University of Mississippi—an impatience with the purely theoretical, a willingness to compromise and to help others achieve their goals, a refusal to bear grudges, and a lasting belief in the power of education—are to be seen in her career and in the politics of the organizations in which she held sway.

In 1922 Howorth was admitted to practice law in the state in the chancery court at Oxford and was then introduced to the Washington County Bar by LeRoy Percy, the ranking Democrat and so-called king of the county. According to her, he said, "Gentlemen, we have something unusual today. We have for the first time a lady lawyer." And then, she recalled, "he stalked out." It was, she surmised, a sign of displeasure and irritation. Percy had reason enough to dislike "lady lawyers" based upon his confrontation in 1907 by Mary Grace Quakenbos, a talented attorney who had directed a federal Department of Justice investigation of Percy's employment of Italian peasants on his Sunnyside Plantation in Arkansas.

Even though no charges were filed, Percy's reputation, along with his esteem for women attorneys, suffered.[1]

Described by the local newspaper as "thoroughly educated in the law," possessing "a strong analytical mind," and "here in her hometown," Howorth hung out her shingle in Greenville that summer of 1922. She argued her first case in court in late June, but she confronted curiosity and no clients willing to trust their estates or lawsuits to her. Taking a break from the disappointment of her initial foray into law, she and some cousins left the Delta for Monteagle. This, their first overland automobile trip, took them over creeks and some trails formed in creek beds, adventure enough to divert Howorth's mind from the hard question of her future. Once on the mountaintop, in what was surely an accommodation, Eleanor's husband, Audley Shands, offered Lucy a position in the Cleveland firm of Shands, Elmore, and Causey.[2]

In Cleveland Lucy joined her three siblings, Bob, Abram, and Eleanor, and their families, each with a lawyer. She was to live at Bob and Keith's home on Victoria Street. The law offices were downtown, on the top floor of the Masonic building, where for the next four years she "learned to be a lawyer." Her starting annual salary was eighteen hundred dollars. She described the practice as one of "country law . . . a very interesting one and a very human one." Her brother-in-law, "a great lawyer" in her estimation, invited her to witness his interviews with clients, assigned her research, and, as he gained confidence in her ability, had her argue cases and work on briefs. "Those were some days," she later said; she described arising before daylight and driving an old Model T to "make the courthouses in the circuit." While she recognized the monopoly men held in her profession, after ten years of practice she concluded, "People generally have been exceedingly kind and considerate of me, however, and I cannot and would not complain."[3]

She learned much in those early months of "hustling in the law," as she described her work, not all of it relating to law. When she first appeared in court, her bright print suit drew snide remarks from the men at the bar. "I never made that mistake again," she said. "After that I always wore something plain, like navy-blue serge." Initially she wore a hat in the courtroom, but as one judge recounted, "She may have come into court with a hat but when the argument gets hot, that hat flies across the table." In October 1922 she argued her first jury case; it was for a woman client, a plantation owner who had brought suit against a man she accused of illegally cutting timber from her land. Howorth failed to win over the jury but won the accolades of her client; she also won the case when it reached the state supreme court on appeal. It was her first appearance there.[4] The first will Howorth drafted that disposed of considerable property was for Mrs. Ben F. Saunders, a prominent suffragist, feminist, and past president of the Mississippi Federation of Women's Clubs. Mrs. Saunders made it a point to travel from her home at Swan Lake, some forty miles from Cleveland, to hire Howorth.[5]

In mid-1923 Shands began to assign Howorth full responsibility for important cases. Still, she did not have the confidence of the larger community, especially that of a husky Swede in need of a lawyer who found her alone in the office and told her, "I will tell you my troubles but I will not pay you a cent." She did not litigate criminal cases. Almost all such cases involved hapless citizens with few resources. "I felt like I'd be taking the bread out of the mouths of poor children."[6]

Keenly aware that she needed to get to know Cleveland's citizens, male and female, Howorth plunged into civic organizations. She joined the Eastern Star, open to men and women with Masonic affiliations, where she was certain to meet potential male jurors. She helped the Cleveland Woman's Club secure public garbage collection, although she could not attend its daytime meetings. She could now accept Eva Horner's earlier invitation to chair the Mississippi District YWCA, and she was named to the Student-Industrial Committee of the southern division of the National Student Council. In 1923 she became chair of the Mississippi Board of the Girl Reserves, and she retained the position until she left the state in 1934. She spoke at fall conferences in four districts and at statewide summer conferences on the Gulf Coast. At the spring YWCA vocational conferences she talked about being a lawyer and was gratified to learn that more women were entering the university law school.[7]

Through YWCA work Howorth became friends with Polly Graham (later Babcock, then Feustal), executive director of the YWCA in Mississippi, where work was ongoing in 325 communities. Howorth described Polly as "pure Yankee, never before in the South but full of enthusiasm and glow."[8] Polly, only twenty-four years old and one year out of Monmouth College, celebrated her birthday at a YWCA conference at which Howorth presided. When Polly described Howorth's leadership of the Girl

Reserves and its "indelible mark on the life of Mississippi," she pointed to the vocational conferences and Howorth's effort to have girls who had never left their counties of birth attend the Gulf Coast programs. Under Polly and Howorth the number of clubs grew to 350, the membership grew from two thousand members to nearly ten thousand. and the budget from nothing at all to ten thousand dollars. Howorth credited the success to the work done by paid secretaries working under her direction, although Mollie Heath Conn, state secretary of the Girl Reserves for a decade, credited Howorth "more than any other single individual . . . for making the work possible."[9]

Both Howorth's law practice and her YWCA work often took her away from Cleveland. When a Mound Bayou bank failed, the State Banking Commission hired the Shands firm to oversee the court-approved receivership. An all-black town ten miles north of Cleveland, Mound Bayou had been founded by Isaiah Montgomery, a former secretary of Joseph Davis, the brother of Jefferson Davis.[10] Shands did law work for Montgomery. The "detailed, grimy work" of foreclosure fell to Howorth, who became acquainted with the local receiver, a black man, and with Eugene Booze, husband of Mary, Montgomery's daughter and a prominent black Republican. Some of the Mound Bayou citizens she met during the foreclosure later became her clients.[11]

In November 1922 a Clarksdale woman contacted Howorth for advice about what local women's organizations could do to combat lawlessness in the town. The matter had come to a head with a morals charge against a local doctor accused of raping a thirteen-year-old stepdaughter. Townswomen wanted advice about the efficacy of a mass meeting. In response, Howorth penned a four-page letter describing the law as it related to rape and adding that the crime was "almost impossible to prove." Howorth was skeptical of the value of a mass meeting because "people go and get their feelings wrought up and fool themselves into thinking they have really done something, and go home and forget all about it." Her frank assessment was that Clarksdale's reputation as "a wide open town" attracted many criminals, "making it difficult to tighten up in one respect and not in others." Women voters were the most potent force for social reform and moral sanctity, she said, an argument Nellie Somerville had often used. Such a shocking matter as the reported rape, Howorth added, should arouse people to the danger of "turning the town loose."[12]

Clarksdale was the home of one of Howorth's best friends during the 1920s and the site of one of the state's most ambitious feminist experiments in advancing women as voters. Minnie Brewer, daughter of former governor Earl Brewer, began publishing a newspaper for Mississippi women in August 1922. The aim of the *Woman Voter* was to educate the new women voters in political matters.[13] Nellie and Lucy Somerville were Brewer's major sources of information on women's activities and had a strong influence on her editorials on women's issues, although Lucy thought that Brewer "knew her politics" and "had more ideas in fifteen minutes" than anyone she had ever known.[14]

Both Howorth and her mother wrote solid, detailed articles for the *Woman Voter*. Howorth prepared a study outline for a series of League of Women Voters programs on women in industry that treated topics such as wages, hours, health, labor organizations, and opportunities for advancement. As chair of the League's Committee on Women in Industry, she recommended broader promotion of League goals by the state legislature: inclusion of women on the state textbook commission, jury service for women, and improved child-labor and age-of-consent laws. The paper printed as "a practical study of citizenship" the text of a speech Nellie made to a convention of the Mississippi Federation of Women's Clubs at Indianola. The now aging suffragist suggested that women study laws, talk to probation officers, and interview chancery clerks to learn about county finances.[15] In its chronicle of the activities of the Somerville women the *Woman Voter* remains a valuable source for understanding their political life during the paper's brief existence. Howorth's initial appearance before the state supreme court in April 1923 received full coverage.[16]

Howorth and Brewer had in common their youth (in 1922 Brewer was twenty-four, Howorth twenty-seven), their political family backgrounds, their avid absorption in politics, their verbal skills, their sense of humor, their conviction of having been called to their professions, and their feminist viewpoint. In other ways they were vastly different. Brewer was flamboyant, loved a party, had many suitors, and was engaged to be married three times. Her sister frankly said that she "ran with a wild crowd," wore "short skirts," and drank but never smoked in public.[17] Howorth, however, never witnessed Minnie's "wild moments" and presented a complete contrast. "We were an incongruous pair . . . devoted however and both good operatives in the political field," she later wrote. Their mutual delight lay in political plots; an example was Howorth's plan to launch an advertising campaign for the *Woman Voter* with the slogan "Bilbo says you shouldn't read the WOMAN VOTER, SUBSCRIBE TODAY." Despite Theodore Bilbo's support for woman suffrage, his moral lapses alienated women voters and were a target of the paper. Bilbo, who styled himself "The Man," was a factor in Mississippi politics from his election to the state senate in 1907 through his term as a U.S. senator from 1935 to his death in 1947. Personal and political scandal swirled about him whether as a state legislator, governor (1916–20 and 1928–32), or U.S. senator. During the brief life of the *Woman Voter* Bilbo was out of office, and his alliance with U.S. Senator James K. Vardaman and his support of Vardaman's candidacy for the Senate in 1922 made Bilbo anathema to Brewer, Howorth, and her mother.[18]

Howorth and Brewer mixed business with pleasure. In Minnie's Ford they drove to the levee, where a barnstormer took them on their first airplane ride (two dollars for fifteen minutes in the air) and gave them a bird's-eye view of the Mississippi River.[19] Professionally, Howorth was Brewer's legal counsel and drew up a contract for the paper that so impressed former governor Brewer that he stated, "If a girl drew up this contract I would be willing to let her make my contract to go to heaven."[20] One of Howorth's contracts temporarily saved the paper for Brewer. When two Jackson businesswomen, Earlene White and Ligon Forbes, proposed to handle circulation for the *Woman Voter*, Howorth included in the agreement a clause that their lists of subscribers and prospects would become Brewer's if the subscription drive did not meet expectation within a specified time. White and Forbes encountered difficulties, but their unwillingness to forfeit the lists created a dilemma for Brewer. "Minnie will get along alright . . . but I am sure the others will try to start another paper," Howorth wrote an old associate in the suffrage movement. She advised League members to "stand with Minnie" and negotiated a legal victory for Brewer based upon the contract. Howorth and Earlene White later formed a friendship through the Business and Professional Women's Club in Jackson that became even stronger after White became postmistress of the United States Senate after 1933.[21]

The years 1922 and 1923 were rife with political issues that involved the Somerville women. By 1922 the National Woman's Party (NWP) had drafted an Equal Rights Amendment, which opponents among women's groups, including the new League of Women Voters, formed in 1920, argued would negate hard-won protective legislation for women. Nellie was openly antagonistic toward the NWP for its claim to be a greater force in victory for the Nineteenth Amendment than the National American Woman Suffrage Association. In addition, Nellie viewed protective legislation as a positive gain. Howorth too, at least in the 1920s, believed that after initial passage of the legislation "for twenty-five years or so, women did have improved conditions in industrial plants."[22]

The NWP arranged in February 1923 for Mary Winsor, a dynamic member from Pennsylvania who had been among the NWP members arrested in 1917 for picketing the White House, to speak in Mississippi. Through Minnie Brewer and Mrs. B. F. Saunders, a League of Women Voters opponent of the NWP, the League arranged for Howorth to respond to Winsor in a debate on equal rights to be staged in Clarksdale. The debate, presided over by Oscar Johnston, a prominent Delta planter and civic leader, became the media event Brewer had hoped for. Howorth rebutted Winsor's advocacy of the NWP's equal-rights program with the rejoinder that the party misrepresented remaining legal disabilities against women. She warned that equal-rights legislation would take away women's right to demand support from husbands as well as their right to homesteads and alimony.[23] The debate was well attended by an audience that concluded Howorth to be the winner, but of course the local crowd had already been in her corner.[24]

Howorth was not happy about the publicity the debate drew because she thought the media depicted any disagreement among women as a "cat fight." She determined not to be drawn into any such debate again because it was important that women present a united front. She later called the debate with Winsor over the ERA a "political mistake" and regretted her arguments; she described the debate as "the one public action I would like to have expunged from the record." Howorth surely did not know that at the NWP's national convention in 1917 Winsor had said, "Don't let's get respectable" in alluding to the possibility that the party might cooperate in a program for social reform with the Women's Bureau, the National Consumers' League, and other groups that she put down as "uplift organizations." The statement suggests that the two women held divergent views on protective legislation and the go-it-alone strategy of the NWP.[25] The truth was that even then Howorth was ambivalent about the Equal

Rights Amendment. She learned one good lesson from the experience: after her marriage she made it a practice that her husband respond to arguments of an opposing woman counsel, and she would reply to the male associate.

The Somerville family's acute awareness of Nellie's intense interest in politics prompted one of the brothers to remark to Lucy, "Can't we get mamma elected to something?" In 1923 the Somervilles did just that. Nellie announced her candidacy for one of three Washington County seats in the Mississippi House of Representatives through the columns of the *Woman Voter* on 23 June. Her single platform was embodied in her affirmation, "My life and character are an open book before the people of this county. I am a law-abiding God-fearing Christian woman. This I have been for many years and this I shall continue to be." She was at the peak of her power, but her husband had fallen ill and was in bed most of the time, though he still valiantly kept up his flood-control work, issuing directions by telephone during a threatening flood in 1923.[26]

Summer 1923 was an exhilarating time for Howorth and Brewer as they promoted Nellie's campaign for the state house of representatives and that of Belle Kearney, the temperance and suffrage leader, for the state senate. Issues of the *Woman Voter* point to the high level of energy the two expended. Kearney had to campaign with a broken arm and the proffered help of Brewer, who wrote Howorth, "Ole sister Belle is a good sport and I know we could elect her."[27] Howorth had broken bones of her own, ribs damaged in an automobile accident that sent her to the renowned Campbell's Clinic in Memphis. She was working hard at her practice also and won a decision from the state supreme court that named her receiver of a pool room. "Nothing like variety to make life interesting," she concluded.[28]

The summer's political fare included a gubernatorial election of consequence to Lucy. She advised Brewer not to endorse young Martin Sennett "Mike" Conner because he would not win. Conner had claimed an exemption from service during the war under the draft law and had thus alienated veterans and women whose sons had gone into the conflict.[29] Presumably those mothers read the *Woman Voter*. In the paper's straw poll in July Henry L. Whitfield defeated Conner, and there was no mention of the third candidate, Theodore G. Bilbo, the nemesis of former governor Brewer and his successor as governor after Brewer's term ended in

1916. Interestingly, Bilbo's platform offered more promises to women than did those of the other candidates, including a pledge to appoint women to all state boards and the construction of a home for "fallen women." Although the latter was almost comical in view of Bilbo's reputation for weaknesses of the flesh, it at least gave attention to the issue of prostitution, one of the targets of Nellie and other progressive reformers. Ironically, Conner's future hold on the governor's office would coincide with Howorth's tenure in the legislature, but whether he knew of her objections to his candidacy in 1923 is not certain.

Political rallies provided an opportunity to solicit subscriptions to the *Woman Voter*. Brewer, Howorth, and Brewer's cousin Emy Lou Gillespie, of Jackson, worked the crowds in Cleveland with moderate success.[30] The *Woman Voter* counted on a large turnout of the newly enfranchised women, reported to be sixty-five thousand strong and inimical to Bilbo and favorable to Whitfield, the recent president of the women's Industrial Institute and College in Columbus. Indeed, in the first primary there was an increase of almost one hundred thousand votes over the number cast in 1919, when women had not voted. Whitfield achieved a plurality but faced a runoff with Bilbo. As Howorth had predicted, the first primary eliminated Conner. "We've got to hop in now and elect Whitfield," Howorth wrote a Clarkdale woman partisan. "It's not going to be an easy thing to do. The Bilbo forces are organized and going strong." But after the second primary she and Brewer could rejoice in Whitfield's victory as "the women's candidate." They anticipated his appointment of women to office. Howorth believed that she, Brewer, Blanche Montgomery Ralston, of Clarksdale, president of the Mississippi Federation of Women's Clubs, and other women activists were building Mississippi women into "a political power structure."[31]

Much closer to Howorth was her mother's race. Four men were running against her for the three Washington County seats.[32] Opposition to Nellie from the political faction led by LeRoy Percy was formidable. His considerable strength as a political operative was demonstrated that summer, when his candidate for sheriff defeated the Ku Klux Klan's popular contender. Percy, the wealthy, aristocratic, and powerful head of a respected Greenville family and a former short-term U.S. senator, was too much a part of Mississippi's conservative political element to condone the election of a woman to a major office. Since at least 1910 he had been the undisputed leader of one faction of Washington County Democrats, while Nellie had been the recognized leader of the opposition.[33] Howorth was elated but amused when Earl Brewer, living nearby in Clarksdale, asked Percy to vote for Nellie. She knew Percy's vote was lost, "but every evidence of strength on her part keeps him from fighting her." Nellie and LeRoy Percy had grown up in Greenville together and had "fought all their lives."[34] The origin of their animus Howorth never explained.

As the race heated up, Howorth wrote Brewer, "The fur is flying in Washington County." She thought her mother would win, but "there may be a row before it is over." Her mother was playing a lone hand, financing and managing her campaign independent of any other race. "I'm a wreck of my former self," Howorth admitted.[35] Bob monitored the vote count on election night, while Lucy supplied coffee and sandwiches to the men canvassing the vote in an all-night session. Nellie ran third among the four, thus assuring her nomination. Belle Kearney won her race in the second primary, but Nellie's victory in the first gave her the distinction of being the first woman elected to the Mississippi legislature.[36]

Howorth's practical experience in college politics, in her law practice, and in Mississippi's turbulent races of 1923 shaped her less-than-idealistic view of politics, which she expressed in "Politics As It Is," an article for the *Woman's Press*. Howorth wrote that despite the definition of politics as the "science of government," women did not perceive politics to be "scientific." Women need to know that the "key to this real kind of politics" (one overlooked by men as well as women) is the beat, or precinct, meeting. An important rule is to "know your friends and stick to them" and to be aware that "no one gets something for nothing." "The basis of progress is trading and log rolling," which did not necessarily mean an engagement in unethical practices; it simply meant that compromises would have to be made. There was "no such thing as a clear issue ever presented to voters." Educated people should cease to view politics "as something either of little consequence or wholly bad." Women, above all, should remember that "in politics as in international relations your enemy of today may be your ally of tomorrow, and regardless of that we all have to continue to live in the same country."[37] By the age of twenty-eight Howorth had discovered what was imperative to be a winning candidate.

In late summer 1923 Minnie Brewer moved her paper to Jackson and hoped that Howorth would join her there. Brewer and her father recommended to Mississippi Attorney General Rush H. Knox that he name Howorth as assistant attorney general even though there was little chance of an appointment. Howorth wrote Knox that she had already endorsed his nominations for assistants and did not pursue the matter further even though she knew she had the endorsement of Mrs. B. F. Saunders, of the Mississippi Federation of Women's Clubs, and the League of Women Voters.[38]

Meanwhile, Howorth accompanied Eleanor and Audley Shands to Minneapolis for the American Bar Association meeting. She was present at the organizational session of the National Association of Women Lawyers (NAWL). She remained a member thereafter, served as a vice president from Mississippi, and published in the NAWL journal.[39] In the early fall Howorth was in New York for a national Girl Reserves committee meeting. Subsequently for a special YWCA issue of the *Woman Voter* she described the YWCA as the "greatest single contribution to the community." It offered a "cross section of American community life" in its diverse ranks. The high-school girl and the college student, the industrial worker and the clubwoman, the business woman and the foreign-born woman were all "studying and working, eating, playing together."[40]

Howorth's commitment to her community led her toward a cooperative undertaking of permanent benefit to Cleveland. To entice the Illinois Central Railroad to locate its shops in Cleveland rather than in Clarksdale, she and Audley Shands, convinced that education and industry were beneficial to each other and to a town's growth, promoted the idea of a local college. Their campaign was timely because Willard F. Bond, the state superintendent of education, was then seeking legislation to locate a teachers' college in the northern part of the state. Shands and Howorth had no difficulty in persuading Mrs. Ivy Hill to donate her property for a college after the land she owned reverted to her when the Bolivar County Agricultural High School closed.[41] Galvanized by the proposal, local citizens formed committees, petitioned legislators, raised funds, and lobbied in Jackson. Mrs. Hill and Howorth were the only female committee members who traveled to Jackson to argue for the college. Robert and Nellie both joined the crusade, he with his pronouncement that Cleveland was less subject to floods than other communities vying for the college, Nellie as one of the legislative sponsors of the act that established Delta State Teachers College in 1924.[42]

That year a series of circumstances brought Joe Howorth back into Lucy's life and gave new promise to her career as a lawyer. Early in 1924 Joe became an associate editor of the *Woman Voter* when Minnie Brewer left with her sister Claudia to study journalism at the University of Wisconsin. He took the job despite Lucy's warning that trouble would ensue and his law practice would suffer. When he endorsed Alabama Senator Oscar W. Underwood for the Democratic nomination for president, Howorth found himself in a hornet's nest after Underwood's stand against prohibition made him anathema to many southerners. Belle Kearney was shocked at the *Woman Voter*'s supporting "a notorious friend of the liquor traffic."[43] Nellie was no happier.

Joe was likely the author of "Super Woman," an interesting editorial that appeared during his editorship. The piece refuted the German philosopher Friedrich Nietzsche's assertion that motherhood was the only solution to the riddle that is "woman." Lucy surmised that Joe wrote the editorial because it concluded that women should have a choice in the matter of motherhood and home vis-à-vis a career and profession.[44] Lucy surely presumed that Joe was sending her a message that such an option should be hers.

A precipitous drop in the cotton market and Earl Brewer's inability to continue to support the *Woman Voter* led to its demise later in 1924. The loss of her father's income forced Minnie to return from Wisconsin and left her at loose ends. Correspondence between Minnie Brewer and Lucy ended when the Brewer sisters left the state and their mutual endeavors with the newspaper ended. Thus an association that had brought much pleasure and frivolity to Howorth and a venue for her own political expression was never again as constant. Contact between the two women became less and less frequent as the years went by. Although Brewer visited Howorth in Jackson during the latter's legislative term in 1934, it was likely their last time together. On leaving for Washington in 1934 Howorth told Brewer, "You had better save up your money and come up to see me," but there is no indication that Minnie made the trip. Lucy's correspondence with Brewer family members lapsed until 1939, when Minnie's father and sister wrote to tell Lucy of Minnie's hospitalization at Whitfield, the state's mental institution, where she died in 1978. Lucy wrote of her friend's decline, "She has seemed to me for a long time like a very fine race horse tied to a plow. It is a great pity that someone of her extraordinary ability would not somehow have become adjusted to this life. . . . Minnie Brewer is one of the tragedies of our state." When Earl Brewer wrote that his daughter's physicians had advised against further communication between the two women, Howorth had no choice but to comply.[45]

In 1924 Nellie Somerville was a delegate to the ten-day Democratic National Convention in New York City. Lucy attended for two days and met Mississippi Senator Pat Harrison, who respected Nellie's political acumen and would become a valuable ally for Howorth.[46] Both the press and the Mississippi delegation credited Nellie, who was a member of the Committee on Permanent Organization, with maintaining the backing of southern delegations for William Gibbs McAdoo, a Californian whom Senator Harrison believed at the outset to be the strongest contender. "A little frail aristocratic looking woman with soft eyes and a plaintive voice turned the tide in Southern delegations back to McAdoo today," one New York newspaper reported.[47] It was Howorth's first opportunity to see a Democratic convention, and through her mother she met national figures who were later to move in and out of her life.

After the convention Howorth sailed to England from New York with the Audley Shands family to attend a joint meeting of the British and American bar associations, having been named a delegate of the Mississippi Bar Association at its May meeting in Jackson.[48] En route to a breakfast with British women barristers, Howorth was shocked to see "poor dilapidated women" sleeping off a drunken debauch. The scene brought to mind the YWCA's position that the destitute circumstances of many of the world's women accounted for their despair and strengthened her conviction that social reform was a continuing concern beyond the United States.[49] From England the Shands and Lucy went to Paris, where French barristers entertained them, and then on to Rome, Florence, Milan, and the Low Countries.[50] It was Howorth's first trip aboard.

There were other personal rewards in 1924. Howorth became the first woman to address the Mississippi Bar Association, speaking on the subject "Laws about Lawyers." The fact that of the total of 120,000 lawyers in America only about 1,800 were women did not discourage her, nor did the fact that among Mississippi's some 1,300 lawyers only 6 were women. Indeed, Howorth thought the field of law was ripe for women intrepid enough to undertake its study, and she had great respect for the women pioneers who preceded her.[51]

A more substantial impetus to Howorth's career came with Governor Henry Whitfield's appointment in 1924 of both Joe Howorth and Lucy Somerville to the State Board of Law Examiners for a four-year term beginning in February 1925. Lucy chaired the four-member panel that included two other males, Frank Scott, of Jackson, and Goode Montgomery, of Laurel. National-press notice came to her because she was the first woman in the country to be named a law examiner.[52] Authorized to administer and evaluate examinations of candidates for admission to the state bar, the new board won kudos from the state bar association for its rigorous testing of applicants. When Whitfield died in office in 1927, Howorth mourned the loss of an official whom she considered to be an "unselfish person, ambitious only for the state of Mississippi."[53]

Howorth had lost her father two years earlier. Increasingly ill and confused, Robert Somerville had been admitted to live at Rural Sanitarium, a Seventh Day Adventist Hospital and retirement home in Madison, Tennessee. He died there on 19 October 1925 and was buried in Greenville.[54] At the time, her mother was at the midpoint of her term in the state legislature, where she was able to deliver passage of significant components of the reform agenda of the state's organized women. As chair of the Committee on Eleemosynary Institutions, she succeeded in having the hospital for the insane moved to the new facility at Whitfield, where treatment of patients vastly improved and a major reorganization was implemented. She won modest factory-inspection laws for working women. It was said that "she knew each political figure, his interests, his record, his motivation, his family, his friends, his supporters, and his probable future actions."[55] Her formula for success was not lost on Howorth.

While drawing up a bill of complaint in 1926, Howorth's first impulse was to have Audley Shands examine it. At that moment she realized that she needed to free herself of dependence upon him, and she decided to establish a solo practice elsewhere. She had remained on salary and believed that a partnership was in the offing; nevertheless, she wanted to be on her own.[56] In the fall she moved to Greenville and went to live in her mother's house, a decision based partly on her father's death. She shared office space and expenses with another lawyer, S. Bun Thomas, a popular, unhurried man who welcomed her practice. Howorth's love of the law continued to grow.[57] Long after retirement she said, "I never got tired of pulling down books. . . . Each time there was a caress in my heart when I handled the law books. It was just what I wanted."[58]

In 1927 U.S. District Judge Edwin R. Holmes appointed Howorth U.S. commissioner for the Southern District of Mississippi. The position bore the title "judge"[59] and led to her lifelong epithet "Judge Lucy." The work enhanced her reputation as a lawyer and boosted her practice. She was one of the attorneys for the Federal Land Bank and the Greenville Commercial National Bank, she represented the Mississippi Rehabilitation Corporation, and she built a solid general practice ranging from replevin suits for livestock to receiverships of corporations.

Helped by friends and the "family prestige [that] wrapped you around in a safety net," she was only beginning to build a practice when the Mississippi River rose above its banks. It was soon obvious that this was not the usual slow spring overflow of the river that brought topsoil from thirty-six states and created what Tennessee Williams's character Big Daddy boasted was "the richest land this side of the Valley Nile." Deltans had seasonably enjoyed the romance of the river, living at time like Venetians, with boats, moonlight serenades, and swimming parties.[60] The great Mississippi River flood of 1927 developed into one of the most ravaging natural disasters in the nation's history. Howorth's actions during the crisis demonstrated her alacrity in meeting challenges in ways that advanced her own interests while at the same time offering sustenance to others.

The historian Pete Daniel would write that Union General William T. Sherman did less damage to Mississippi than the flood of 1927.[61] Herbert Hoover, secretary of commerce and Red Cross relief director, called the flood "the greatest peacetime catastrophe in the history of the U.S."[62] The deluge displaced six hundred thousand people and washed over sixteen million acres in seven states, with waters covering a width of one hundred miles in some areas.[63] Sixty-two years after federal troops burned Myra Smith's home, Nellie and Lucy faced not fire but water, as well as the patriarchy that dominated the power structure of Washington County.

Lucy Somerville's personal history intersects with that of the flood and the river in a number of ways. After a devastating flood in 1844, Abram Smith, her great grandfather, introduced a bill in the Mississippi legislature in 1846–47 that authorized planters to construct levees on their land and legislated instruction on how to build them, presumably the first attempt at flood control in the Delta.[64] As a member of the Levee Board Howorth's father had spent most of his professional life trying to control the river. He traveled to Washington every year to lobby Congress for flood-control funds, a difficult task in view of congressional opinion that flood control was a local matter. When Congress finally funded a program in 1917, World War I delayed implementation.[65]

Lucy Somerville's account of the 1927 flood illustrates the energy and courage that characterized her immediate and practical response to crisis, her ambition, and the influence of her mother when both Somervilles were tested by the LeRoy Percy family in the realm of public power. Before the levee broke, Howorth and Ben Wasson crossed the river to Lake Village, Arkansas, to observe the rise in the river from that vantage. Wasson, Howorth said, was still "battling his literary instincts and trying to make a lawyer of himself." He and Howorth had produced a type of Spoon River anthology of Greenville that editors at Alfred A. Knopf deemed showed talent, although they declined publication. Wasson had come into Howorth's office to suggest that they catch the *Burney Swain*, a large commercial boat now riding surreally on a risen river. In Lake Village they saw what seemed to be the whole population of the town on the levee, the men stacking sandbags, the women serving coffee and sandwiches. They commented on the relative lack of activity on the Mississippi side.[66]

A habitual river watcher, Howorth had been uneasy all spring about the readings from Cairo, Illinois. She had learned from her father to take notice of the water's behavior during winter, spring rises, and snowfalls. From the deck of the *Burney Swain* she and Ben saw the rolling muddy water. Convinced that the levee would soon break, Howorth located the best carpenter she knew; he was to be at her house the next morning. On 21 April at 7:45 A.M. the siren sounded, signifying that the river had broken through at Mounds Landing, near Scott, Mississippi, eighteen miles north of Greenville. Water from that single break flooded more than 2 million acres, pouring through the crevasse with such a volume as rushed over Niagara Falls in the same time frame. When the alarm sounded, William Alexander Percy was at home completing a poem; Howorth was at the lumberyard buying material for a boat.[67]

The carpenter arrived as promised and worked quickly to build a boat and paddles. He built a ramp to the house so that Howorth could drive her Ford up on the porch and nailed the steps to stakes to prevent their washing away. Oldtimers on the river, the Somervilles had a "high water house" built four feet above ground. While the carpenter worked, Howorth bought a supply of soap, disinfectant, and cleaning supplies at the drugstore, feeling, she said, like the biblical prophet Noah. She then drove to the grocery for food. She telephoned her mother, who was in Jackson for the 1927 legislative session; Nellie arrived in Greenville on the train that afternoon as special trains carried away hundreds of people who were fleeing the Delta—the "rabbit folk," William Alexander Percy called them.[68]

Alerted to an even more serious flood than expected, the Somervilles prepared for an eventuality of eight feet of water. In the dead of night they placed furniture in higher areas of the house and packed all that could be packed. "Houses along their [the Somervilles'] street were as gaily lighted as the Rue de la Paix after the Opera," Howorth wrote in an account of the flood for the *Woman's Press*. Bright lights did not change the foreboding that this flood was significantly different from the annual "overflows" that were a part of the natural life cycle in the Delta. "We respected the River," she wrote of pre-1927 days, "but somehow we never feared it." Now she feared it; this flood was different.[69]

The waters arrived in the Somerville neighborhood at 5:30 A.M. on 22 April, only a day after the levee broke above the town. "So long as I may live, I know I can never forget my first sight of the water in town. . . . I saw a glittering, slimy mass wriggling along the street like some horrid, merciless serpent stifling the breath from the body of its victim." A block over, Will Percy stood on his porch and saw the water gliding, "dirty and filled with snakes and eels and it covered mother's blue larkspur."[70] The water rose for a week, covered 80 percent of the town, and then stopped short of entering the Somerville home. Flood water would remain in Greenville until August.

Red Cross personnel were in town almost immediately with instructions to locate the center of community power and work through it.[71] Although Nellie Somerville had defeated the Percy faction in 1923 with her election to the legislature, Red Cross officials did not consult her, deferring instead to the Percys. An all-male emergency committee formed with William Alexander Percy as chair, a logical choice for he had worked with Belgium relief efforts before the United States entered the war. While he began to make policy decisions, Howorth learned to maneuver her boat, no easy task at a time when the water flowed so swiftly that in Greenville streets it took rescue boats four hours to proceed a mile against the current.[72]

The human dimension of the disaster, the incomparable loss of life and property and the displacement of black and white sharecroppers and tenants, was ominous. Most survivors never recovered their livelihood or spirits. Animals suffered also. Howorth wrote, "One of the saddest things I have heard was the lowing and mournful baying of the livestock as they drowned the first few nights of the flood."[73] It was imperative that emergency food and shelter be provided for sixty thousand refugees and thirty thousand head of stock already lining the levee in the Greenville area. All told, some 330,000 persons were rescued from atop houses and trees and taken to refugee camps along the length of the flooded river.

After the Red Cross and the relief committee confiscated all the motorboats and food supplies available in town, civilians rich or poor could obtain food only through the Red Cross. When Nellie refused to eat "charity bread," Howorth "scrounged" food from the Red Cross and told her mother she had bought it. What Nellie perceived as the heavy-handedness of the Red Cross provoked her throughout its presence. When the town's water supply became infected, Howorth found that her best source of water was that in which canned tomatoes were packed. The gas supply had been turned off, but electricity remained, as did the telephone service, which served as a vital link to the community for the Somervilles. The telephone prevented the dreaded sense of isolation from other citizens, but it could not assuage the Somervilles' isolation from the place they most wanted to be, namely, at the center of policy and decision making. It was over the telephone that they learned of Will Percy's intention to evacuate women, children, and the infirm.[74]

Howorth and Will Percy had contradictory perspectives on the evacuation plan. She remembered it as a gender issue, while Percy wrote of it as a racial matter. In his *Lanterns on the Levee* he wrote of ordering women (whites only) to leave early. According to him, many did leave, except his own mother and a few older women who, having seen floods "come and go," were "similarly disdainful and insubordinate," among them, of course, Nellie and Lucy Somerville. Lucy vehemently disagreed with Percy's statement and maintained that only a few white women left, among them the sick and those with small children and those who had relatives elsewhere to provide shelter.[75] Will Percy then ordered all blacks to be evacuated to Vicksburg, but the committee countermanded his order. It infuriated him that rescue vessels were turned back because he knew that the planter aristocracy had placed their economic interests and fear of the dispersal of their black laborers above their welfare. Later he learned that his father, LeRoy Percy, had led the committee to resist the order. The elder Percy was among the first to question the wisdom of stripping the area of its labor force, and at least on that matter Nellie agreed.[76]

Both Nellie Somerville and LeRoy Percy had vested interests in rescinding the order to evacuate both the white and black population, but Nellie's name appears in none of the widely read accounts. Although she wanted the community preserved, her major concern was Howorth's future, not the planters' fortunes. As for herself, Howorth determined that she would not obey the order that white women leave. "Who wants a lawyer that in the midst of a crisis has to go running off and take shelter?" she asked. Nellie contacted the relief committee to challenge Will Percy's order to remove the blacks from the levee. She feared, as did LeRoy Percy, that if they left, they would not return, and the economic basis of the Greenville community would be destroyed, and with it Howorth's profession.[77] The Somervilles knew that the evacuation order had been revoked, but they could not know that LeRoy Percy had been behind it. His son Will claimed that he did not learn the truth for two years. Howorth knew Will, ten years her elder, but she "never had any feelings" about him. She did not see him as a political figure. "First place," she said, "I didn't think he had any political sense."[78] Regarding Will Percy's romance with the medieval, she thought "the man was frozen into a world that didn't exist."[79]

A six-mile-long tent city sprang up after the decision to retain the population that refuged on the levee. Home-demonstration agents and Red Cross workers provided practical instruction and health care.[80] When Howorth found that refugees were camped in her office, she was able to relocate her quarters in a room outside the offices of the health department, a dry, well-lighted space on the second floor. Nellie secured those accommodations for her daughter after a timely telephone request to the county health officer. Howorth reached her new office in a motorboat operated by a neighbor. She had no clients, but she observed the hard labor of men in the vicinity and devised a scheme to create a relief post for them.

With the help of a neighbor, Beth Mayhall, she secured bread, coffee, and tins of potted ham from the Red Cross, and soon the two women had a distribution center for hot coffee and sandwiches. Lawyers, bankers, and businessmen continued to flock to her office for the duration of the flood. With her office as a gathering spot, Howorth was able to hear the latest news about the flood and ongoing relief decisions of the Red Cross.[81]

There she learned that the local Red Cross director who specialized in emergency relief was to be replaced by a new director to oversee long-term reconstruction. Neither Howorth nor her mother had been pleased by the failure of the Red Cross to involve women in decision making or to make full use of their abilities. They attributed some of the neglect to use women's services to the condescension toward women they were certain the Percy men harbored. Will Percy even admitted at one point in his autobiography, "We are the ones I suppose who doubt despairingly the fitness . . . (under our breath be it said) of women." More to the point, they were miffed that they had been ignored. When Howorth learned that a new director would arrive in Greenville, she telephoned the Washington, DC, headquarters to contact a woman she had first met at the Red Cross office in New Orleans during the war. Howorth convinced her that some citizens had been denied help because they had failed to support the Percy faction. The discrimination "was not extensive but it existed," and she had her own "ideas of community help." But as she later admitted, she was "ambitious" in seeking to be employed by the Red Cross "in a position of responsibility."[82]

When a female Red Cross official arrived in Greenville, she sought out Lucy Somerville and placed her on a committee to inspect refugee camp tents and the care extended to children, the elderly, and the disabled. The woman may have been Margaret Wells Wood, Howorth's friend from New York days, who arrived in Greenville in early July as a Red Cross social-hygiene inspector and instructor. The work was "grubby" but also "instructive," Howorth said. As months passed and the water receded, she inspected houses before residents returned. That work involved the risks in entering dwellings infested with insects and snakes, but she considered the assignment a victory because it permitted her to do the public service she earlier had been denied. Lucy and Nellie also began a clothing-distribution project independent of the Red Cross. Nellie's lack of patience with Red Cross procedures prompted her to issue a call through the Women's

Christian Temperance Union, in which she held a state office. Clothing poured in from across the nation, including two freight loads of blankets and quilts and "clean country clothes" from Iowa and Kansas. The Somervilles used a vacant store building as a distribution center and launched their modest program with none of the Red Cross's strict stipulations for recipient eligibility.[83]

In July Lucy went by boat to Vicksburg, where Joe Howorth met her for the drive to Jackson. As chair of the Board of Law Examiners, she intended to be present to administer an examination to aspiring lawyers. In August, when she returned to her office in the Weinberger building, Ben Wasson dropped by to tell her he was off to New York, where as an editor he would have a hand in publishing the work of William Faulkner.[84]

The flood of 1927 marked the end of an era in Howorth's life. Joe had remained a good friend, seemingly more than a friend. He had broken his engagement, the details of which Lucy never questioned. He had been on Army Reserve duty in Vicksburg during the flood and unable to persuade the Somerville women to leave Greenville. "A box of chocolate candy—that's all she'd let me do for her in the flood," he recalled.[85] Six months after the flood was over, Lucy and Joe married and moved to Jackson. She hoped to launch a flourishing legal practice in the capital city, where all kinds of new opportunities existed.

4

Howorth and Howorth, Attorneys-at-Law, 1928–1931

MARRIAGE IN 1928 and a move to Jackson placed Lucy at the hub of professional and political activity in the state's capital city. She became acquainted with a lively group of activists in professional women's circles and continued affiliations with organizations she had first joined in New York. Professionally her firm floundered at the onset of the Great Depression in 1929, but politically she fared well, being elected to the state legislature in 1931.

"And So Cupid Wins" ran the headline over Lucy Howorth's picture on the front page of the *Memphis Evening Appeal* on 17 February 1928. The story, which Lucy attributed to Minnie Brewer, told of the marriage of Lucy and Joe on the previous day in Greenville. "Cupid" had been Governor Whitfield, whose appointment of the two lawyers to the Board of Law Examiners in 1924 had reunited the couple after the year their friendship began at the University of Mississippi Law School. Although Joe had left Ole Miss without receiving a degree, he had been admitted to the bar and was practicing in Jackson.[1] The news story reported that the newlyweds were honeymooning at the famed Peabody Hotel in Memphis and would leave for Mobile and Florida. It did not report a less pleasant fact, namely, that Nellie Somerville had refused to attend the ceremony, which had taken place before the fireplace at the Wils Kretschmar home in Greenville. Eleanor and Audley Shands were witnesses for the simple exchange of vows that Lucy downplayed as "a plain ole marrying."[2] Nellie's refusal was not based on an objection to Joe but rather on her conviction that Lucy was destined for a brilliant career and that marriage would derail it.

Virginia Drachman's findings on the outcomes of marriage for women lawyers suggest that Lucy's union with Joe was atypical. Nearly half of the women lawyers in 1920 thought that marriage and a career were incompatible; nevertheless, "personal sacrifice was not a universal reality for all married women." Success or failure "depended on the type of man a woman married,"[3] and in Joe Lucy won a prize. At the outset she told him that when he returned home each evening, briefcase in hand, she would be returning beside him, her briefcase in hand. She made it crystal clear that she had no domestic talents and did not intend to develop any. Throughout their more than fifty years together Joe did most of the cooking on the nights they did not eat away from home. Lucy's stated her point of view as follows: "It has always seemed to me that the best thing for me was to do as well as possible the things for which I have some talent and leave the rest alone."[4]

Joe accepted her conditions and even appeared to welcome them. If Joe initially held the traditional views of his Lutheran minister father and family, he changed his outlook. He told Lucy that he wanted their marriage to be a "freeing experience" for her. "I think that human beings are made to go in pairs," Lucy said, "and I think that each supplements the other and if they are really congenial and devoted [there is] none of this stupid domination."[5]

From all accounts their marriage produced no conflicts. Years after they married, a friend wrote, "For the first hour I saw the two of you together, I thought you were the most unlikely couple I'd ever seen—and after that, the most inevitable couple." Of Joe the friend wrote, "The man had the gentlest manner, the most open smile and the most matter-of-fact inner serenity of anyone I've known."[6] And yet Joe was a stereotypical male who liked to hunt, fish, smoke, drink, cuss, and soldier, and Lucy had no objections.

Joe, like Lucy, loved literature, and he tried his hand at writing. His black notebook contains primarily short stories and sketches that appear to be plot lines for longer writing projects. Themes of the pieces, dating from the 1920s and 1930s, are for the most part love, race, and relationships. One that was completed, "Brothers under the Skin," about the friendship of two World War I soldiers, one white and the other black, appeared in the University's *Mississippian* in 1920 under the byline "Marion Mississippi." Later, rejection letters apparently discouraged him, and Joe gave up fiction in the mid-1930s.[7]

Joe was unabashedly in love with Lucy and admired her. A year after their marriage he wrote in his journal, "Valentine day—this year I have

Lucy for a Valentine—and am grateful indeed." Forty-five years later, when she returned from an AAUW trip, he wrote of buying a bottle of champagne to "welcome Lucy home."[8] He was proud of her achievements and affectionately seldom called her anything but "The Judge."

Few people ever had nerve enough to ask why the Howorths had no children. To interviewer Constance Myers, Lucy retorted, "That's my private business."[9] Lucy told a child who knew no better than to ask, "There was insanity in Joe's family," but one of Nellie's half-brothers suffered from mental illness as well.[10] Then, too, Nellie's mild deformity of her hand could have been a concern. One family member thought that Joe and Lucy would have had children if they could.[11] In the realm of speculation the fact can be added that Lucy was almost thirty-three when she married, and by the time she may have considered a pregnancy the Depression was already under way in Mississippi and the firm of Howorth and Howorth was struggling. According to Virginia Drachman's research, almost all women lawyers found that children took a greater toll on a woman's legal career than marriage.[12] Lucy and Joe may have made a conscious decision not to have a child.

The couple formed the firm of Howorth and Howorth and discussed the possibility of Joe's joining Lucy in Greenville but dismissed the idea. They may have wanted to distance themselves from Nellie; moreover, Lucy feared that some people might think that Joe had attached himself to her successful practice.[13] She had a legal legacy in Jackson through William L. Nugent, her grandfather, and other family members. The state capital was a logical place for a flourishing practice and for a political animal such as Lucy.

Lucy and Joe set up housekeeping at a small place in Jackson but were often at the home of Audley Shands's brother Harley and his wife, Bessie Nugent Shands, Nellie's much younger half-sister. While Harley recuperated from tuberculosis in Colorado, the Howorths stayed at the Shands home to care for the children. Couprey, then six, adored Lucy, commenting nearly seventy years later, "I have loved Lucy since I was six years old."[14] Later the Howorths built a house in the developing Belhaven district, whose best-known new homebuilder was the father of the writer Eudora Welty.

At an early stage in the marriage the Howorths discussed whose career would receive the greater effort and agreed that Lucy's should. Joe was frank to admit that she was the smarter of the two and, as Lucy often said herself, "ambitious."[15] But both were deeply involved in public affairs. Whereas in Greenville Lucy had built a bridge to the town's males through the Eastern Star, Jackson, with a population of sixty thousand, was not so easy a place to "bridge." Now she had Joe to help reach the community. When Joe joined the American Legion, Lucy joined its auxiliary.[16] All in all, she joined nineteen organizations while a Jackson resident. But she was interested in more than just advancing herself professionally. Lucy often spoke of an organization as "a tool to accomplish social objectives, to develop people," and she maintained practically all of her earlier associations, particularly with the YWCA. Her reputation as a champion for young women drew requests that she assist advocacy groups, including the North Carolina–based Southern Summer School for Women Workers, which sought, through Lucy, Mississippi enrollees for its programs.[17]

With the help of her Jackson friends and family, Howorth quickly found her way into women's groups. Since 1926 she had been the legal adviser for the Mississippi Federation of Women's Clubs, and she joined the BPW and the Jackson branch of the AAUW.[18] She considered her Jackson "debut" as a leader to be her position as chair of the November 1928 local program of the National Committee on the Cause and Cure of War (NCCCW) sponsored by the AAUW, the BPW, the Temple Sisterhoods, the federated women's clubs, and the Mississippi YWCA.[19] When Carrie Chapman Catt, a strong supporter of Woodrow Wilson's war efforts, turned to a crusade for world peace after the suffrage victory, she organized a consortium of organizations to focus upon a permanent peace. It included, among others, the Council of Women for World Missions, the League of Women Voters, the WCTU, and the Women's Trade Union League.[20]

Lucy enlisted Martha Catching Enochs, a BPW colleague, to help plan the conference to be held on 16 and 17 November at Jackson's King Edward Hotel and Galloway Memorial Methodist Church. Members of her planning committee included Enochs, who served as program chair, and Ellen S. Woodward, chair of attendance. Woodward, then the director of civic welfare and community development of the Mississippi State Board of Development, had been an acquaintance of Lucy's since their residence in Greenville in the early 1920s.[21] As general chairperson, Lucy gained the spotlight when she launched the conference with an explanation of its purpose. She described as "marvelous" the keynote address, "The Road to Understanding," given by Mrs. Anna Pennybacker of Austin, Texas, the past and then honorary president of the General Federation of Women's Clubs.[22] After leaving Jackson, Pennybacker wrote to "My dear, dear little chairman" that the conference was "one of the most artistic" of the programs held around the country. The two women had no further contact, but in the 1950s Lucy refuted accusations that Pennybacker was a Communist or fellow traveler.[23]

Among program participants were representatives from each of the colleges in the state. The State Teachers College at Hattiesburg sent Kate Brown, a history professor and past president of the Mississippi Education Association, whose study in Europe of the World Court at The Hague, Netherlands, had been sponsored by the Carnegie Foundation. Brown's speech was entitled "What the World Does to Prevent War." Henry Bobo, a Clarksdale high-school student and Boy Scout who had won a trip to Geneva through a national competitive examination on the League of Nations and had met Mrs. Pennybacker there, spoke on his personal impressions of the League.[24] It gratified Lucy that her native Delta was represented at the conference and that she had the opportunity to present herself well before a large number of prominent women. She remained interested, although not active, in Mrs. Catt's NCCCW and attended its session in 1935. When German and Japanese aggression proved that the League of Nations was powerless, the NCCCW ceased to exist.[25] By then Lucy was in Washington, and her perspectives on neutrality and defense preparation echoed those of the administration.

The Howorths' tenure on the Board of Law Examiners ended early in 1928, when the Bilbo administration "reorganized the board out of existence," reputedly after a friend of the new governor failed the examination. By tightening requirements after three-fourths of the applicants in 1924 failed, the board no longer had to deal with an excessive number of examinees from outside Mississippi. In describing an examination conducted by Lucy, a leading Jackson lawyer stated in 1933 that "she had given the hardest examination he had ever seen and he had taken both the New York and Connecticut Bar examinations."[26] Many young lawyers who were examined by the Howorths became prominent, including Mississippi's future U.S. senator James O. Eastland.[27] Meanwhile, Lucy continued as the U.S. commissioner for the Southern District. The court met periodically and could finish its business within a week. Litigation, which included some criminal offenses, often bootlegging, liquor smuggling, or the illegal sale of stamps or theft of registered mail, was generally noncontroversial and did not attract publicity.[28]

The firm of Howorth and Howorth grew steadily, with legal work on deeds, contracts, guardianship cases, and the general run of an office practice. Asked if they ever had differences over litigation, Lucy replied, "My husband and I didn't quarrel over cases. After all, we were paid to quarrel for other people."[29] A number of factors helped the firm to expand: the Howorths' contacts through the organizations they joined, knowledge of Lucy's legacy in law from Colonel Nugent, her connections through Dr. Harley Shands and her mother, Joe and Lucy's service on the Board of Law Examiners, and above all, their growing reputation as lawyers. "They do say you are a bearcat in court," one client told Lucy.[30] When asked what was most important to a lawyer's success, Lucy said simply, "Reputation is the greatest thing."[31]

Lucy knew she had a gift for public speaking and an ability to persuade others to her way of thinking, but she had no thought of public office for herself. "I wanted to be a good lawyer; that's all I wanted to be," she said.[32] Economics forced her to look at other options with the onset of the Great Depression in 1929. Soon the Howorths had to barter legal work for goods and services such as stationery, printing, and dry cleaning. But barter could not pay the rent on the entire floor of the office building they had leased, and the Howorths had to reduce tenants' rent to keep them. As Lucy put it, "We were going down in a financial hole." Lucy confided to her brother Bob, "All our clients are broke. We are practicing just to keep our hand in apparently."[33]

Harley and Bessie Shands anticipated that their political favorite, Mike Conner, a former speaker of the state house of representatives, would be elected governor in 1931 and set about finding candidates for the legislature who would support him. Her two relatives were the first to suggest that Lucy run. Shands had a good medical practice, and his wife was a popular socialite. Trial balloons they launched for Lucy were encouraging.[34] Hence, the need for added income, a show of family support, her own ambition, and a conviction that she could contribute to the public good were all factors in Howorth's decision to announce her candidacy on 28 June 1931. Her candidacy seems to have had a positive effect on a potentially strong female electorate, for four days later the *Clarion-Ledger* reported that there was an "almost continuous line" of women registrants at the courthouse. Seventy-five percent of all persons seeking to vote were new registrants. Moreover, they appeared "unaccompanied" and "without guidance or solicitation of male members of the household."[35]

In a formal announcement of a slogan of "Honesty and Fairness in Office," Howorth set forth her platform. The people of Hinds County would come first; she would study the state's financial problems and try to solve them; she opposed the hodgepodge of "nuisance taxes," but she did not promise to vote for lower taxes; and she would work to restore the academic integrity of the colleges and universities that had lost their accreditation because of Bilbo's disruptive interference. Only Delta State Teachers College in Cleveland had escaped his mass firing of administrators and faculty.[36]

Howorth vowed that she was not running "for the exercise"; she had every intention of winning. She considered two among the large field of candidates to be the most formidable. One was L. L. Posey, a Jackson lawyer and "fixture" in the legislature, who she was certain would be elected, and the other was Walter Capers, a popular, brilliant young man, an attorney who that year had founded the Jackson School of Law. His father was rector of St. Andrew's Cathedral, and his family well respected. Other serious contenders were Samuel Key, a Jackson druggist who had been president of the Mississippi State Pharmaceutical Association, and Carl Chadwick, a young, first-time political candidate. Five other men rounded out the ten-candidate field.[37]

Howorth knew that organization was the secret to winning in politics; she had written a blueprint for success in her *Woman's Press* article. Knowing she could not see all the voters, she sought to build a volunteer committee in each of the county's thirty-nine precincts.[38] "I got very uptight," she said, and thus Nellie Somerville came to Jackson to help organize women voters. Somerville operated from a room in the King Edward Hotel, famous in Mississippi history as a headquarters for political brokers; however, she did not remain long, for she soon realized that she would become an issue to the detriment of her daughter's campaign.[39] Somerville had not fared well when she sought reelection to the Mississippi legislature in 1927. She had announced her candidacy, remained in the race less than a month, and withdrawn after four men entered what was certain to be a bitter race. Moreover, she had been exhausted by the devastating flood of that summer and dreaded the prospect of a brewing fight with proliquor interests. She knew her popularity had declined in Washington County because of inroads made by the LeRoy Percy faction. In fact, early in 1931 Nellie moved from Greenville to Cleveland and built a house adjacent to the home of Bob and Keith. Not content to live there, she frequently traveled, for she found Cleveland to be too languid. In Greenville she could merely walk down the street and "stir something up," but not in sleepy Cleveland.[40]

When Nellie realized that her adamant stand on prohibition and other unpopular issues made her a liability in her daughter's campaign, she decided to return home. "Don't you come to the train," she told Howorth. "I'll keep in touch by phone and a few people I can trust." Leaving Howorth a check for five hundred dollars, Nellie left Jackson and did not return until after the election. Explaining her mother's absence, Howorth said: "You have to have your antennae out. If you don't you are sunk."[41]

Lucy had other antennae up that summer. WJDX, Hinds County's only radio station, beamed her spot appeals to voters.[42] She was canny enough not to interrupt the soap operas, the noon farm and market reports, and other favorite programs of listeners with her ten- to fifteen-minute broadcasts. She placed advertisements in all the small county newspapers and created candidate cards and pocket-sized ink blotters. The Howorths had little personal money to contribute to her campaign chest, which came to fifteen hundred dollars, a handsome sum at the time. She had her mother's five hundred dollars and the few sums that Joe raised from men in the community. There is no record that organized women provided any substantial contributions, but Lucy knew that women candidates always were at a disadvantage when it came to raising funds.[43]

With Joe at the wheel, the Howorths canvassed the electorate along the back roads of the county, where the population was sparse and where she sought to reach voters other candidates seldom saw. When Joe and Lucy found men clustered on benches before a small country store, they resorted to instinct to determine the leader. In one instance, when Lucy approached a man and handed him her card, he paid no attention and continued to whittle during her appeal. Finally, he stood up and held out his hand to shake hers. "Lady, if I hadn't seen you, I wouldn't have voted for you, but I will." His response strengthened her conviction that victory could come from contact with rural voters. After buying a sack of sugar at the store, Joe and Lucy left behind a group of farmers and a store owner whose votes they counted upon. It was a scene repeated at crossroads throughout the county. Lucy knew that she was suspect as a woman candidate and exercised her quick wit to offset potential opposition. When one doubting voter asked why she had two last names, she replied that she was "the proud possessor of two names only through the honorable state of matrimony." The skeptic seemed to be impressed with that answer, and she left believing she had won another vote.[44]

Unable to afford a bid for items auctioned at charity and church bazaars and fairs, the Howorths devised a winning plan. Lucy waited until the women were cleaning up and offered perhaps ten dollars for leftover food, which she then donated to an orphanage or a neighboring needy family. In another display of her "down-home" approach to rural voters in Hinds County, at a Lutheran church raffle in which the minister's wife won a ham and Lucy won a sack of flour, candidate Howorth gave the flour to the minister's wife, saying that ham was no good without biscuits. She won cheers from the crowd, whose votes she thought would be in her column. She attributed the boxes she won in the county precincts, particularly in the southern tier of the county, to her carefully crafted appeal to voters.[45]

Still, Howorth campaigned vigorously in urban Jackson, where prominent citizens remembered Colonel Nugent. She had identified herself in her announcement for office as "the granddaughter of Col. W. L. Nugent, who fought with the Confederate troops in the defense of Jackson." She probably knew little of his many appearances in court, but older voters knew that he had argued before the state supreme court the unconstitutionality of the Mississippi Reconstruction legislature's civil rights measures. If Lucy held serious reservations about the conservative, even regressive, legalisms of her grandfather, she was not above using them for political gain.[46]

Joe, a favorite in Democratic party circles, was a decided asset in the campaign. One of Lucy's legendary tales was that he wore the brim off a new Panama straw hat by tipping it to women. Joe's brother Carl was a Millsaps alumnus, a former baseball player in the Cotton States League, and a Jackson realtor.[47] Popular and amiable, he was an asset as a campaigner with Jacksonians unlike those the Harley Shandses could influence, Bessie among the social crowd and Harley among his patients and colleagues in the medical profession. Dr. Shands reportedly was instrumental in Lucy's win in the pivotal box at Utica, where the vote was sizable.[48] The most influential among the women's organizations and women friends were the BPW and the AAUW. College graduates formed a small element; Lucy credited a Randolph-Macon alumna for her majority in the small town of Pocahontas.[49]

Lucy knew that the central labor council in Jackson opposed her because nonunion and black laborers had built the Howorth home. She met with the council's head to explain that Joe had not known whom their contractor employed. Surmising that her explanation was not convincing, she "doubled back" to unionized railroad employees and via Carl Howorth identified key leaders among them.[50]

The campaign was fatiguing; Howorth found the house-to-house canvass in Jackson's impoverished sections depressing. She met people "all beaten down," but she knew she must canvass voters from all socioeconomic levels not only because some could possibly be voters but also to hear the views of people in need. New York had made her sensitive to the poorest citizens. And from the standpoint of practical politics, she needed to combat the idea that she was of the "State Street socialite crowd," which her family, but not she, represented.[51]

Posey was a clear winner in the first primary, but Howorth was one of four candidates who vied in the second primary for the remaining two seats. Her principal challenger was Walter Capers, who had run second in the first primary. She herself had run third, but they both had to face the runoff election.[52] As the second primary neared, Lucy feared her support was slipping away. She was reluctant to seek an endorsement from the two leading Jackson newspapers, both extremely competitive and bitter rivals, for fear that support from either could alienate partisans of the other. In particular she avoided Fred Sullens, the mercurial editor of the *Jackson Daily News*. Two days before the election the crusty editor wrote her a personal letter that astonished her. In spite of her failure to show any interest in his vote, he and his wife would vote for her because of the "dearth of talent among the candidates!" Whatever his justification, Lucy was relieved to have his support.[53]

Throughout election night Lucy remained awake, uncertain of the outcome. As expected, Walter Capers won handily, but Howorth defeated the other two men in the runoff to gain the third Hinds County seat.[54] Thus, throughout the fall she prepared for the 1932 legislative session. Constituents who had supported her and those who had fought her hard began making contact to press their interests. She knew that not all women had supported her, among them Henrietta Mitchell, a former Mississippi Democratic committeewoman. Mitchell had held the post in the early 1920s, lost it to a rival, and then blamed Howorth for not supporting her. Howorth had not been involved in the scrap that cost Mitchell the post; she had not even been playing the game of politics at the time. Thus it surprised her that Mitchell was the first person who confronted her on the opening day of the legislative session with a bill that she wanted introduced. Mitchell was likely the subject of Howorth's account of a woman who had not voted for her but "now came around to give instructions" about what she should do in the legislature. When Howorth asked why the woman had not voted for her, she replied, "I was afraid I'd lose my vote." "The varmint," Howorth thought to herself, although she maintained her composure. It always disturbed her to hear people talk about "losing their vote": "You don't lose your vote if you vote for what you think is right. It may not win that time, but it may win maybe fifty years later. But, anyhow, you've done your duty, and you've done what in your judgment is right."[55]

While Lucy groomed for a legislative term to begin in January, Joe Howorth was active in organizing the Young Democrats in Mississippi for the presidential election in November. Neither Howorth knew the promise that election would hold.

Nellie Somerville, campaign photo, 1923.
Courtesy, Mississippi Department of Archives and History.

The Somerville children, circa 1898.
Left to right: Abe, Eleanor, and Robert. Lucy is standing in back.
Howorth Collection, Delta State University, unprocessed. Used by permission.

Marionettes, from the Ole Miss yearbook, 1921.

Florence Simms, 1923.
The Schlesinger Library, Radcliffe Institute, Harvard University. Used by permission.

Lucy, 1924.
Howorth Collection, Delta State University, unprocessed. Used by permission.

Joe and Lucy, 1938.
Howorth Collection, Delta State University, unprocessed. Used by permission.

Mary Agnes Brown, 1942.
The Schlesinger Library, Radcliffe Institute, Harvard University. Used by permission.

Lucy as Vice President of AAUW, 1952.
Howorth Collection, Delta State University, unprocessed. Used by permission.

Lucy, 1980s.
Howorth Collection, Delta State University, unprocessed. Used by permission.

Radcliffe honorees, 1983. Seated: Chien-Shiung Wu, Lucy Somerville Howorth. Standing, left to right: Eudora Welty, Dr. Mary Steichen Calderone, Jean Fairfax.
Howorth Collection, Delta State University, unprocessed. Used by permission.

5

"I have a few things to say"
The Mississippi Legislature, 1932–1934

LUCY HOWORTH'S premier standing with male classmates in her 1922 University of Mississippi law class and her status within the Mississippi Bar Association enhanced her authority as a member of the Mississippi House of Representatives. She was far from the stereotypical southern woman legislator who served as a surrogate for a deceased husband.[1] A comment in the *Literary Digest* in 1925 that "the widow in politics is becoming a somewhat familiar phrase" had nothing to do with Howorth.[2] To the contrary, her much alive and lively husband was her strongest supporter during her legislative tenure, just as he had been in her campaign.

Howorth's arrival at Mississippi's lower house was an occasion of note. Friends in the Jackson BPW placed roses on her desk on the opening day, and the national media noted that she and Nellie Nugent Somerville were the first mother and daughter in the nation to be elected to a state legislature.[3] She was one of three women in the 1932 body. The others were Madge Quin Fugler, a former suffrage leader, and Mildred Spurrier Topp, a Greenwood businesswoman. Both Fugler and Topp, like Howorth, served only one term.[4]

Howorth based her views on how women legislators should present themselves on her mother's caution to her own colleague, Ellen S. Woodward, in 1926 that they should not occupy adjacent seats nor appear as feminist allies. Howorth, Fugler, and Topp remained on cordial terms, but they pursued their own causes and did not vote as a clique on all measures. It was Howorth who most often went her own way in quietly establishing close ties with the power structure in the legislature, principally Speaker Thomas L. Bailey and the respected members Walter L. Sillers, chair of the powerful Rules Committee, who was from Howorth's native Delta, and Laurens Kennedy, of Natchez, chair of the Appropriations Committee. She determined at the outset that in order to maintain her own independence and integrity, she would not wear the governor's "label." She made friends among colleagues by assisting them in drafting legally sound measures, and she granted them access to secretarial assistance in her law office. The no-nonsense demeanor exhibited by the three women members and their businesslike brevity in addressing the House won them the respect of male colleagues. "Women [legislators] are not as inclined to prep and prank; they do not make long speeches; they are inclined to attend to business and get it behind them," Howorth once wrote. She recalled no animosity toward her nor any belittlement of her efforts. "We were certainly not pushed around," she said years later, and she pointed out that all three women served as committee chairs.[5]

The Mississippi legislature that convened in January 1932 faced almost insurmountable odds in trying to please disgruntled voters, whose confidence in their government was at low tide. In the 1931 election they returned only 31 of the 189 members of the previous legislature. The state, plain and simple, was dead broke. The administration of outgoing Governor Theodore G. Bilbo had left the state in shambles, with a treasury balance of $1,326 and debits of more than $50 million. State warrants and certificates, that is, IOUs, totaled at least $13 million.[6] As a bold and unprecedented remedy, the new, young governor, Mike Conner, proposed a sales tax, thus assuring a strong debate in both the state senate and the house. Consumers rebelled at the idea of the tax, although many of the state's citizens, whose low income dropped the state per capita average to $126, did not vote and could not likely do political damage to sales-tax proponents. Major opponents were Jackson and Hinds County merchants, backed by the city's two newspapers, who soon began steadily to beat editorial drums against the tax.

Howorth was subject to conflicting pressures. Her associates in the BPW appealed to her in tears to resist the tax. They had been warned by one of their employers, R. E. Kennington, owner of the large Jackson department store where Howorth most often shopped, that they would lose their jobs if the tax were enacted. Kennington expected a customer rebellion and silent cash registers. Like most of the state's retailers, he did not want to deal with the bothersome collection of the tax tokens. "Hinds County was just hot against it," Howorth recalled.[7] The influential editor of Jackson's *Clarion-Ledger* thundered that for Mississippi "Sherman's invasion was not more disastrous" than the sales tax. In the *Clarion-*

Ledger daily "honor roll" of legislators who opposed the tax Howorth's name was noticeably absent.[8]

House Speaker Bailey staunchly supported the tax, as did representatives of beleaguered public-school teachers, many of whom in 1932 were paid only by warrants. The state superintendent of education rallied four thousand teachers to protest cuts in school funding and to support a 3 percent sales tax.[9] The practical Howorth recognized that there was no option but to levy the tax to save the state's fiscal structure from unmitigated disaster and to support education, however poorly. In her thinking "the reestablishment of the credit of the state was the first and most important problem before the Legislature." Before the legislature even met, she had served on the Tax Committee of the Mississippi Bar Association, which recommended a sales tax.[10] Hence she had no qualms about voting for the tax throughout its checkered path toward final passage. Late in February 1932, when Jackson citizens assembled in a mass public meeting to steer their representatives toward opposition, Howorth was alone among the three Hinds County delegations in her unequivocal support of the tax. She did not attend a second protest because she had already made her position clear. To cast one of her votes for the tax, she left home with influenza, waited in Speaker Bailey's office until the roll call reached her name, and returned home immediately afterward.[11] By a change of one vote, the emergency-revenue measure became law in April 1932, making Mississippi the first state in the nation to enact a general sales tax.[12]

As Bailey organized the legislature, he intended to name each of the three women members a committee chairperson. He appeared dismayed that Howorth chose to chair the Public Lands Committee. When he informed her that it had not met at all in the preceding session, she retorted, "That's all right, it'll meet this time." Under Howorth the committee became one of the most active in the session and produced significant legislation. Working with the state forester, it created a state parks system and authorized the federal government to create national parks and forests within the state. Howorth later boasted, "I wrote most of those laws." In addition, the committee reorganized the Public Lands Office, enabling it to handle the volume of land the state gained through delinquent taxes.[13] Howorth "scored a notable victory," according to the *Clarion-Ledger,* when she called up a bill from the Public Lands Committee that created a state mineral board, the Mineral Lease Commission, to control drilling for gas and oil on state-owned land. The measure passed without dissent.[14]

In 1928 Bailey had suggested that a committee on conservation be created, and he saw to it in 1932 that Howorth became a member. The appointment complemented that of her position as chair of Public Lands. Howorth customarily dismissed requests that she become the secretary of groups dominated by men, but she welcomed the opportunity to be secretary of the Conservation Committee. She knew that the office conferred upon the secretary the post of ranking member in the absence of the chairperson. She made the most of the position as its public voice and floor manager on several occasions.[15] Impressed by what other states had done to preserve forest lands and wildlife, Governor Conner in his inaugural address in 1932 called for the creation of a game and fish commission. Howorth joined sixteen other House members in cosponsoring H.B. 116 to establish the commission. The bill drew widespread support for its potential to create jobs, provide recreational areas, and pay for its functions through licenses and fees. The measure passed the House by a vote of 79 to 51; Senate concurrence followed.[16]

Howorth offered an amendment to the bill that individuals be permitted to grow and sell game, including fish, taken on their own property. "I thought our minds should be on creating business, an opportunity for people to make money to stop starving," she said years later. Subjected to ridicule by some legislators who questioned, "Who's going to grow fish?" she insisted on her amendment and won what reporters described as her "first floor skirmish."[17] Although it was long in coming, she lived to see her native Delta become the capital of the nation's catfish industry.

Early in the 1932 session a *Jackson Daily News* writer observed that "women members . . . have served notice they are to be reckoned with." The comment came after Howorth and Fugler introduced a bill requiring that voters present poll-tax receipts for the preceding and current years in order to vote. At a time when the transient population was increasing, the measure allegedly aimed to prevent fraudulent voting by voters who had not lived in the state for two years as required by the state constitution. When Howorth called up the Senate's companion bill in the closing days of the session, the House accepted it by a vote of 108 to 7.[18] Which of the two women originated the restriction does not appear in the record. Fugler, president of the McComb League of Women Voters from 1922 to

1926, viewed the measure as a means of "cleaning up" elections. In none of her oral interviews or written memoranda did Howorth mention her actions in 1932 regarding the poll tax. There is no way of knowing who influenced her or what motivated her to strengthen a measure that from the beginning was designed to prevent voting by blacks and poor whites.[19]

When Mildred Topp's bill repealing the prohibition of the teaching of evolution in Mississippi schools fell by the wayside, Howorth lost an opportunity to enter a debate she surely would have enjoyed. Similarly, an adverse committee report ended further action on a bill aimed at removing the disqualification of women for jury service. Inaction by the University and Colleges Committee on a bill to prohibit coeducation at Mississippi State College choked debate on that proposal and thus foiled another good fight Howorth would have relished.[20]

Howorth always enjoyed tackling issues relating to governmental structure. She and Hooker Coen, of Copiah County, devoted long hours to the reapportionment of Mississippi's congressional districts mandated by the 1930 census. Their bill, based upon an equitable division of the population into eight districts, ran counter to many entrenched interests; consequently, the Committee on Census and Apportionment dismissed it in favor of a scheme that Howorth opposed and that Conner permitted to become law without his signature.[21]

A move toward assembling a constitutional convention to replace the state's 1890 document, which was woefully inadequate for the exigencies of 1932, drew Howorth into another attempt to modernize Mississippi's government. Her work on the Mississippi Bar Association's Economic Survey made her appointment to a House-Senate Joint Committee on the Reorganization of State Government a natural outcome. Committee members concluded that constitutional revision was imperative, and to that end Howorth and six colleagues introduced a bill calling for a convention; inaction by the Constitution Committee blocked any House consideration in the 1932 session, and the matter carried over into the 1934 session, by which time Howorth had changed her mind.[22]

Virtually no social issues came before the 1932 legislature. Those that did, including a bill Howorth offered on behalf of the Mississippi Federation of Women's Clubs and the Mississippi Art Association, were soon dismissed. Howorth knew that her measure to require the teaching of art in the public schools would be reported unfavorably by the Education Committee, but she managed not to lose face with the women who had lobbied the bill. She needed to regain the favor she had lost by her support of the sales tax. "You know, it's a hardball game," she recalled, "and those women, I wanted to please them." She said that "Mr. and Mrs. Average Citizen" viewed a session of the legislature as "a cross between a comic opera and an attack of the hives," and so she sought to maintain a middle course between supporting legislation that was practical and feasible and supporting legislation that was mere grandstanding.[23] If circumstances warranted it, however, she could play the game either way.

Howorth supported creation of staggered terms for the board of trustees of the state's institutions of higher education to rectify the loss of regional accreditation of the state's universities resulting from former governor Bilbo's usurpation of power over the schools. Despite her obvious disagreements with "The Man," she had managed to avoid alienating him. In 1930, when his administration had authorized the creation of a Research Commission to launch a study of the fiscal and governmental structure of the state, Bilbo had refused to appoint Blanche Montgomery Ralston, president of the Mississippi federated women's clubs, and an outspoken Bilbo critic. With Bilbo's blessing, Howorth, as legislative chair of the Jackson BPW, became one of the three women members of the Research Commission. The appointment resulted in contacts and polite correspondence with Bilbo, but Howorth took pains to leave for the record a statement that she "never voted for, supported or in any other way did anything to help Mr. Bilbo. . . . He is one of the worst things that ever happened to the State of Mississippi." She compared him to a porcupine, saying that he "would sting anyone who came near."[24]

The Research Commission met only four times; its major decision was to engage the Brookings Institution, of Washington, DC, to conduct an extensive study of the state's functions. The Brookings team produced a detailed blueprint of some two thousand pages. When Governor Conner requested that the 1932 legislature order a printing of the Brookings report, he easily won House consent, but Howorth personally placed little value in the merits of the plan. She was disappointed that the vast effort devoted to the study had resulted in a report that replicated recommendations made by the Brookings team to a number of other states that had called for similar studies, and as of late 1933 she could attribute no change to the commission report and did not see its application to Mississippi's particular needs. Of the report she said, "It was a nice fat book. Nobody read it."[25]

Service on the Research Commission had one positive outcome for Howorth; it placed her in the company of Ellen S. Woodward, executive director of the quasi-public Mississippi State Board of Development. Howorth's suggestion that Woodward be named secretary of the Research Commission solidified a friendship that lasted for forty years, until Woodward's death in 1971. Woodward had been a neighbor in Greenville in 1920–22, when her husband was Greenville's city attorney. In law school at the time, Howorth had only known of Ellen Woodward, who was eight years older, as her mother's protégée in the Civic Improvement Club and as her legislative colleague. It was not until their associations in Jackson that they became fast friends.[26]

The legislative session ended on 18 May; the second longest in history to that time, it was described as one of the most "colorful" on record.[27] Even before adjournment, the legislators were absorbed in the politics attendant to the approaching state Democratic convention and the national convention in Chicago in June. Howorth needed to devote considerable time after adjournment to stacked files in the firm of Howorth and Howorth, but she knew that the political stakes were too high for her to remain uninvolved in the electoral process. First, Hinds County Democrats selected her as a delegate to the state convention. Second, she knew that both Madge Fugler and Mildred Topp were to be alternates-at-large at the Chicago convention. With no intentions of being overlooked, Howorth wrangled an alternate's slot for herself from the incoming Mississippi national committeeman, Louis Jiggets. Her friendship with Ellen Woodward, Mississippi's new Democratic committeewoman, was an advantage for Howorth in the Windy City. As an alternate, Howorth voted in place of absent delegates and steadily supported Roosevelt's run for the nomination, as did both Mississippi senators, Pat Harrison and Hubert D. Stephens. One reporter noted that she was "full of confidence that women, after all, have earned their place in politics" and was out to carve a place herself.[28] As president of the Young Democrats in Mississippi, Joe had some visibility at the Chicago convention. Just what personal advantage they hoped would result from an active role in Democratic politics was not a matter either articulated, at least in public.

Less than a month after the convention ended, Senator Pat Harrison wrote Lucy Howorth a glowing tribute for her "fine friendship and loyalty" and "steadfastness" in Chicago. Soon James F. Farley, Democratic presidential nominee Franklin D. Roosevelt's campaign manager, contacted her. "You are so well organized and doing such splendid work in Jackson and elsewhere," wrote one of Farley's staff. Even candidate Roosevelt was writing Howorth: "You know how much I appreciate your services in 'notifying' me and how much I shall continue to appreciate your loyal support during the coming weeks."[29]

In October Mary W. "Molly" Dewson, head of the Women's Division of the Democratic Party, enlisted Howorth in her campaign to win over women "on the fence" and even Republican women. Dewson considered the appeal to women of the Republican candidate, Herbert Hoover, "flagrant and cunning." Howorth distributed Rainbow fliers, the Democratic promotional leaflets that were the hallmark of the women's campaign, served as chair of the Democratic speakers' bureau in Mississippi, and made three broadcasts in early November on the Jackson station WJDX. She made certain that Molly Dewson knew her name and recognized her work for Roosevelt. Dewson remembered that she had met Howorth in the company of Nellie Nugent Somerville at the national convention of the National American Woman Suffrage Association in Washington in 1915, but it seems that Howorth had not conversed with Molly in Chicago. "I made no effort while in Chicago to see you, because your time was needed elsewhere," Howorth wrote. She reminded Dewson that they had met again in New York in 1919, when Howorth was the "youngest and therefore a less important member" of the YWCA industrial staff. Howorth used her widespread associations with women's organizations to urge their participation in the campaign. She appealed to Mississippi BPW members through their club bulletin to "rise to their responsibility and opportunity" to effect "the power that comes with organized effort."[30]

Howorth and Dewson's correspondence was even livelier after the Democratic victory in November as women scrambled for the federal jobs that seemed promising under the new administration. Dewson's role in placing women in the new administration was already a matter of public knowledge. Her initials, M.W., the journalist Bess Furman joked, stood for "More Women." Howorth's letter to Dewson two weeks after the election left no doubt that her strategy was to make herself useful to Dewson and perhaps eventually land a job for herself or for Joe. She urged that women's aspects of the party apparatus be "promoted and encouraged" and that national committeewomen have a voice in patronage if they were to maintain an "efficient organization." Her strong ties to Ellen Woodward could only mean that Howorth would hold an advantage should committeewomen be given a role in patronage. In complying with a request from Woodward, who held high hopes herself for presidential favor, Howorth contacted the new president-elect early in 1933 to endorse Wyoming Governor Nellie Tayloe Ross for a cabinet post.[31]

Dewson was especially anxious for Howorth to organize Democratic women at the county level in Mississippi to study and support the plans of the party. Dewson concluded that in the overwhelmingly Democratic South, women were "almost as conservative as the unawakened Republican strongholds in Vermont, New Hampshire and Maine." She thought it "a forlorn hope" that the Mississippi Federation of Women's Clubs would "study and do active work in connection with economic matters" and advised Howorth not to "bother too much with the business and professional women" because most of such women she knew "have taken a most restricted view of economic matters." Doubting that federated women could be politicized, Dewson advised Howorth to engage organized Democrats in a study of government.[32]

Howorth had greater personal interest in what possibilities existed for Joe in the new era. She inquired of Senator Harrison and Will Whittington, a congressman from her Delta district, about a post as an assistant U.S. district attorney. But, she added, "I feel Gov. Roosevelt is interested in appointing some women." Thus, she thought it likely that she would be given preference over her husband, although she demurred, "I prefer him to have the place."[33] What she did not know was that both Senators Harrison and Stephens, in answering queries by the Federal Bureau of Investigation (FBI), had advised that Howorth was a better candidate for employment than was Joe. Harrison held the opinion that she had "considerable more sense than her husband," while Stephens termed her "a very brilliant woman" and said that compared with Joe, she was "far superior in intelligence and ability" and "very aggressive." In the opinion of the senators she was a stronger office lawyer than she was a trial lawyer, but then she had never preferred trial law.[34]

The job quest continued, with overtures for Howorth from James B. Frazier, the father of Howorth's sister-in-law and a former U.S. senator and

Tennessee governor, to his fellow Tennessean Cordell Hull, already slated to be Roosevelt's secretary of state. To be sure, Howorth was angling for a federal job in either Washington or Mississippi.[35] She was more aggressive than Molly Dewson thought she was. Dewson mistakenly believed Howorth was somewhat self-effacing, as she found many women seeking jobs to be, particularly after Howorth wrote that she preferred a less important job in Mississippi, where she could maintain her "connections," to one based in Washington.[36] In all probability Dewson did not know that Howorth had already written Senator Harrison in February 1933 of her decision to apply for a place as an attorney in the office of the U.S. attorney general or in the Internal Revenue Division of the Treasury Department. The senator replied that he "went up to the Justice Department . . . and am urging them to find something for you," apparently without results.[37]

Senator Harrison's job canvass for Howorth continued throughout 1933 as he contacted General Frank Hines, of the Veterans Administration (VA), while Howorth sent her credentials to U.S. Attorney General Homer Cummings. Dewson continued to concentrate on placing scores of women in administrative jobs, and she wrote Howorth of her contact with General Hines, although she feared that a spot on the VA Board of Appeals was "far too good to be given to a mere woman."[38] Harrison and Dewson's most notable success was Woodward's appointment as director of women's relief work in the new Federal Emergency Relief Administration. When FERA chief Harry L. Hopkins flew into Jackson in August 1933 to make the official announcement, Howorth arranged for a group of Woodward's friends to accompany her to the airport.[39]

Meanwhile, Howorth still had obligations to her Hinds County constituents, which she took very seriously. The second session of the legislature convened on 2 January 1934, and Howorth was as energetic in that three-month session as she had been in 1932. She played a prominent role in several significant legislative moves. Early in the session she voted against a measure by which the House legalized the sale of 4 percent beer and light wines. She had, after all, enjoyed support in her 1931 election from the WCTU and other prohibition stalwarts, and in the 1920s she had written pamphlets on prohibition enforcement for the WCTU. Nellie Somerville, an old warhorse for temperance, was in Jackson to witness the first successful assault against the state's prohibition law.[40] The retreat from a quarter-century of bone-dry prohibition began when Conner signed a bill in February calling for local option by county voters. When the House voted in late March for the statewide referendum on county-controlled liquor stores under state supervision, Howorth voted nay, although she did not speak on the bill that drew affirmative votes from both Topp and Fugler.[41]

Lifting strictures against the sale of alcoholic beverages was, at base, a vain effort to raise revenue when the state was laid low. Howorth took the lead in a number of moves to alleviate Depression conditions and bring more relief work assistance to unemployed Mississippians. As chair of the Public Lands Committee, she called up a bill authorizing county supervisors to allocate land for state parks and reforestation. Passage made possible the establishment of five to ten additional Civilian Conservation Corps facilities.[42]

Howorth had learned much through her law practice about the developing gas and oil industry in Hinds County and elsewhere in Mississippi. As noted earlier, during the first session in 1932 her Public Lands Committee had driven to passage a measure that created the Mineral Lease Commission. (Longevity permitted her to see the Mineral Lease Commission assume responsibility for the mineral rights on state property, particularly offshore deposits. In 1978 it was merged with other agencies into the Department of Natural Resources, and in 1989 reorganization placed its original functions in the new Department of Environmental Quality.) In 1934, during House debate on a bill to authorize the commission to drill on state property, Howorth sensed that she was under personal attack by a colleague who was attempting to shut off the debate. "You sit down. I have the floor, and I have a few things to say," she retorted in the only time during her House term that she was known to raise her voice in anger. Observers reported that she was heard all across the capitol rotunda and in the senate chamber. At least one person confronted her about her encounter with the colleague. After a woman stopped Howorth on a Jackson street and said, "I didn't know you had it in you. You don't look like much," Howorth decided that "laying low, not 'looking like much' and then pouncing on the blind side of the opposition" ought to be "one of her main methods" in achieving her goals. Henceforth, standing five feet tall and weighing approximately 120 pounds, she made the most of her short stature and unimposing appearance as a surprise factor that disarmed potential opposition.⁴³ Despite Howorth's success in the House with her measure to extend a grant of new powers to the Mineral Lease Commission, the Senate killed the measure. Still, her work on the Public Lands Committee had been so vigorous that her champion, House Speaker Bailey, wrote of her efforts as "worthy of the best traditions of Mississippi legislative history."⁴⁴

Howorth played a significant role in the passage of another Depression-related measure, one designed to lessen the hardships that befell families who lost their property to foreclosure. She submitted a bill, based upon a Minnesota law, that permitted property owners to apply to a chancery court to postpone foreclosure. Bailey, in a move to foster a moratorium, referred the measure to Howorth's own Public Lands Committee rather than to the Judiciary Committee, which he feared would kill it. The powerful Walter Sillers pronounced the bill "perfectly fair," and it passed the House by a vote of 87 to 40. Howorth was adamant that property owners needed relief from their creditors even though banks, loan companies, and insurance firms were among the clients of her law firm. She got her bill passed by the Senate by permitting the chair of the Judiciary Committee to claim authorship of the measure, and the governor signed the bill. Enactment of her measure brought immense satisfaction to Howorth, who recalled that it "was like a flying trapeze getting that through."⁴⁵

Howorth bore no personal animosity toward Governor Conner during her legislative term. She described him as "able," the "smartest man around," but also extremely "egotistical." Despite her service in 1928 on a Mississippi Bar Commission on the Study of State Government and her recognition that the state constitution was badly outmoded, she resisted the governor's request that the legislature call a constitutional convention to draft a new document. She believed the governor was motivated by a desire to make possible successive gubernatorial terms not permitted under the 1890 constitution. As a member of the legislative Joint Constitutional Committee, she based her opposition on the grounds that conditions in the state were "too upset and disorganized [and] unbalanced." Moreover, her Hinds County constituency was "dead set" against tampering with the constitution. Howorth's argument probably had little effect on the legislature's decision not to propose a new constitution. Stronger opposition came from entrenched courthouse rings and "drys" who feared the repeal of prohibition.⁴⁶

Historic preservationists within the state's women's clubs backed efforts of the Mississippi congressional delegation to get President Roosevelt and Congress to authorize a survey for eventual construction of a Natchez Trace Parkway along the roadbed of an antebellum trail from Natchez to Nashville. From January to August 1934 Howorth served on the executive board of the Natchez Trace Military Highway Association. The board met in Jackson sporadically, and members were assigned clusters of counties in which to promote the parkway's development. Howorth, who had little time for such work, wrote a Delta friend, "I am not keeping house and the Legislature and other things have me on the run."[47]

Howorth used her legislative prerogatives to tout the work of other women's organizations whose agenda her mother had also attempted to legislate into social reform. During 1934 she escorted to the podium the national executive secretary of the YWCA, who spoke on her organization's "good work" in the state, and Howorth also introduced to the House her close friend Martha Catching Enochs, state president of the YWCA. More important, she was responsible for the appearance in Jackson in 1934 of Lucy Randolph Mason, of the National Consumers' League, who came to lobby the legislature to ratify the Child Labor Amendment, proposed by Congress in 1927.[48]

In 1933, the legislative off year, Howorth wrote to the National Child Labor Committee to request promotional literature for reviving interest in a national Child Labor Amendment. In 1927 an earlier amendment had failed to achieve ratification when the requisite number of states voted against it, but advocates hoped that another strong push would bring victory in 1934. Ratification by the Mississippi legislature was not likely, for there was stiff opposition in the judiciary committees of both houses. Molly Dewson wrote Howorth in January 1934 of her deep disappointment that the House had so far failed to ratify the amendment. Remembering Nellie Somerville's hard fight for suffrage, Dewson declared that "we need a leader like her to stop the exploitation of children." She apparently did not know that Somerville had turned against the amendment because she feared the loss of state control over the terms under which child labor would be banned.[49] Howorth sidestepped Dewson's idea to enlist Nellie by responding that her mother was past seventy years of age and that although she was still "alert and adroit as ever, I try to keep her out of heated contests."[50]

Prior to Lucy Randolph Mason's visit, Ellen Woodward contacted Mississippi legislators to ask that they give considerate attention to Mason; at the same time, she told Dewson that Howorth, whose influence with Conner both counted on to win his support for ratification, had "not been voting with the Governor on a number of measures."[51] The Mississippi Senate passed the amendment in early March, but it faced "hard sailing" in the House, where a majority of the Committee on the Constitution were irrevocably against it. Howorth attributed the intense opposition among legislators to their fear that ratification would prompt Congress to pass a law "so that negro families can no longer be used in making a crop."[52]

Howorth and Sidney Roebuck, of the House Constitution Committee, brought out a minority report favoring the amendment that went nowhere. Howorth explained to Dewson that the staunch opposition was due to "the promiscuous spreading of prejudicial and foolish suggestions as to what Congress might do." Because ratification faced a certain defeat if voted upon, Lucy Randolph Mason advised its proponents to let it die on the calendar. Thus the Child Labor Amendment was dead in Mississippi. Apprised of this by Howorth, Molly Dewson acquiesced but hoped that Howorth and Woodward "could make men uncomfortable in the primaries."[53] After the legislature adjourned on 4 April, Dewson asked Howorth, "What is the matter with the women of Mississippi that they cannot get for themselves and mothers all over the country the ratification of the Child Labor Amendment?" Howorth expressed her regret at the failure, which she blamed on the "general lack of interest in public affairs accompanied by the Depression."[54]

Adjournment in April 1934 marked virtually the end of Lucy Howorth's legislative service, although the term would not officially end until January 1936. She had thoroughly enjoyed her one term, during which she had made a mark among a powerful group of legislators, with whom she had stood her ground and made of herself an equal. On at least one occasion she had even gotten the best of the powerhouse Walter Sillers when she enlisted older, more experienced lawmakers to thwart the speaker's attempt to promulgate a rule that his Rules Committee could set the House calendar and determine bills to be placed upon it. He did not gain the power until Howorth was no longer in the legislature. She had stayed "as busy as a switch engine" and was justifiably proud that House Speaker Tom Bailey had given her his gavel so that she could preside over the House for a full week.[55]

Howorth later remarked, "I am a born parliamentarian. . . . I was brought up at meetings where my mother was presiding." Years of experience convinced her that a knowledge of parliamentary law was a key to advancement within organizations: "I've seen so many young women join a club, learn to speak, learn a little parliamentary law, and become an effective force." Of the three functions of government, legislative, executive, and judicial, in which she had served by the time she retired in the late 1950s, she described the first as the one that was "really fun." "It gives an opportunity to maneuver, to persuade, to study people, and to get a sense of accomplishment." There is no doubt that she enjoyed the way she could manipulate the Senate to debate and deliver her House-initiated bills by her delay in calling her own committees into session to deliberate measures that the Senate wanted to have passed. She learned early how to play the game, and she played it well, but she knew that winners used more than their wiles. "You can't take a club and make somebody do something—you have to push and tug and try to change hearts and minds."[56]

Even as Howorth began her second legislative term in January 1934, the ploys continued to land a job for her with the VA, although Molly Dewson was also approaching officers of the Federal Home Loan Bank. "Do not think for a minute that I have forgotten about you," she assured Howorth. Pat Harrison continued his efforts to place her on the Veterans Board of Appeals but asked her to "say nothing about it, as there are plenty of other Mississippians who are on my back for assignment to that Board."[57] Although surely unknown to Howorth, Roosevelt in January 1934 discussed with Missy LeHand, his personal secretary, his decision to include women among the new members slated for the VA Board of Appeals. Dewson, who was present at the exchange, reminded LeHand that the names of specific women had been recommended, among them lawyers, including Mrs. Joseph M. Howorth. Finally, on 7 March Dewson wrote Howorth that she was "delighted beyond measure" to notify her of her placement on the VA Board of Appeals at an annual salary of fifty-six hundred dollars. Two other women would also be placed on the board: Mrs. Carroll Lee Stewart, of California, and Mrs. Thornton Lee (Laura) Brown, of Missouri. Dewson attributed her success to having won over General Frank Hines, whose opposition to women board members she was convinced had been the roadblock in the delay. "I had to fight for it like a bag of cats," she wrote Howorth.[58]

Howorth received notification also from both Mississippi senators and understood that the matter was confidential until General Hines informed her officially. But Dewson's victory boast to Howorth was premature. To Howorth's dismay, by the end of March the appointment of additional members to the appeals board lay in suspension because of amendments attached by Congress to an economy bill, but at least Dewson was encouraged that Hines was "rather inclined" to accept the "new departure" of including women on the board.[59] Acting on Dewson's advice, Howorth approached the Home Owners' Loan Corporation, and shortly later Dewson recommended that she apply to the National Recovery Administration, although "dealing with manufacturers who are pretty hard-boiled [would be] a difficult position for a woman." At that point Howorth wrote Dewson that she did not wish to be "a nuisance" or "flood" offices with "a raft of endorsements," nor did she want to "hang around Washington."[60] By June Howorth was reconciled to dismissing the so-called appointment to the VA as "another one of life's funny experiences," and so she began to explore the rumor that Harry Blair, assistant attorney general, had expressed a need for attorneys.[61]

But in another month an appointment for a six-month term on the VA Board of Appeals came through, an opportunity Howorth was convinced she should accept. Nellie may have influenced her, writing to a friend, "She thought best to accept as the salary is fine and it would give her prestige even if she does not stay more than six months."[62] Although Howorth went to Washington and took up residence at the Hotel Roosevelt, she did not resign from the legislature. Since it met biennially, there would be no session in 1935 and thus Howorth could accept the temporary appointment. She took for granted that her legislative work had ended, although she did not comment on what obligations she might still have toward her constituents. At least that was her conviction, although her brother-in-law Audley Shands advised her that acceptance of the post in Washington was tantamount to resignation from her seat in the House. Yet he added, "I think I would sit and say nothing."[63] As late as September 1935, after Howorth had resided for fourteen months in Washington, Mississippi Attorney General Greek Rice remained in contact with her regarding legislative matters even though there was no regular session that year.[64] Howorth did not attend a short special session of the legislature in the fall of 1935, although she obtained a "pair" for a crucial vote on a highway bill.[65] Howorth took pains to have Rice place on record her return of the salary requisitions she automatically received. He replied that the "Newspaper boys" to whom he showed her letter said that this action on her part was "just what they expected of you." Other absent legislators had accepted their pay.[66]

Earlier, in late April 1935, Howorth had announced that she would not be a candidate for reelection in the summer race for the next legislature.[67] She had learned that the additional new positions for members of the VA Board of Appeals had been made permanent, but only time would tell whether the new women appointees would be able to retain those positions at the end of the six-month assignment. Howorth anticipated the work and hubbub as a New Deal appointee. "What change and excitement," Augusta Marshall wrote. "You'll love being in the thick of it." "As you say," her old friend added when the six-month assignment neared an end, "[it is] a sort of juggling merry-go-round and certainly no place to put your faith in."[68] But, as time would tell, Howorth remained in Washington and threw herself into new ventures not only in government work but also among a new group of Washington-based women enmeshed in public affairs and determined to advance women's place in government.

6

A Watchdog for Women, 1935–1946

BEGINNING IN 1933 Congress ruled that the VA's civilian Board of Appeals would be appointed by the president rather than by the VA administrator, as it had been in the past. Numerous complaints and disability claims of veterans from earlier wars swamped the VA and prompted the decision to increase the board's membership to thirty, including the chair and the vice chair. Having three women on the board was unprecedented until 1934, and the practice of having women on the board was ended by the end of World War II. "The 3 women were always disliked, not personally, but because war was men's business," Lucy Howorth explained as she recalled her nine-year tenure ending in 1943.[1]

Women lawyers, however, were not alien to the Veterans Administration; the first was appointed in 1917. By 1934 Mary Agnes Brown, who became one of Howorth's closest friends, was among the women lawyers in the Washington office. Soon after Howorth's arrival in Washington, Brown and the other VA women attorneys welcomed the new Appeals Board members with a breakfast aboard the four-masted *Constellation*, tied up at the Potomac River bank. Howorth credited the placement of women on the Appeals Board to the work of those women lawyers in the VA.[2]

Howorth's official document of appointment directed the Board of Appeals to make final decisions on appeals of adverse decisions involving benefits under all laws administered by regional boards of the VA. The board members worked in groups of three, assigned on a rotating basis. Eventually, Howorth was designated as a section chair, a role enhanced by her legal expertise.[3] But initially, despite their qualifications, she and her two women associates met with neglect and indifference on the part of superiors who allocated cases for deliberation. Howorth became incensed, as did the other two women on the board. Neither of the other two had a legal education, but they were, in Molly Dewson's words, women of "balance and understanding." Mrs. Thornton Lee (Laura) Brown, of Missouri, had been a special representative of the Federal Deposit Insurance Corporation with jurisdiction over six states and had organized Democratic women's clubs in twenty-seven states. Mrs. Carroll Stewart, a widow of a Spanish-American War veteran, had known Franklin Roosevelt since he was in her state of California in 1920; she was serving on the Los Angeles Civil Service Commission when she left for Washington.[4]

Although the *Washington Post* bleated that the three women now sitting around "a man-sized table" had "blazed another pioneer trail," their table remained empty of work. "Nobody came near us," Howorth said about the first weeks of service. "We weren't dumb people, we'd been around." And so the women began to "cultivate" the staff while they remained "in that deep freeze." Finally, after three weeks the women sought a conference with the Board of Appeals chairperson, a former Virginia governor, John G. Pollard, who then assigned them to three different panels, where each would work with two men. When they learned that a new male member of the Board, P. D. Gold, of North Carolina, had received an unlimited appointment, whereas theirs was for only six months, Brown, Stewart, and Howorth requested a second conference with Pollard and came away with unlimited terms. Recalling those first weeks on the board, Howorth boasted, "We just used our heads and figured out how to beat the game."[5]

The work of the Board of Appeals, dealing as it did with affairs relating to veterans' financial resources, physical and mental disabilities, terms of service, and other private matters, has remained confidential to this day. Howorth never revealed any specifics on just what she did during the years on the board, nor were there ever any newspaper accounts of board decisions. Other than specific items in her letter of appointment, her official work on the board remains opaque. Her work did not put her in the limelight as did that of other administration women whose work could be discussed at Eleanor Roosevelt's press conference and other venues that boosted the New Deal.

While Howorth was touted as one of the "Women of the New Deal," she was not employed in a New Deal agency. Nor was she in a position to be an advocate for New Deal reforms as were other women among the Democratic coteries for officeholders. For example, Ellen Woodward in the Federal Emergency Relief Administration and the Works Progress Administration (WPA), Katharine Lenroot at the Children's Bureau, Nellie Tayloe Ross at the U.S. Mint, and Hilda Worthington Smith in the Workers' Service Programs of the FERA and the WPA were among the women expected to be effective spokespersons for New Deal programs. Howorth had no reason to count upon Eleanor Roosevelt to enlarge the authority of her office. Howorth's work with the VA Board of Appeals was of little or no interest to the First Lady, and their contacts were limited to social gatherings of women's professional organizations in Washington or at the Women's National Democratic Club (WNDC). Nonetheless, Howorth became well acquainted with the wide range of women drawn into the Roosevelt administration.

Howorth was, however, highly visible on the Washington scene as one of the new women in town under presidential appointment. Neither Brown nor Stewart was as extroverted as Howorth, nor were they as eager to know other women in New Deal circles and, more important, to be recognized by them. Many of the connections were social, and most involved some matter related to the advancement of women. Howorth had to curb her tongue on policy matters subject to congressional division and Republican criticism. Holding an executive position proscribed comment. Her job "had its disadvantages," she told Randolph-Macon students in 1935. "It's rather like taking the veil, for no matter how exciting the current scene, we make no comment." But then Howorth eschewed certain organizations and issues by choice. Like her mother, she never warmed to the League of Women Voters, although she had served for a short time in the Mississippi League in the early 1920s. "I didn't see much I admired," she said in 1983. "It has done a great many good things but its philosophy just wasn't my philosophy."[6] Her antipathy was due to the nonpartisanship of the League, which ran counter to the intense partisanship of the cadre of Democratic women in Washington, and the League position that members could not run for public office. She found the League to be "a studious, ladylike group that wouldn't really tangle."[7] Nor did she join or even speak of any of the peace movements that attracted many reformist women in the 1930s and 1940s.

Women in the New Deal network were not constrained, however, in their advocacy of greater participation of women in government. Soft-spoken yet forceful, imbued with southern charm, a quick wit, and a pleasing personality, Howorth won friends easily and soon made her mark. "I like your little Lucy Howorth," Molly Dewson wrote Ellen Woodward. "I knew I would."[8] Howorth was a standard figure at the clubhouse and at the gala functions of the WNDC, a fashionable structure on New Hampshire Avenue built in 1892. A dinner in April 1935 honoring the women of the New Deal was attended by all the luminaries, and Howorth was delighted that she was among them. She was right at home in Washington, thinking of herself rather like "Brer Rabbit in the briar patch," with many friends from college and New York in the city. In October the three women on the VA Board entertained the coterie of New Deal women at a lavish tea at the WNDC clubhouse for which Molly Dewson returned to Washington to attend. Other activities placed Howorth among prominent women in the city. She was among a dozen women, including Eleanor Roosevelt, Sue Shelton White, and Ellen Woodward, who took instruction from Elizabeth von Hess, who had come from New York to Washington to give lessons in speech improvement.[9]

It was politically safe for the women to discuss and debate public issues among themselves, and as a lawyer Howorth was often involved in debates staged by the WNDC Education Committee. For regional conferences of the Democratic Women's Division she was a prime target in Dewson's program planning. "[H]ave Lucy Howorth come down from Washington," Dewson once advised her assistant, May Thompson Evans. "[B]eing a lawyer she can work up [the] subject," which happened to be reciprocal trade treaties. But in the 1936 presidential race Dewson could not call upon Howorth. It made her "froth at the mouth . . . that we could not put you out as a speaker." Later that year Howorth had to decline Dewson's request that she help form a group in Mississippi to work toward a constitutional amendment to protect New Deal labor legislation. Howorth was not "free to act," she told Dewson.[10]

Lucy remained at the Hotel Roosevelt without Joe until he joined her in the summer of 1935. By then Joe had wound up the cases in Jackson for which the firm had responsibility. "So you've decided on Washington. I think you and Joe will have a wonderful time there," Augusta Marshall wrote. The couple made the Hotel Roosevelt their home for two years, then moved into the Kennedy-Warren complex, located on Connecticut Avenue at the edge of Rock Creek Park. Described as the "finest Art Deco apartment house ever built in the city," it was the handsome home to many New Deal newcomers, including Harry Hopkins, the relief "czar" of the

Roosevelt administration, and Congressman and Mrs. Lyndon B. Johnson. Its spacious public dining facilities relieved Howorth of the cooking she boasted she never did and presented a gracious aura when the Howorths entertained guests, although they engaged the Army-Navy Club "if they really wanted to put on the dog." "In Washington you have to entertain," Howorth said. They sometimes held parties at a studio that Joe rented after he began to paint.[11]

Washington was an exciting place to be in the 1930s, populated with a bevy of southerners, many of them professionals from Mississippi thanks to the influence of Senator Pat Harrison. The national newscaster David Brinkley later wrote that "the New Deal newcomers, with good reason, did not regard themselves as socialites."[12] Most drew modest incomes, but they had a good time after work hours. Joe was admitted to the Washington, DC, bar in 1936 and received a law degree from George Washington University in 1940. Still, the Howorths never missed a function of the Mississippi Society, which elected Joe president in time for all the elaborate arrangements for the throng of Mississippians who arrived by a special train for the Roosevelt inauguration in 1937. Howorth never talked much of her social life outside that among the coterie of New Deal women whose WNDC, BPW, and AAUW functions, dinner programs, and teas feting one another supplied society columns of the Washington press with steady copy and enough to fill Kathleen Sexton's chatty weekly column in the *Jackson Daily News*, "Mississippians at the Capital," which described an active life for the home-state migrants.

Howorth made permanent friends among many of Washington's Democratic women. She had known Sue Shelton White, of Tennessee, since the fight for woman suffrage and from the time the two had served together on a panel discussion titled "Women in Politics" at the 1933 BPW convention. White wrote to Howorth then, "You made quite a hit with me." They remained close friends and often entertained friends together with clever theme parties. Howorth enjoyed Sue's company and admired her many good qualities: "She could instill strength into a reed."[13] When Sue was job-hunting in 1935, Howorth pulled with other WNDC members to "make a definite drive [to find paid employment] for Sue." White, a former executive secretary of the Democratic Women's Division, lived with Florence Armstrong, another woman Howorth admired. Howorth and Armstrong became joint executors for White, and Howorth would make all the arrangements for White's funeral at her death from cancer in 1943. Armstrong, like Howorth, was a watchdog for women in government work and had experiences similar to Howorth's in dealing with male coworkers. Armstrong wrote of an able officeholder who "had had her troubles from some of the little boys who were not so competent."[14]

Howorth was close to Eudora Ramsey Richardson, head of the WPA's Virginia Federal Writers' Project and a frequent guest in Washington. They had many mutual interests, particularly the national BPW.[15] But, without a doubt, Howorth's closest woman friend was Ellen Woodward, her Mississippi ally in public affairs and an assistant administrator of the FERA in 1933 and, then, the WPA after 1935. They were often thrown together at public events and at the WNDC, but Howorth regretted that Ellen was too consumed by work to join her and Joe on their weekend getaways to Maryland and elsewhere. Howorth enjoyed hiking, golfing, and her pleasure trips. Woodward traveled widely, but always on work-relief business. It was through the Washington BPW and the WNDC that they had most of their mutual contacts. The two friends were extremely close until Woodward's loss of memory made it impossible to communicate sometime around 1964. Howorth recalled in her own late years that she had "admired and respected many women but I loved Ellen first among women." In 1941 both Howorths sought to have Millsaps College in Jackson confer an honorary degree upon Woodward, a move thwarted primarily because of an unnamed prominent Millsaps trustee's opposition to WPA programs in Mississippi.[16]

In 1939 and 1940 Howorth became acquainted with a number of women dignitaries in various enterprises to celebrate women's achievements. She was one of the initial sponsors and a director of the Washington committee for the World Center for Women's Archives, launched by the historian Mary Beard in 1939. When the archives evolved into the Arthur and Elizabeth Schlesinger Library at Radcliffe College, Howorth began depositing collections there relating to the woman suffrage movement in Mississippi.[17] Howorth's attendance as a representative of the YWCA at the Woman's Centennial Congress, convened in New York City in 1940 by the aging suffragist Carrie Chapman Catt, placed her in the company of women leaders from all walks of life. A number of women's organizations to which Howorth belonged, including the BPW, the YWCA, and the AAUW, sponsored the celebration of a century of women's progress in what was little more than a media event.[18]

Lucy Howorth was an inveterate joiner who seldom missed a convention. Recalling that she was three months old when her mother took her to a convention, Howorth confessed, "I have been a convention goer ever since." She enjoyed conventions because "you meet people who are surfacing as leaders." She was active in the Southern Society of Washington, the Washington Alpha Omicron Pi Alumnae, the Washington Women's City Club, the American Newspaper Women's Club, and the Mississippi Society. After a meeting of the Southern Society for which Lucy had made the arrangements, the president wrote to her, "Permit me to say that I have never had so many congratulatory messages about any meeting of the Society."[19] She joined the Soroptimist Club upon invitation in 1941 and served for a time on its Committee on International Understanding and Goodwill.[20] The international aspects of service clubs increasingly interested her.

Of all her organizational affiliations, the National Federation of Business and Professional Women's Clubs had the earliest appeal, although the AAUW would claim more of her time after 1943. Howorth had first become interested in the BPW when she met its founder, Lena Madesin Phillips, in New York in 1919. Since there was no BPW club in Cleveland or Greenville, Howorth did not become a member again until after her move to Jackson, where the BPW was one of the strongest in the federation. Howorth threw herself into its activities and attended the national convention in Chicago in 1933. In 1934 Howorth, described in the local newspaper as "identified with every progressive and worthwhile movement in Jackson," became president of the local club.[21]

Membership in the Washington BPW reunited her with Earlene White, and in 1936 White asked Howorth to manage her campaign for the national federation presidency. At the 1937 convention in Atlantic City Howorth assigned a Mississippi member to each state delegation to show strangers that "Mississippians were nice people [and] not barefoot morons." (Nellie Nugent Somerville shared her daughter's sensitivity to the perception some people had of Mississippi women. In 1938 she wrote Ellen Woodward, "You are living proof that Mississippi has as good brain power as New York which we know but they do not.") Howorth's tactics and the influence of Ellen Woodward, better known throughout the country than Howorth, succeeded, and White was elected. The 1937 convention was notable for its endorsement of the ERA, which had been bruited about since its first submission to Congress in 1923. Howorth joined the victory procession on the boardwalk immediately following adjournment of the session.[22]

White named Howorth the program coordinator in her "cabinet" and assigned her to several smaller tasks.[23] Most important, she asked her to represent the federation at the meeting of the International Federation of Business and Professional Women's Clubs (IFBPW) in Trondheim, Norway, in May 1939. The BPW office staff gave Howorth "quite a send-off" from New York City, and she made the most of opportunities to meet interesting people aboard ship. The assembly offered new opportunities for her to make friends, with whom she kept in touch for years. She wrote home to her mother that the European delegates "are particularly grateful for my praise or favorable comment on their own activities and you know I am always strong on that sort of thing." "Such journeys as this were among your youthful dreams," Augusta Marshall reminded her.[24]

The IFBPW's three-year objective, "More Women in Public Office," was in keeping with her own growing personal crusade to get women in office and her sense that a new approach was needed to educate girls and young women to have a "more courageous attitude toward work." She had the opportunity to meet the Swedish sociologist Alva Myrdal, who had supervised the federation's first paid research to gain authoritative evidence of women's abilities to advance. Myrdal's report offered proof that women's organizations had helped women attain elective or appointive office.[25] The convention ended with a successful reception that Howorth planned for Florence Harriman, the U.S. ambassador to Norway.[26]

Howorth's account made no mention of the absence of delegates from countries already threatened by German aggression and the talk at Trondheim of how women should serve their countries in the event of war. Lena Madesin Phillips's biographer has written of the "chill" in Norway that summer, where host federation members "donned masks to make their visitors feel at ease."[27] Howorth was alarmed enough by the talk of war and a potential gasoline shortage that in 1940 she and Joe left their Kennedy-Warren quarters and moved to the Pall Mall, an apartment building one block from the White House and within walking distance of her office at the VA.

Elected president of the Washington club before her trip abroad,

Howorth was installed the day after her return and then left to attend the national convention in Kansas City, where she joined with Sarah T. Hughes, president-elect of the Texas federation, in maneuvering election to the national presidency of Dr. Minnie Maffett, a Dallas physician. In a postconvention letter Louise Franklin Bache, on behalf of the BPW professional staff, praised Howorth for her "splendid leadership" at the convention in "this critical year," a convention Howorth deemed to be "one of the most important ever" and one that set a decade-long course of action. Molly Dewson wrote to Howorth of her satisfaction that a Democrat was elected BPW president; Dewson was pleased that "hard-boiled females" who "seem to forget the virtues of generosity and sympathy for the underprivileged" had not succeeded at Kansas City.[28] Howorth knew that Dewson was looking toward the 1940 presidential campaign, as she herself was, and she was relieved that BPW delegates appeared to be less conservative than Dewson had thought they were in 1932.

Although the printed proceedings of the 1939 convention give no indication of any discord, there had been an effort to turn back the clock on the BPW's earlier affirmation of the right of married women to work. The recession of 1937 had renewed attempts made by some states earlier in the decade to ban the employment of married women. Howorth and Margaret Hickey saw to it that the BPW launched a counterattack by proposing a federal constitutional amendment stating that no one should be barred from employment because of sex, race, or marital status. The convention adopted the amendment, drafted by Howorth and the BPW legislative chair, but nothing came of it after the onset of World War II opened the work force to married women. Also, early in the convention Howorth and others worked to replace an Iowa woman who, as vice president, was in line for the presidency. The Iowan's moves to "fight" the 1939–40 nationwide program alarmed the more progressive BPW leadership, who were unhappy about the opposition to the New Deal administration of conservative businesswomen, particularly their antipathy to the Social Security amendments of 1939.[29] It was this conservative bent that had earlier disturbed Molly Dewson.

Howorth continued as a member of the national board when Maffett appointed her chair of the Public Affairs Committee.[30] New duties thrust upon Howorth in the VA after the outbreak of World War II caused her to resign her committee post because she could not make visits to clubs, a function she considered vital to the promotion of her committee's work.[31] Other than confiding in Ellen Woodward, who agreed with her, she kept to herself her private view that Maffett had become too much of a "prima donna" and increasingly difficult to work with. Howorth became troubled by the "growing habit" of the national staff to handle matters in such a way that national chairs "are left with no opportunity to exercise their judgment." The issue came to a head when a member of the national staff drafted a report for her Public Affairs Committee, although Howorth had had no opportunity to read reports from state federations.[32]

Howorth began to think about "the comforts of a back seat" and chose not to attend the 1941 convention in Los Angeles. No convention was held in 1943 due to government strictures on wartime travel, but in 1944 in New York Howorth was again a campaign manager for a successful, no-contest election of a new president, Margaret Hickey, of Missouri. Hickey, who held a law degree from the law school of the University of Kansas City, was the owner and administrator of the successful Miss Hickey's School for Secretaries in St. Louis, which prepared women for employment as administrative secretaries and executives of small businesses. Hickey was a BPW leader who in time would fill a number of important advisory positions in wartime and postwar federal agencies.[33]

Hickey and Howorth were close professionally, especially as the former was drawn more and more into government circles, and they remained personal friends long into retirement. During World War II Hickey chaired the Women's Advisory Committee of the War Manpower Commission, and in 1945 she was in England on assignment for the commission to study postwar employment and reemployment of women. As Hickey's term as president of the BPW ended, admirers of Howorth tapped her as a candidate for the national office, but her own personal job status led her to decline the honor. An earlier bid to Howorth to seek the national presidency had come in 1940, when the Mississippi BPW sought to advance her candidacy, but she had declined then for the same reason she gave in 1946. She could not expect to receive official leave from the VA to perform a president's duties, and she could not jeopardize her career, which was at a turning point. To a supporter she wrote, "I should have to eat a good many of the things I have said about employees of the Government serving as National President, and this would be indigestible for one of my makeup."[34]

The 1946 convention at Cleveland, Ohio, was a subdued event for Howorth because it took place immediately after funeral services for her brother, Robert, who had died suddenly from a heart attack while attending a meeting in Jackson, Mississippi. Furthermore, at the same time she was rising to leadership in the AAUW, one of whose officers, Gillie A. Larew, that year described her as "a subject of wonder and admiration" possessing "almost super-human powers."[35]

Howorth remained dedicated to the BPW even though her years as a national official were ending. Goals refined at the New York convention in 1944—consolidation of women's gains in wartime work and office places, greater emphasis on equal pay for equal work, and the election and appointment of qualified women for public offices—were all vitally important to her.[36] Her most active years in the BPW, in the 1930s and 1940s, "were important to American women," she concluded. "Without the National Federation of Business and Professional Women, they might have been devastating."[37]

Aside from the BPW's strong advocacy of professional and business women's interests, Howorth admired its egalitarianism. She held "great respect and affection" for the BPW. "The lowliest clerk and the owner of a business stand on an absolute equality," she wrote in a long reflection on the organization. She valued the associations with working women that she had through the federation. "Your friendship has meant so much to me," a Washington, DC, member wrote to Howorth upon completing a year as local president.[38] She was only one of the young women rising in their profession who looked to Howorth and her BPW friends for encouragement.

Marguerite Rawalt, later a national president, who joined the BPW in 1944, remembered that Lucy Howorth and Ellen Woodward "were always pointed out" to her as women leaders. Active in her own bar and women's lawyer affiliations, Rawalt wanted to know women in government positions. Howorth won Rawalt's affection also for the support Howorth gave her in her election as third vice president of the Federal Bar Association. Rawalt knew that Howorth, whose position in government carried weight with "all the men she worked with," had said about Rawalt, "We ought to have one woman [FBA officer] . . . and she's a good one." Rawalt had been present when Howorth had broken a barrier in 1934 as the first woman to address the Federal Bar Association.[39]

While Howorth's interest in the BPW did not waver, in 1943 she had to devote herself to a personal challenge, as a consequence of which she joined a broad crusade to seek and protect jobs for women in the federal government. In 1943 new policy decreed that only veterans could serve on the Board of Appeals, thereby reducing the number of board members. It seemed to Carroll Stewart that the "line of least resistance was [to decree] the 'military preference'" for removing women members. In Howorth's opinion, it was a "policy reduction in force," and she was "riffed," as were the other two women on the board, along with the one man who was a nonveteran. Laura Brown chose the retirement for which she was eligible. Carroll Stewart, who was given a position in a California veterans' office, wrote later to Howorth that it was unfortunate that they had "encountered" R. L. Jarnigan, chairman of the Board of Appeals, for "he had no toleration for women." In ousting the nonveterans, Jarnigan prevailed over VA administrator Frank Hines, who had given Howorth high marks. The one man affected by the ruling moved to another position in the VA, as did Howorth. She became an attorney in the Office of the Solicitor of the VA.[40]

Howorth performed legal work related to veterans' legislation and served as a member of the Fair Employment Hearing Board. Between 1943 and 1949 the VA legislative office dealt with increased compensation of veterans relative to the cost of living, problems deriving from demobilization, housing, hospitalization, and oversight of the GI Bill of 1944. By the time Howorth left that position for a more attractive one in 1949, her salary had reached $7,900. While she had protested the removal of nonveterans from the VA Board of Appeals in 1943, she had made the most of her dismissal, and while the work in her new position was heavier, she was appreciative that she had been given "shelter in time of storm."[41]

Howorth's work in veterans' affairs directed her energies toward the role of women in the military. She was galvanized to action in 1943 when Joe, then an army captain working at the Pentagon, handed her a publication and quipped, "Here is something to get your blood pressure up." It was a Civil Service Commission booklet entitled *Operations Manual for Placement of Women and the Physically Handicapped.* Determined to get it "killed," she immediately arranged a meeting with Sarah Hughes, of Texas, who was in Washington to chair a meeting of the AAUW Committee on the Economic and Legal Status of Women (CELSW). Kathryn

McHale, the AAUW general director, wrote the Civil Service Commission that the brochure would be "laughable were it not deplorable in the attitude which it conveys toward women in American life." The committee took quick action that led to removal of the offending publication. The incident, Howorth later said, "marked a shift in my own organizational activities," and she began to move her emphasis from the BPW to the AAUW. As a result of another conversation Howorth had with AAUW leaders, Hughes's committee turned to the recruitment of women for the armed services and the failure of Congress to grant women in the military the full recognition accorded men.[42]

A subsequent polling of national and state leaders resulted in the adoption of a strong AAUW stand that women should be subject to the draft. Howorth wrote in an AAUW report that "the obligation rests upon all citizens alike to serve the country."[43] Apparently, Howorth attempted to join the Women's Army Corps (WAC) sometime in 1943 or 1944. Oveta Culp Hobby, head the of WAC, wrote her in May 1944, "I remember that you thought seriously of joining us at one time and I wish that it might have been possible," and a month later Colonel Mary Agnes Brown wrote from her post in Australia, "Gosh, I wish I'd been more coercive in trying to get you in. Still think it's not too late."[44] At the age of forty-seven or forty-eight, depending on just when she sought to enlist, Howorth could have barely met the qualifications for officer enlistees that they be no more than fifty years of age, but she fell under the height requirement. She may have learned also that basic training was required of all recruits, with almost no exceptions, and the prospect of that was daunting. Whether any of the requirements could have been waived in her case is not certain.

For whatever reason, Howorth took an avid interest in the treatment of women in the military, basing some of her advocacy on statements from Colonel Brown, who wrote candidly of her own observations: "I've put in some long hours in the Army and fought many a battle to get the idea over that women are people, even when in uniform."[45] Howorth had known Mary Agnes Brown through the BPW as well as the VA and the camaraderie among women lawyers in Washington, and she took an active role in securing for her through Colonel Hobby a ranking command in the WAC as it was taking shape in 1942. Brown, who became director of the Eighth Service Command, stationed in Australia, wrote from there of the "regular Army[, which] had not been exposed to successful business and professional women." Howorth took immense pleasure in Brown's eventual appointment to the VA Board of Appeals once membership was opened to women veterans after the war.[46]

Unable to join the military, Howorth threw herself into civilian work with the Red Cross, heading up its drives and coordinating VA civilian volunteer work. She felt resplendent in the Red Cross uniform she could wear on occasion and performed with such competency that at the close of her work in 1945 VA Administrator General Omar Bradley wrote that her able leadership had "contributed to the morale of the employees during the war and to the prestige of the Veterans Administration." Of Bradley, Howorth said years later, "He had the quickest mind of anybody I knew."[47]

Howorth was a graduate of the first Red Cross class in accident prevention and lectured to each class in the VA series. She received an award for her more than five hundred hours of volunteer work. Her report at the end of 1945 described how six thousand employees of the VA had been organized into a variety of Red Cross training programs. Her interest in the Red Cross stemmed also from her niece's work with the organization in Africa and Italy. Dorothy Shands, Eleanor's daughter, wrote her aunt letters full of the excitement of a Red Cross worker near the field of battle.[48]

Howorth's own struggles to keep a job, her association with other anxious women officeholders, and her knowledge of the ways in which the BPW and the AAUW monitored women in government all motivated her to take aggressive action. With the end of the New Deal, the heady days of women as federal appointees had waned. The onset of war had not resulted in appreciable gains for women, and as prospects for peace heightened in 1943 and 1944 a number of women's organizations coalesced to push for the appointment of women to the innumerable peacekeeping agencies being formed.

Howorth was curious in early 1944 when Charl O. Williams, a former national BPW president (1935–37) and at that time director of field services for the National Education Association, invited her to lunch at the AAUW tearoom. Soon Williams turned the conversation to her idea that a consortium of women's organizations should conduct a conference at the White House to demonstrate that a handful of competent women were already performing admirably in international peace agencies and that many more should be appointed. When Howorth asked, "Who's to spark it?" Williams replied, "You." Thus, Howorth became the keynote speaker at the widely covered White House Conference on Women in Post-War Policy Making held at the White House on 14 June 1944 with the warm endorsement of the First Lady. Eleanor Roosevelt had already written on the subject in April in the popular *Reader's Digest,* and in May she entertained at a White House luncheon a select group of concerned women, including Dr. Maffett of the BPW, Kathryn McHale of the AAUW, and Charl Williams, to explore the appointment of women to commissions in the planning stage that would deal with postwar problems. Howorth was not there, but since she had an uncanny knack for always knowing what was going on, she wrote a lengthy letter to McHale delineating specific qualifications that women delegates, advisers, and technical staff should possess. And she took pains to see that Mrs. Roosevelt received a copy. With the First Lady's blessing, the June conference gained wide acclaim and presented Howorth the opportunity of her dreams.[49]

The idea of the conference struck a responsive chord with leaders of women's clubs, among whom a plan of action had been brewing since the midwar years. In 1943 Margaret Hickey had written Howorth, "How I wish that the National Federation would move into this very important issue with resounding leadership instead of tiptoeing through the tulips." In 1943 AAUW's CELSW had held a summer workshop titled "Women in the Post-War World." By 1944 Howorth and Sarah Hughes were engaged in a feverish exchange with Hickey and others over just what recommendations should be made for women as peacekeepers. Hughes, by that time a Texas district court judge, endorsed Howorth's views that care be exercised in making specific recommendations to the Department of State, the agency that would appoint most peacekeeping officers.[50]

Reminiscing about her preparation for her keynote address at the White House on June 14, Howorth said, "I gave myself a shake and I did it." Introduced by Eleanor Roosevelt, Howorth spoke to a distinguished group: Samuel I. Rosenman, special counsel to the president; Jonathan W. Daniel, administrative assistant to the president; representatives from the ten Cabinet departments; and 213 women representing seventy-five national women's organizations. Also present was the handful of women who had attended international conferences in some official capacity. Howorth must have taken a special delight in the presence among women representing Cabinet departments of Helen R. Carloss, a special assistant to the attorney general and Mississippi native.[51]

Howorth declared at the outset, "World conditions demand even more of women today." "Women," she asserted, "are the natural preservers of the human race"; according to the 1940 census, they outnumbered men, owned more than 50 percent of the country's property, and participated widely in public endeavors. There would be no single peace conference at the end of World War II, as there had been at Versailles in 1919; rather there already had been and would continue be a number of conferences to address specific issues and human needs. Women with education, experience, and competence would be "ineffective in this hour of destiny" unless they were to hold positions that allowed them to make policy. She could point to those women present who would follow her to the podium and provide briefings on the work they had already done at international conferences: Ellen Woodward and Elizabeth A. Conkey, Cook County (Illinois) Commissioner of Public Welfare, who had been advisers to the U.S. delegates at the United Nations Relief and Rehabilitation Administration (UNRRA) conference in Atlantic City in 1943; Josephine Schain, a delegate to the United Nations Conference on Food and Agriculture; C. Mildred Thompson, dean at Vassar, who had been the U.S. delegate to the Conference of Allied Ministers of Education in London; and Secretary of Labor Frances Perkins, an official delegate to the International Labor Conference in Philadelphia.[52]

To deal pragmatically with just how women could gain appointments, Howorth called for a roster of qualified women to be forwarded to appointing authorities. She was frank in stating that women whose names were on the list must be eminently qualified and must "not be obnoxious to the public." Organizations represented at the conference were to "comb their rolls for capable women." And she warned that women's organizations must be "broad enough, bold enough, generous enough, patriotic enough to rally behind suitable women without fear of disunity . . . or of actual strife." Without providing details, she said she had seen too much competition and jealousy among women seeking important posts within their own groups. She was optimistic about the task that lay ahead. She said that "the prestige of the great lady who is our hostess supports our endeavors" and she was convinced that the government was "friendly to our cause."[53] Maine Congresswoman Margaret Chase Smith, former

U.S. minister to Denmark Ruth Bryan Rohde, and Women's Bureau chief Katharine Lenroot added their support to the movement, but the most important voice was that of Eleanor Roosevelt, whose influence could weigh heavily in the appointment process.[54]

In later years Howorth thought her speech seemed "dated," but it "took hold" even if it "didn't thrill my soul" some forty years later.[55] It gained immediate national press coverage, particularly in continuing columns written by Malvina Lindsay, of the *Washington Post*, who penned the hard-hitting column "Top-Notch Women." Lindsay continued her journalistic crusade for women as postwar planners and wrote Howorth that she had appointed her "Member No. 1 of my brain trust." Augusta Marshall wrote praising the speech: "That's what I like about your brains; they cut right through the generalities with which most people stop."[56]

The message of the day reached a few men who held appointive power. Herbert Lehman, director of the UNRRA, told Ellen Woodward that a roster of qualified women "may be of value to us in our work."[57] Others showed little or no interest in women's efforts to secure positions. When Howorth in the company of other women went to see Alger Hiss in the State Department, she found him "arrogant and rude." She wished to be a "Committee of One to get Alger Hiss out of government." Margaret Hickey responded that Hiss's argument was "well worked out and is what is known as the 'State Department line.'" She thought the State Department relied too much upon a few women who were "academically trained technicians" and neglected to consider women for posts who had "broad training."[58]

A Continuation Committee, headed by Charl Williams, persisted in pressing the State Department to consult the roster under preparation that eventually produced 260 names. In reality, however, there is little way to know whether the few women who did receive posts in Cabinet departments could credit the December 1944 roster for their appointments. Evaluating the effectiveness of the roster is made more difficult by the decision not to release any names to the press nor to provide copies of the list to anyone but President Roosevelt and the State Department. Charl Williams, in explaining the decision to members of the Continuation Committee, cited five women, including Howorth, who wished to have their work in preparing the roster remain anonymous.[59] Howorth did not include the list in the otherwise full record of the White House conference that she placed in the AAUW Papers.

Women leaders continued their campaign at a forum conducted by the *New York Herald Tribune* in October 1944. That same month Howorth led a symposium at the AAUW clubhouse on women's participation in postwar policymaking. From 1945 into 1947 the White House Conference of 1944 was replicated in some twenty states. Among the most notable were those in Texas, where Sarah Hughes and Minnie Maffett spearheaded the drafting of a roster of women to be forwarded to an incoming governor. Howorth praised a series of conferences in South Carolina, where she gave a keynote address in 1947 stressing the general themes of her 1944 speech.[60] At the time she was gratified by the "whole progressive program" of Governor J. Strom Thurmond, who stated in his inaugural address his support of "equal rights for women in every respect," adding that women should serve on juries, be given equal pay for equal work, and occupy positions of importance in state governments. Mary E. Frayser, president of the South Carolina White House Conference, agreed that Thurmond's "forthright stand" on women's role in government was encouraging.[61]

Sarah Hughes had not known Howorth well until their discussion in 1943 about the Civil Service Commission publication that had been so abhorrent. Shortly after AAUW general Director Kathryn McHale invited Howorth to become a member of the AAUW's CELSW and Howorth submitted her questions for consideration at the September 1944 meeting, Hughes wrote to her, "You are certainly one of the clearest thinkers I know."[62] Hughes chaired the committee during the war and immediate postwar years (1941–46), when it set an ambitious agenda that was the focus of work throughout the 1940s: open recruitment and access of women to all branches of the armed forces, appointment of women to policymaking positions at all levels of government and to United Nations commissions, increased numbers of women as elective officials, and the removal of discriminations against women in jury service, pay, and Social Security benefits.[63]

Meeting with the committee in 1944, Howorth joined a group that included, among others, her Randolph-Macon mentor Gillie A. Larew, the anthropologist Ruth Benedict, and the future AAUW general director Helen Bragdon. Howorth led committee consideration of the necessity of full employment as a government policy in order to ensure the full utilization of women.[64] Howorth and Margaret Hickey had had long discussions on the threats that working women faced as the nation moved toward peace. In 1940, when Howorth had been chair of the BPW Public Affairs Committee, she had issued a pamphlet analyzing the status of married women workers and employment policies in small communities. Its conclusions reinforced what thinking people (i.e., all but employers) seemed to know, namely, that married women worked out of necessity.[65]

Wartime employment erased the ban against married women workers only temporarily. Hickey, as chair of the Woman's Advisory Committee of the War Manpower Commission, kept in close contact with AAUW officers, who monitored women's employment conditions and who attended meetings of the Women's Advisory Committee. Esther Cole Franklin, an AAUW research specialist, advised Hickey early in 1944 that a high-ranking Department of Labor official was "probably interested . . . in the withdrawal of women from the labor market." She was alarmed by his promotion of a nationwide campaign based on the social value of the family that would "appeal to women to consider home responsibilities."[66] Apprehensive about the fate of women workers, Howorth placed a proposal before the CELSW that it go on record to support revisions in the Social Security law to recognize women's work in the home by providing compensatory benefits. She was, of course, much too visionary about the extension of Social Security to cover housewives for their work in the home.[67] Writing for the April 1945 issue of the *AAUW Journal,* Howorth applauded the CELSW for furthering victories in "the bitter battles of bread for women."[68] The committee adopted her resolution that women be appointed to the Surplus Property Board. Her reasoning was that government agencies and boards that handled financial affairs were "where the real power lies."[69] Whether such an appointment was ever made is a matter that seems to have fallen by the wayside.

Before the committee met in 1945 Howorth began to explore the neglect of women in training for the sciences. It disturbed her that the War Department's official history omitted women's role in the development of the atomic bomb. "There is an evident backlash on every side against women's opportunities for advancement," she said.[70] She repeated her concerns at the 1946 meeting, when it was apparent to her that male veterans were crowding women out in education programs in science and law. "We don't want a generation of women losing opportunities in college education."[71] The education of women and girls in science and mathematics became a major initiative of the AAUW as the cold war progressed.

There is little evidence that women made perceptible gains in the federal or state governments, for all their activity. The death of President Roosevelt in April 1945 and the beginning of the presidency of Harry S. Truman exacerbated their concerns. Once again Lucy Howorth assumed the role of watchdog. In a later description of the transition from Roosevelt to Truman she deplored the "remarkable speed" with which there occurred a "complete change of atmosphere throughout the Government." "Petty persecution of women began, they were denied access to phones, they were pulled off interdepartmental committees, they were denied promotions." The end of the war meant that "women were the first to go." Only a month after the Japanese surrender in September 1945 Doris Fleeson headlined a grim column "Influence of Women Seen Nil in Washington Events Today."[72]

Howorth soon decided that it would be prudent for women in government to assure the new president that they were interested in him and his problems. Once again, Malvina Lindsay joined the fray, calling upon Howorth for column ideas: "I should have you help me every time." In August Howorth joined eleven other women representing national organizations in a meeting with President Truman, ostensibly to discuss a proclamation for the twenty-fifth anniversary of woman suffrage and support for a congressional measure decreeing equal pay for women.[73]

From the beginning Howorth had been in the inner circle of women who were on the alert during the transition from war to peace and from president to president. In 1942 she met with a committee initially set up by Mary Wooley, president of Mt. Holyoke, and then chaired by Emily Hickman, of the New Jersey State College for Women. Howorth had "fascinating experiences" with colleagues in the federal government in the group first called the Committee on the Participation of Women in Post-War Planning. One of the groups behind the White House Conference, in November 1945 it adopted the name Committee on Women in World Affairs (CWWA). Members worked assiduously in writing letters and creating rosters of women to recommend for appointments, especially after 1944.[74]

Still another group, the Committee of Ten, composed only of Washington-based women, met from time to time when it seemed necessary to bolster a specific appointment or to save a woman's a job that was on the line. Howorth and Ellen Woodward were members, as were May Thompson Evans, a Democratic Women's Division worker since the early New Deal, and Jewel Swofford, a Truman friend of long standing and chair of the United States Employment Compensation Commission (USEC).[75] Howorth took the initiative in meeting in June 1945 with Swofford, a Missouri Democrat who had managed to save her appointment to the USEC while Truman was still vice president. The session, Howorth thought, "marked the initiative of a constructive, planned drive [for] women in policy making positions."[76] Swofford secured what Howorth called a "beachhead," reporting that First Lady Bess Truman would transmit the women's messages to the president. "We got to Mrs. Truman," Howorth said, "and people don't know it, but she wielded a good deal more power than is thought." Swofford, "as fine, loyal a person as ever lived," in Howorth's estimation, proved to be just that in her mediation with President Truman after he issued an executive order in 1946 calling for reorganization of the executive branch.[77] A sympathetic Malvina Lindsay wrote bluntly that executive reorganization was "the old nemesis of the career woman."[78] The struggle for women in government was now in earnest.

To Howorth and her band of vigilantes, the most serious outcome of reorganization was the abolition of the Social Security Board, and with it Ellen Woodward's position as a member of the board since 1938. No other effort of Howorth to protect the position of a woman in government equaled the letter-writing campaign she organized on Woodward's behalf. Woodward had been touted as the second highest ranking woman appointee in the Roosevelt administration (after Cabinet member Frances Perkins) when she had been a WPA assistant administrator. An essential member of the women's network, she had, in Howorth's view, served "the progressive program of the party most brilliantly."[79]

The loss of Woodward would be grave, Howorth knew, for should she be "bumped," "no woman above a [civil service] Grade 10 was safe."[80] In a long memorandum in May 1946 Howorth pointed out to Emily Hickman the jeopardy in which reorganization placed positions held by Woodward, Swofford, Bess Goodykoontz in the Office of Education, and Katharine Lenroot in the Children's Bureau. In June, Howorth whirled into action by drafting, with May Thompson Evans, a letter to be sent to the presidents of twenty-five women's organizations spelling out the effect of Reorganization Plan No. 2 and recommending that Woodward be given a divisional directorship in the new Federal Security Agency.[81]

The efforts paid off, at least for Woodward, who was made the director of the Office of Interstate and International Relations in the Federal Security Agency. At the end of the year, Howorth reported to colleagues on the AAUW board that progress had been made by the CWWA and a coterie of Democratic women in saving and creating jobs, but she gave no names, nor did she specify positions created. She was certain that "had not women worked as they did much that had been gained in the Roosevelt administration would have been swept away." She was proud of the way women had pulled together. "We didn't call it sisterhood then," Howorth remarked years later, but "we knew that we were all in the same boat."[82]

Howorth remained a member of the CWWA until her resignation in 1954, when she retired from her federal job. She cited also the apparent dissolution of the Washington-based Committee of Ten and "the end of [CWWA] usefulness." A "new approach is in order," she believed, but she gave no clue as to what it might be. Dorothy Kenyon, then CWWA president, agreed that the organization "is going into moth-balls."[83] Howorth remained devoted to Emily Hickman, who had died in an automobile accident in 1947, and in 1958 Howorth placed in her own papers a moving tribute to Hickman, whom she described as "indefatigable . . . patient, wise, and persistent."[84] To rebut those who "sniffed" at the CWWA, Howorth cited the "plethora" of meetings, commissions, and conferences held as World War II was ending in which the presence of determined women had resulted in the accomplishment of CWWA goals.[85] Still, she admitted that "it is always difficult to assess with accuracy" the result of the kind of activity in which the CWWA had engaged.[86]

Howorth herself was the subject of a drive by friends when a death in 1945 opened a judgeship on the Municipal Court of the District of Columbia. After Gladys Tillett, head of the Democratic Women's Division, appealed to Attorney General Tom C. Clark to appoint a woman, he agreed. Before she wrote either Clark or Robert Hannegan, chair of the Democratic National Committee, Tillett garnered support for Howorth from Mississippi's congressional force, prominent Democratic state committee women, and Emily Hickman of the CWWA. "Everything looks exceedingly encouraging," Tillett wrote Howorth in early December 1945.[87] In February, Clark recommended Howorth's appointment to President Truman, and presumably the nomination was to be forwarded to the Senate for confirmation.[88]

At that point Howorth's nomination hit a snag and "was withdrawn at the last minute," according to the *Washington Evening Star.* Howorth knew of opposition from the District Bar Association because she did not practice law locally, although the law permitted outside appointments. Moreover, President Truman was having problems with Senate confirmation of two other Mississippians, George E. Allen for the Reconstruction Finance Corporation and James K. Vardaman for the Federal Reserve Board. Publicly Howorth took the stance of "holding the fort while the cards [were] reshuffled."[89] Meanwhile, letters of support continued to flood into the offices of Clark and Truman, including a strong endorsement from Malvina Lindsay. Margaret Hickey wrote Howorth of her dismay at the "depressing" news. She thought Howorth had been "so grand" at the time of the VA Board reduction, for she had been willing to "overlook" the manner in which "the political boys play what they think is a wise game."[90]

Howorth thought it best to withdraw her name, an act, she said, that "was probably making a virtue of necessity." Joe did not stand in her way, but he advised her that work on the Municipal Court, where he often had legal business, was demanding and unrewarding in cases involving both criminal and civil law. She confided to a relative her embarrassment over the hubris but knew she had "learned a good deal about back stage Washington." As the matter ended, Attorney General Clark maintained his commitment to appoint a woman, paying deference to Howorth's recommendation. Upon conferring with Gladys Tillett, Howorth selected from the membership of the Woman's Bar Association a Washington, DC, native, Nadine Gallagher. Writing to the president on 22 June, Howorth conveyed her "sincere gratification" at the appointment and assured him, "I fully understand the circumstances surrounding the withdrawal of my name." Her attitude, Tom Clark replied, was "a work of real bigness."[91] The affair closed at the Restaurant Madrillon in late June, when Howorth joined Gallagher, U.S. Court of Tax Appeals Judge Marion J. Herron, and other judicial women for a luncheon celebration.[92]

Late in 1946 President Truman's office received a flood of endorsements, mostly from women's organizations, for women who could be named to key administration positions, including assistant secretary of state, positions in bureaus within the State Department, and special assistant to the president. For special assistant to the president a roster of six names included those of Margaret Hickey, Gladys Tillett, and Lucy Howorth.[93] Nothing came of the recommendation; records remain silent. Howorth never spoke of the endorsement, and she may not even have known of it.

Thus, in 1946 Howorth remained as a legislative attorney in the VA. With her six-month absorption in the Municipal Court appointment behind her, she was ready to move on in her continuing advocacy of women in politics and public affairs.

7

"I glory in being a feminist," 1947–1954

HER "THREE interlocking interests," Lucy Howorth told Randolph-Macon College alumnae in 1948, were "the study and practice of law, participation in government, and the advancement of women."[1] While she was always involved in the last of these, her extensive work with the AAUW Committee on the Economic and Legal Status of Women, or CELSW, later the Committee on the Status of Women, absorbed much of her boundless energy in advancing the status of women after 1943. Becoming chair of the committee in 1947 presented an even larger venue for her enormous vitality, especially at a time when the AAUW board and membership were struggling with postwar dilemmas about racism, communism, and conflicting views about feminism. And while she became involved in promoting opportunities for women as a group, she remained in the inner circle of the other organizations devoted to placing individual women on national and international councils of authority. For Howorth herself, a new job in 1949 led her to the most prestigious position in her twenty-year career in federal service.

As optimistic as Howorth was at the end of President Harry Truman's first year in office, obstacles remained, originating primarily among his advisers. Part of the problem was the antipathy within the administration to Gladys Tillett, head of the Democratic Women's Division. By late 1945 Tillett must have sensed that she was on her way out when Doris Fleeson wrote of "grumbling" among Democratic women "over what is termed a lack of force" in her. Howorth remained in Tillett's camp and enlisted friends to support her when a push was under way to have her named to the United Nations General Assembly.[2] Nothing came of that, but Howorth believed "a good measure of credit" was due Tillett for the appointment of Barnard College Dean Virginia Gildersleeve to the American delegation to the San Francisco Conference in 1945, which established the United

Nations. "She always tried to deliver the goods," Howorth said, including assisting in placing women on the VA Board of Appeals. "We were in and out many a stunt."[3] She had worked closely with Tillett and "had more respect for her than some who put her down as a lightweight."[4]

In 1948 India Edwards, an outspoken Truman partisan from Missouri, replaced Tillett as head of the Women's Division. The president's confidence in Edwards and her dogged persistence in promoting women in government helped bridge the gap women had perceived when Truman first entered office.[5] By the time Edwards left office in 1953 several women had achieved firsts by way of presidential appointment. In his first three years as president Truman had named only three women to posts high enough to warrant Senate confirmation. After Edwards succeeded Tillett, the appointment of women to office so increased that Truman surpassed Roosevelt in the number of women appointed, though not necessarily in terms of the importance of the offices to which they were appointed. Women achieved enough of a breakthrough that Doris Fleeson could write in 1957 that a fair proportion who eventually won appointments from Truman were still in government work.[6]

One of the firsts among the Truman appointees was Lucy Howorth, the beneficiary of congressional passage of the War Claims Act of 1948, which authorized the president to appoint three members to a War Claims Commission. One was Daniel F. Cleary, at the time a staffer in the Legislative Office of the VA, who had worked easily with Howorth and become her good friend. Cleary, intensely Democratic, was named chair of the commission. Another member was Georgia L. Lusk, a former New Mexico congresswoman (1946–48) and the only woman to serve on the commission. Members had the authority to name the commission's legal staff, and Cleary wanted Howorth as assistant general counsel, a selection easily approved in President Truman's office. When the fiasco over the municipal judgeship ended in 1946, Attorney General Clark had written Howorth, "There will be another day for you, I am sure." Thus Howorth moved into yet another federal office where she would deal in administrative law.[7] Friends who feared that Howorth had been "bounced," as Molly Dewson put it when the word was out that Howorth was leaving the VA, were gratified that she had landed an even better job. Colleagues in the VA gave her high marks, one affirming her as "an excellent lawyer . . . very straightforward in all her dealings" with associates, while another stated that there had been "no conflict of personalities." Thus she left on good terms.[8]

Mary Agnes Brown, Howorth's friend and a former officer in the Women's Army Corps, was among women who won federal promotion in 1949. After her discharge, Brown returned as an attorney in the Legislative Office of the VA and was put in charge of women's affairs. Her appointment to the VA Board of Appeals in 1949 fulfilled the desire Howorth had harbored that women veterans be named to the board. The appointment was achieved after "a good many knocked heads," Howorth recalled. Brown, whom she considered to be "a woman of extraordinary mental and staying power," was a close personal friend. Before Brown's marriage and move to Florida, she and Howorth spent much time together, including a vacation trip to the Canadian Rockies in 1949.[9]

Early in 1949 Howorth gloried in another victory for women following the "thumping majority" Maine voters gave Margaret Chase Smith, the first woman to serve in the Senate since the retirement of Hattie Caraway, of Arkansas, in 1946. "The power was there and this seemed to be the spark it was waiting for," Howorth believed. She spoke at a breakfast meeting of the women who had arrived in Washington on the "Women for Public Office Special" sponsored by the Multi-Party Committee of Women, Inc., a New York–based organization. The bipartisan committee had as its goal securing local and state appointments for women.[10] On that third of January not only did Smith enter the Senate but eight women entered the House of Representatives. Just as she had done in her White House keynote in 1944, Howorth called for a definite plan of action: women's attendance at ward and precinct meetings, a search for able women who could be developed for public office, encouragement of women's organizations to further citizenship programs, "nailing" male candidates on the issue of appointing women, and the start of a drive to raise money to staff an office in four major cities to coordinate activities. "The girls are just not there when the boys are planning how to run everything," Howorth stated. But she was convinced that "the great women's organizations can carry the ball at this point."[11]

Howorth's involvement with the Multi-Party Committee was transitory. She was first contacted by a New York judge, Anna K. Kross, when the idea was in its incipient stage under chairperson Mary Bollman, of New York. "We must wake up our dormant women," Kross wrote. "The women of the extreme Left are not asleep—that is an additional reason for those of us who still believe there is a middle course to get busy." Later, when she applied for a postretirement position in Washington, Howorth explained that the Multi-Party Committee had never achieved national status but was limited to New York. In fact, the breakfast in January 1949 had resulted in a financial deficit, and such inadequacies made it impossible for the committee ever to move ahead. Howorth withdrew and by 1956 doubted the committee still existed.[12]

Probably women's most concerted effort to secure a major spot for one of their own was that exerted to have May Thompson Evans named one of several assistant secretaries of labor. Evans had been a dedicated worker in the Democratic Party. Once an assistant director of the Women's Division (1937–41), she had moved on to become a wartime assistant to the director of the Office of Civilian Defense in 1941 and an employment specialist for the War Manpower Commission (1942–45). At the time that women coalesced to win the Labor Department post for her, she was with the Federal Security Agency in another position dealing with employment. Howorth saw the appointment as "about the biggest chance we will get as things seem to be going now." She was straightforward in approaching Secretary of Labor Maurice Tobin: "Women of the United States are keenly aware that they have practically no voice in government policy making." It was a condition, she argued "that must be remedied." Despite a barrage of letters to the president and to Tobin from numerous women's organizations, both North Carolina senators, and the entire state congressional delegation, Evans failed to secure the appointment, which went to a man.[13]

By far the most notable appointment of a woman came in 1949, not in policymaking but in the judiciary, when Truman placed Burnita Shelton Matthews on the bench of the United States District Court for the District of Columbia. She was the first woman ever appointed to a federal district court. Howorth had known Matthews, a native Mississippian, since the 1920s, when Matthews earned her law degree at the National University Law School in Washington, DC, and then worked as a legal researcher and counsel for the National Woman's Party. Their paths had gone separate ways, but Howorth had always admired Matthews and appreciated her efforts in the 1920s and 1930s to lobby the Mississippi legislature for the removal of legal disabilities of women, including strictures against women as jurors.[14]

The struggle for women's rights in her home state during the thirties, forties, and fifties was a fray that Howorth chose not to enter, either from fear of going into a losing battle, a conflict with her positions in government, or because she lacked the time to pursue homestate reforms. Howorth and Matthews were cordial but never personal friends. Nonetheless, Matthews's appointment pleased Howorth, and she expressed her gratitude to Truman and his attorney general, J. Howard McGrath. The latter agreed with her that Matthews's selection had been "wise and popular" and would bear "great meaning to professional women . . . serving to encourage them in their efforts toward the recognition of able women in important public service."[15]

In 1947, when Howorth became chair of the AAUW's CELSW, the name was changed to the Committee on the Status of Women to reflect the broader concerns that she wanted to pursue. In the years that followed, Howorth expanded the scope of the committee to include a number of problems that women confronted in the postwar years, and she used her position as chair to speak out about both positive developments and those that continued to hinder women. One of Howorth's first open statements was a letter to the editor of the *AAUW Journal* lauding the opening of jury service for women in North Carolina, Maryland, New Hampshire, and South Dakota, victories for which AAUW members claimed major credit.[16]

Although the committee usually met in the fall, the 1947 meeting was held in January 1948. It was evident that Howorth's outspokenness during the four years in which she had been a member would be curbed now that she was chair. The new committee members, Melanie Rosborough, of the University of Miami, the sociologist Rosamonde Boyd, of South Carolina, and Colonel Jessie Pearl Rice, of Indianapolis, assured a lively discussion of such perennial topics as the ERA, women in the military, and women in policymaking. "You had the programs for the day planned so well that it was no wonder so much could be covered," Rosborough wrote upon her return to Coral Gables. In her commencement address at Randolph-Macon in 1948 Howorth reprised, for a general audience, the agenda of the Committee on the Status of Women and challenged the new graduates to devote themselves to a career and to enter public life, where women were still only "a footnote and afterthought."[17]

Howorth sent Augusta Marshall, who was living in Mankato, Minnesota, a copy of the address she would make, and a proud Gus wrote back, "We didn't know when we use [sic] to walk around and around the graveled walks, talking and planning that you would be the one among the very few graduates ever asked to speak at commencement." It was in that 1948 address on the campus of her alma mater that Howorth defined herself: "Briefly, I am a lawyer; I was a politician; I am a feminist." She regretted that average Americans resented being called "politicians" and said that "too many women shudder at being called feminists." She added the memorable line, "With Lady Astor, I glory in being a feminist." Not from that platform but later, in private moments, she was extremely critical of women in government who denied being feminists. That women such as Secretary of Labor Frances Perkins eschewed feminism "was always a pain in the neck to me," Howorth said.[18] She herself was never reticent or apologetic about her feminism, and she was dismayed that the author of a sketch on her that appeared in the *Randolph-Macon Alumnae Bulletin* wrote, "She is in no sense a feminist." "Hogwash," Howorth penned in the margin of her personal copy before she distributed copies to friends.

Following the 1948 meeting of the Committee on the Status of Women, Howorth wrote for the *AAUW Journal* a clear rationale for the direction the committee would take. "The points of emphasis for the study and activity programs . . . affecting the status of women" would include the prevention of discriminations and improvement of opportunities in women's employment, women's increased participation in public affairs, and whatever emphases in government, the work force, and education would "make more effective women's lives and influence." Already alert to new and international issues that had arisen, the committee expanded the AAUW's focus on the status of women to include the agenda of the United Nations Commission on the Status of Women.[19]

On the domestic scene Howorth wrote, "There is little evidence that obstructions to [women's] advancement in professional, scientific, executive, and supervisory positions are being removed." Thus the AAUW had begun to work through the U.S. Women's Bureau to seek remedies. And it continued to lodge protests against the quota system for women in medical, professional, and graduate schools, which led to policymaking positions in government and administrative positions in higher education. At least some satisfaction came with Harvard Law School's decision to admit women, but in the postwar years AAUW's own reluctance to criticize institutions that were assisting veterans limited its effectiveness in combating sex discrimination by colleges.[20]

The AAUW was not immune from conflicts in the immediate postwar years about "domesticity" as a panacea for problems inherent in the nation's readjustment to peace. In 1948 Howorth railed against the "hue and cry over 'momism,' 'smother love,' and the like" at a time when the media glorified the wife and mother.[21] The AAUW board, leery of the call for women to return to the home, was sensitive to the feelings of those women who were being told to choose between marriage and family on the one hand and a professional career and public service on the other, or at best to find some means to have both. Fearful that marriage and family responsibilities would blunt an educated woman's chances to work or further her own education, the AAUW wrestled with how to respond to what was already taking place. Over the years Howorth personally had known women who made choices, and she seemed ambivalent about them. Years later, living in retirement in Cleveland, she was dismayed that a promising young journalist chose to leave work to devote two or three years as a full-time mother to a toddler. "To an extent this is laudable," she wrote to a friend, "but it can be overdone."[22]

Howorth followed with intense interest developments in higher education that affected women. Hallie Farmer, a professor of history and political science at Alabama College, in Montevallo, the state's public college for women only, was responsible for Howorth's appearance at an AAUW conference on campus in 1950, at which she sounded the same alarm that she did whenever she spoke. There would be "very little moonlight and roses in this speech," she warned. In the wake of World War II and the six-month-old Korean War, Howorth exhorted women to step forward in leadership positions to counter the popular myth that "the man is to be dominant." The preeminence of the male "is not the *pattern* of American life," she maintained. She cited the finding of Eleanor Flexner, a scholar on women's issues, that of the more than 50 million women over the age of twenty-one, a vast majority were in the lower-income brackets and were paid less than men for the same work.[23]

Howorth was dismayed that some women's colleges had abandoned a curriculum like the one she had pursued at Randolph-Macon, the equal to that found in men's colleges, and instead had adopted less demanding programs. "There has been already too much talk about the need for a special curriculum for women," she warned the deans of women at their annual conference in 1951. She feared that such curricula would "channel the intellectually able, potential scholar into areas so shallow she would be unable to survive" in an increasingly competitive society. Conversely, that same year Lynn White, president of Mills College, a private college for women, told AAUW members at their national convention that a proper education for women should include instruction in the preparation of a fancy dish that he described. Howorth responded indignantly: "He, like others, has missed the spirit of the leaders of the women's movement."[24]

Howorth regretted that World War II had not resulted in an increase in the percentage of college-educated women; despite the numerical growth of women enrolled in college, the percentage of women going to college was lower than at any time in the past fifty years. Women seeking graduate and professional degrees were not entering the sciences as she wished. Too many sought training in "quickie" programs in technology that offered no promotion and led to "blind alley consequences of educational short-cuts." The demotion of deans of women to subordinate positions under a dean of students, usually a male, was another trend that Howorth found disturbing. She was first made aware of the trend in 1946, when she was invited by the president of the National Association of Deans of Women to a gathering of women in Washington who were alarmed at the increasing removal of women from administrative posts in universities and high schools, resulting in the absence of women in institutional policymaking. At one time the AAUW would not sanction for membership an institution that did not have a dean of women. Years later Howorth regretted that the AAUW had ceased to examine and approve institutions, but she realized that the Department of Health, Education, and Welfare, created in 1953, had taken over many of the AAUW's oversight functions.[25]

In one instance Howorth herself expressed an interest in a college presidency. In 1950, when the Texas State College for Women presidential search committee invited her to apply upon the recommendation of an unnamed person, Howorth submitted her credentials, listing among references Sarah Hughes, Mary Agnes Brown, and Margaret Hickey. In a ten-page dossier she described her own education at a woman's college, her work with women's organizations in the public realm, and her conviction that a public college should combine cultural and vocational education within a strong liberal-arts setting.[26] Her investigation into TSCW as a public women's college, her familiarity with Mississippi State College for Women, and her knowledge of Hallie Farmer's institution, Alabama College, may have tempered Howorth's insistence that women's college curricula should be like that of Randolph-Macon. She seems to have developed somewhat different expectations for private and public women's colleges and compromised her earlier reluctance to endorse curricula that led to the careers for women in the "vocations." Her papers make no mention of any response to her application, and she never commented on the subject.

Althea Hottel was president of the AAUW during the time when the national board debated the question of admitting black members. The application of Mary Church Terrell, an Oberlin-educated advocate of racial justice, for membership in the Washington branch in 1946 led to a protracted debate within the branch.[27] The second oldest AAUW local after Boston, the Washington branch was composed of members who were, as Howorth described them, wealthy, "old guard socialites" and "Seven Sisters graduates" who were opposed to admitting black members. The controversy resulted in a split in the branch, with the formation of the University Club by opponents of integration. Howorth remained in the group that retained status as a recognized AAUW branch.[28]

From 1946 to 1949, throughout the dispute over the admissions policy, Kathryn McHale, general director of the AAUW, and president Althea Hottel took clear positions in favor of integration and stood their ground against the recalcitrant Washington branch.[29] At the Dallas convention in 1947 there was a strong undercurrent about the race issue, and feeling ran high. As parliamentarian, Howorth managed to avoid a bitter floor debate, and delegates left Dallas having mandated to the national board a new policy that opened the AAUW to any graduate of an approved institution. Between 1947 and 1949 board members fanned out over the country to preach open membership, while a committee redefined criteria for approving an institution's graduates. In 1948 fifteen national directors of the AAUW, among them Howorth, Gillie A. Larew of Randolph-Macon, Susan Riley of the George Peabody College in Nashville, and Bessie Randolph, the president of Hollins College in Virginia, signed a statement criticizing the Washington branch for refusing to admit black members.[30]

At the Seattle convention in 1949 membership for black graduates came to a vote. The burden of the argument in favor of open membership was to be carried by southerners. Howorth told the story: "We agreed that the Southerners would carry that burden. . . . So we had to go off and huddle a little, and we named Gillie A. Larew to lead the fight on the floor." Since she was not serving as parliamentarian at that convention, Howorth was free also to be a floor leader. She disregarded the fact that some Mississippi delegates viewed her as a traitor. The resolution passed, and thus the issue of the admission of black members was ended, at least from the standpoint of national policy. Susan Levine, in her history of the AAUW, cites Howorth's role as "important" in guiding the association toward racial integration.[31] Reflecting upon her long involvement in the AAUW, Howorth seemed proudest of her role in the 1949 integration decision.

At the Dallas convention in 1947 delegates complained that there was too much centralization of decision making by the Washington staff, which they attributed to the absence of national conventions during the war. Four years later Howorth did not see that the problem had dissipated. She became testy when Helen Bragdon, AAUW's new general director, declined to pay expenses for secretarial staff to attend the Atlantic City convention in 1951. Howorth viewed the decision as disparaging to the clerical staff. "I am shocked," she wrote Bragdon, "at the caste attitude that seems to prevail at headquarters. . . . The association does a great deal of talking about democracy and . . . a rigid caste system does not fit in such talk." Bragdon was stunned by such a "very serious charge" and, because many of the staff knew of Howorth's letter, she responded that "any decision [will be] difficult and even unpopular." Bragdon said she hoped that as two "forthright persons" with "a sense of humor" they could "talk matters over thoroughly" and "then become fast friends forever."[32] That never happened, but the two managed to remain civil to each other.

Bragdon thought the dissension at headquarters that Howorth described had existed before she took over and had been resolved when disgruntled clerical personnel had left. Howorth, who apparently was determined to have the last word, responded that she had not meant to "be so unfair as to hold a new executive responsible for the atmosphere and attitudes of a long established office." She was concerned that her own confidentiality had been breached and added, "There is much that I might say upon the failure of Board members to develop a cooperative relationship with the Executive Director and I should not like to find myself guilty." On a more conciliatory note she wrote that service on both YWCA and AAUW boards had rewarded her with "some of my finest friendships."[33] What became of the rift is not clarified by additional exchanges, but most likely the two women simply agreed to disagree. Later correspondence with Kathryn McHale suggests that Howorth was cognizant of a situation at the national headquarters that needed to be resolved. After Howorth became second vice president of the AAUW in 1951 McHale wrote, "I do hope . . . you will be able to crusade on the wide gap between the executive committee's ideational support of principles and their actual practices with respect to the staff. . . . You are in a better position than ever before to do this."[34]

While pointing to the differences among individuals in the AAUW hierarchy, Howorth also recognized the gap that existed between the AAUW national board and hundreds of branches regarding both policy and practice. She knew that few branches followed directives from the board that they establish a local Committee on the Status of Women. Some branches were no more than clubs that served as acceptable outlets for the social needs of women who had little or no interest in AAUW goals. Writing to an AAUW leader in Texas, Howorth said that she hoped some instruction could be given the Ada, Oklahoma, branch so that it "should have a broader conception of the opportunities and responsibilities of women and they should not proceed on a program confined to the living room walls."[35] Throughout her term on the national Committee on the Status of Women from 1943 through 1950 Howorth witnessed the reluctance of many branches to adhere to the national position on admitting black members. Not until she returned to her Mississippi branch and the state AAUW after 1960 would she see evidence of her influence in the AAUW at the grass-roots level.

The ERA had been on the study program of the AAUW since 1924. AAUW opposition, first stated in 1938, entered CELSW deliberations at every yearly meeting. In 1941, in a summary of opposition to the amendment, the AAUW stated that proponents evidenced "a naive confidence in the power of legalisms [that] cannot possibly have any important effect upon human conduct or upon the psychological barriers to equality which are the really important barriers that remain. . . . At worst the Amendment would be highly destructive. At best it would be wholly ineffective, leaving the job of piece-meal removal of remaining discriminations still to be done." In 1942, when Sarah Hughes was asked to chair the CELSW, she made clear her support of the ERA lest the national board not wish her to serve. When Howorth succeeded her, she knew that the board had "a knockdown, dragout fight" before it agreed to her chairing the committee. She made no apologies for her support of the amendment.[36]

The ERA drew particular attention in 1946, when it was under consideration by the 79th Congress. Howorth consistently voted in CELSW polls that the AAUW go on record as supporting the amendment.[37] Nonetheless, she respected AAUW's opposition but deplored the division among women's groups. She believed that the AAUW, whose opposition had not been virulent or as offensive as the actions of some other women's groups, could assume leadership in effecting a compromise among women's organizations on a new wording of the ERA and just how to bring about passage.[38] AAUW discussion of the ERA, never extensive, occurred at every meeting of the Committee on the Status of Women, but as long as AAUW conventions went on record against any amendment that did not safeguard "the health, safety, and welfare of women," a majority of the committee voted not to support the amendment. Although Howorth made clear her wish that the AAUW reverse its opposition, as the BPW had in 1939, she did not believe that she should use her position as committee chair to go against convention majorities.[39] There matters stood at the last committee meeting at which Howorth presided in 1950, when a 4–4 poll of the members present maintained the standstill.[40] It was not until 1971 that the AAUW finally endorsed the ERA.

In 1948 Howorth led her committee in backing an initiative of the national board to ask President Truman and his secretary of defense to integrate women into every phase of the national defense-preparedness program. She disliked the absence of women entirely among the forty-nine members of the Office of Defense Planning. From 1948 to 1950 she wrote firm letters to successive secretaries of defense seeking full integration of women into national defense. "Modern war draws no distinction between men and women," she wrote James Forrestal. In 1949 Howorth dismissed as a "brush off" Secretary of Defense Louis Johnson's explanation that no women had been invited to participate in the Joint Orientation Defense Conference because of problems of accommodations and transportation.[41] Her letters were adamant but polite, but she could fire a few salvos when necessary, as she did in her reply to a U.S. Navy captain who had explained that no women had been invited to a defense conference because it was "impractical" and created "problems of accommodation," an oblique reference to the lack of restroom facilities. To that old bromide Howorth replied, "It is particularly important that the Department of National Defense pull itself out of antediluvian thinking and adjust to new conditions." Margaret Hickey confirmed Howorth's exchanges with Defense Department leaders. Basing her comments upon her experiences with the War Manpower Commission, Hickey wrote, "It was almost unbelievable that these young men know so little of the . . . contributions of women."[42]

Most precisely, the AAUW resolved that Congress remove the statutory limitation on the strength of women's components of the armed services, which held them to 2 percent of the regular armed forces. As expected, commanders of the women's branches were enthusiastic about the AAUW stand, the director of the WACs writing Howorth, "If there were no organization like yours, there would be no corps like ours." In a November 1948 press release by the Committee of the Status of Women, Howorth had asserted that "from now on any war will mean total war and plans should be underway now for the utilization of women and men in case of war." When the Women's Armed Services Integration Act of 1948 removed limitations and women were fully integrated into the armed forces, the AAUW believed that it had contributed significantly to the decision.[43]

With the advent of the Korean War in 1950, a number of women's organizations stiffened their opposition to alien ideologies and launched "anti" programs that bordered on hysteria. The AAUW sought a middle road between constructive patriotic support and shrill reaction to the threat of Communism. It was especially difficult for the AAUW to place on government boards members whose liberal views were widely known, such as Kathryn McHale, AAUW's former general director, who was nominated in 1950 to serve on the Subversive Activities Control Board, a position that required confirmation by the Senate Judiciary Committee. Howorth knew its chairman, New Mexico's Pat McCarran, an ardent conservative and outspoken anti-Communist, through her work on the War Claims Commission. It was McCarran's Internal Security Act that had established the Subversive Activities Control Board. Howorth considered

McHale to be "a sensitive, shy person, gifted with a creative mind" and volunteered to coach her about some of the "peculiarities" of McCarran's committee so that she "would not break under the strain that Committee actions might induce."[44]

Although President Truman had appointed McHale in the fall of 1950, the McCarran Committee held up the appointment while it investigated McHale for her support of two AAUW associates, Dorothy Kenyon and Esther Caukin Brunauer, both under investigation by the committee headed by Joseph McCarthy. Wisconsin's red-baiting senator had just begun his probe for fellow travelers and full-blown Communists. McCarthy had named the two AAUW associates as Communist sympathizers because of their work to promote internationalism. McHale, Kenyon, and Brunauer were all cleared, but McHale's confirmation was almost a year in coming. "It was a good thing that you prepared me on the tactics of the gentleman responsible," McHale wrote Howorth, "otherwise my apprehensions would have upset me much more than they did." Howorth left nothing in writing to express whatever opinion she subsequently held about McHale's defense of her Subversive Activities Control Board's vigorous investigation of groups variously described as either left-wing and dangerous or merely liberal and nonthreatening to national security. Where public opinion placed the AAUW on the political spectrum from left to right continued to trouble Helen Bragdon, McHale's successor at AAUW headquarters, and she warned Susan Riley and Lucy Howorth shortly before the Korean War ended that right-wingers were "representing themselves as belonging to some well-established organizations" such as those of churchwomen and the AAUW.[45] And yet some right-wingers carped that the AAUW was left-wing. Such was the dilemma of the AAUW.

Indeed, public opinion about where the AAUW stood on a matter as grave as the Communist threat vis-à-vis one's personal freedom to dissent was matched to some degree by ambiguity among national board members, not to mention local branches. Howorth agreed with Bragdon that the AAUW must deal with its public persona in this regard. Thus, one of the last responsibilities she assumed as chair of the Committee on the Status of Women was to represent the AAUW in a coalition of women's organizations for civil defense.[46]

The new partnership, the Clearing House of Women's Organizations for National Defense, began at the impetus of the BPW convention on 6 October 1950 following an address by Margaret Hickey. Representatives of thirty-eight women's organizations who were present in Washington at the initial meeting resolved to determine vital services women could perform in a period of defense mobilization and, as Howorth quoted General George Marshall to her committee, an "enduring period of tension." Most immediately, Clearing House leaders needed to plan for a crucial meeting with Secretary of Defense Stuart Symington, which most particularly would determine how a coalition of women's organizations could function as a partner to the already established and official women's program within the National Security Resources Board, created in 1947 and superseded in December 1950 by the Federal Civil Defense Administration (FCDA). The high regard that constituent members had for Lucy Howorth surfaced during a rambling and unfocused planning session on how to approach Symington. Unless she "took over" at the meeting, the Clearing House's start might be inauspicious. Or as one worried member, Eleanor Dolan, of the AAUW's national staff, put it, "We would make fools of ourselves." She was relieved that Howorth "was able to see the miserable situation and took the initiative and responsibility in the conference."[47] Once again Howorth demonstrated her unusual ability to get to the point.

Even after the conference with Symington at the State Department, there was a "wrangle" in the anteroom among the delegation about their next move. "It was a sorry spectacle to which Mrs. Howorth soon put a stop," Dolan wrote in her report to AAUW officers. And thus Howorth became a stalwart in the Clearing House and kept her Committee on the Status of Women fully informed about its programs and Symington's assurance that "qualified women could be used at all levels in the defense activity."[48]

With that understanding the Clearing House officially got under way in February 1951 with Lucy Howorth as vice chair and Mrs. Hiram Cole Houghton, national president of the General Federation of Women's Clubs, as chair.[49] Howorth recognized that there was "still a question whether problems could be clarified sufficiently to permit completion of the organization."[50] In March the Clearing House of Women's Organizations for National Defense became the Assembly of Women's Organizations for National Security, indicating that it had moved beyond the planning stage. In June Howorth succeeded to a term as chairperson that she set at six months in the belief that at the end of that time the position could be taken by a woman who could make it her major interest. She was hesitant also to serve longer than six months because she was a government employee, but inasmuch as her agency was not a defense agency, she decided that "that aspect was not too important."[51] "There is no doubt that the forthright common-sense qualities for which Judge Howorth is well known will enable her to set the course of this new organization," predicted a Washington newspaper columnist.[52]

In view of the unstructured nature of the Assembly and the declining membership of constituent groups, not even Howorth's skills and sense of direction could evolve a working program within six months. Most activity seemed to be that of a series of minor gatherings of the leaders of member organizations within the Assembly, composed mostly of Washington-area members. Howorth and the incoming chairperson, Mrs. Wyman Chadwick, a former president of the Ladies Auxiliary of the Veterans of Foreign Wars, recorded a broadcast for the Voice of America, a medium Howorth considered promising in promoting the Assembly's agenda. Other than that, the goals of the Assembly seemed no different than those of other existing groups: a recruitment drive for women's community and social services for armed-services personnel at nearby military installations, the appointment of women regional directors for the FCDA, and the support of women in the military branches. In her final report as chair, Howorth admitted that in the area of internal affairs the Assembly had "made little progress in improving its structure," but she was encouraged by the fact that clubwomen had "learned to know each other and that in itself was helpful." As for specific AAUW defense projects, members had shown films, set up air-warden systems, distributed FCDA bulletins, organized bloodmobiles, and, in particular, extended civil-defense programs into schools.[53]

Her report indicated that the Assembly was little more than a loose federation of representatives from the approximately ten remaining organizations of the original fourteen of February 1951. In February 1953 Pauline Mandigo, of the BPW, wrote Howorth and Marguerite Rawalt, the BPW representative to the Assembly, that "like a fleet in time of peace" the Assembly "can become a mothball program." The last meeting of the Assembly that Howorth attended was in October 1953, when only a handful of representatives of member organizations attended. Although it limped on until its last meeting in 1959, apparently the end of the Korean

War in June had sounded the death knell for the Assembly. It was an idea whose time had come and gone. Given that the Assembly's coffers, based upon contributions by member organizations of a mere one hundred dollars each, were miniscule, it was never fiscally solid.[54]

Still, Howorth was positive about the Assembly because it had been an effort to bring organized women's groups together for a common purpose. Moreover, she was convinced that during the McCarthy era the Assembly shielded from red-baiting extremists women's organizations whose political and social agendas had long been important but suspect in many quarters. She had reminded Susan Riley in 1951 that the AAUW was subject to "loose charges" that it was "the reverse of patriotism."[55] In blunter terms one might be tempted to say that the Assembly had been a "foil." Scholars of the women's movement during the decade conclude that it had "little or no impact on government policy toward women during the Korean War."[56] But there is no way to measure the Assembly's effect in actually mobilizing constructive attitudes and action on the part of the tens of thousands of members of its constituent organizations that promoted a useful climate for national defense.

Howorth viewed the AAUW's participation in the Assembly more as a means of injecting women into important aspects of government than as a matter of what the historian Laura McElnaney has called "atomic housewifery" or the "militarized women's housework" of cleaning, cooking, and family preparedness for an atomic disaster. Howorth surely found little inspiration in the FCDA's preachy bulletins on food preparation, bomb-shelter provisioning, and such, if she read them at all. And just as surely she was displeased by the disclaimers of Katherine Howard, FCDA's deputy director for women's civil-defense activities, and her FCDA women associates that they were not feminists. Howorth's own record of the Assembly and Assembly bulletins makes no reference to the FCDA's emphasis on domestic skills as women's surest line of defense. It remains unclear how much recognition the government's own civilian defense agencies gave to the Assembly, existing as it did outside government supervision. Nor is it certain that other AAUW leaders shared Howorth's enthusiasm for the Assembly. As early as May 1951, AAUW president Althea Hottel confided to Howorth even before Howorth became chair that she was "a bit apprehensive about our spreading ourselves too far on operations that involve more than clearing house information." The AAUW, she continued, "considered there was inadequate information on the part of the Civilian Defense Organization as to the specific contributions which various organizations could make."[57]

Howorth's role in the Assembly of Women's Organization for National Defense, like her role on the Committee on Women in World Affairs, reveals the fine line she learned to walk to avoid groups suspected as leftist organizations. She was careful all her life to dodge them. "I had narrow escapes," she told Constance Myers. "In Washington, or in life, you've got to make sure you don't get into fringe outfits." She had not joined the Lawyers Guild because she did not consider it to be "a bona fide professional organization." She discerned as early as 1935 that "you had to be careful what you joined." Avoiding organizations identified with the popular front of the Communist Party was one of the "most unpleasant parts of my activity with organizations."[58]

Likewise, she took care that the AAUW exercise caution in its endorsements of peace moves. When a Russian-inspired petition known as the Stockholm Peace Appeal, which called for nuclear disarmament of the United States, reached the International Federation of University Women (IFUW), Howorth advised the AAUW general director to warn the IFUW not to become involved, an action the State Department commended.[59] In a Voice of America broadcast Howorth cautioned women about peace programs that included Communists.[60] She knew that women's reform organizations had been dealt a serious blow by the "Spider Web" chart, first published in 1923, which had linked them with a vast international Communist conspiracy.[61] Patricia Carol Walls has described how during the McCarthy era right-wingers linked "sex solidarity" with Communism and thereby intimidated women's groups. The AAUW, aware of the high-profile ordeal of Esther Brunauer's and Dorothy Kenyon's tangles with Senate inquisitors, was sensitive lest it be charged itself.[62]

In 1939 the House Un-American Activities Committee had labeled the AAUW as subversive.[63] Memory of that no doubt gave Howorth pause when she decided upon a leadership role in the Assembly of Women's Organizations and made her doubly determined that the Assembly repel the vigorous attacks of public criticism from the *Chicago Tribune*. In fact, she cited the *Tribune*'s repeated criticisms of the Assembly as indicative of its significance. A rightist pamphlet, *America's Affairs*, assailed the Assembly as a subscriber to the "manufacture of packaged thinking for women" and named Lucy Howorth as one of several government employees involved. "Utter nonsense," was her response.[64]

Thus, it is easily understood that Howorth cast the Assembly as an organization to promote civil and national defense and deemphasized associations with internationalism. She felt secure enough about the Assembly to keep a full record of its work, whereas she destroyed most of her file on the Committee for Participation of Women in Postwar Planning (CWPP) and retained little on the CWWA in order to protect members who might be called before the McCarthy Committee to defend their internationalism.[65] She never stated exactly when she destroyed her CWPP files, but it could have been an action to protect Ellen Woodward at the time of her involvement in UNRRA assemblies. Landon R. Y. Storrs suggests that more than one public figure censored papers destined for archives, although Howorth made her decision before she prepared papers for the Schlesinger Library. Historians who have studied the Assembly view it much as does Joanne Meyerowitz: "In some cases, women (and men) used Cold War rhetoric to promote women's public policy participation. Some mainstream women's organizations adopted the language of the Cold War to strengthen their public mission in the postwar era."[66]

Nonetheless, Howorth's own affiliation with the two groups in the 1940s and 1950s was the subject of FBI queries when she applied for a government assignment in 1956. Interrogators questioned the nature of her association with an unidentified AAUW staff member whose "subversive" activities had later led to her resignation from a State Department job, in all probability Esther Brunauer, who had been the staff secretary of the AAUW's International Relations Committee. Howorth had first met Brunauer in 1932, when she was in Jackson to speak to the AAUW on the work of the IFUW. After being told by interviewees that the CWWA was "a good organization of good purposes" that by 1956 was inactive, the FBI raised no further questions. As to the Assembly, Howorth informed the FBI that her association had only been as a "representative on behalf of the AAUW." All persons interviewed concurred with one who stated that Howorth was "a person of excellent character, associates and loyal to the United States."[67]

Howorth's term on the Committee on the Status of Women ended in 1951, and upon her recommendation the committee leadership fell to Rosamonde Boyd.[68] The top tier of officers for the next four years included two Mississippians. The new president was Dr. Susan Riley, a George Peabody College professor of English who had been educated at Blue Mountain College, a small Baptist college for women in Mississippi. She had risen through the ranks both in her teaching career and in AAUW leadership.[69] The other was Howorth, who became the second vice president. In 1950 Melanie Rosborough had wanted to forward Howorth's name as AAUW national president, but Howorth had declined, citing her long-held credo that government-service personnel should not head national organizations that took positions on public issues. She agreed to serve as second vice president so that she could continue on the board of directors and contribute to "personnel matters." Congratulations came from members of her Committee on the Status of Women and from Kathryn McHale, who returned to the subject of the gulf between the AAUW executive committee's policies and its practice: "There has been a wide gap between what the Association believes in with respect to the advancement of Status of Women and what they have actually practiced."[70]

Howorth's new office entailed a great deal of travel until her term ended in 1955. Most often she attended branch functions throughout the country, later boasting that in one capacity or another she had spoken in every state but Nevada. In an AAUW board meeting in October 1951 Howorth expressed her belief that there was "a growing awareness" among members on matters relating to the status of women and said that she was therefore more encouraged than she had been while chair of the Committee on the Status of Women, although specific gains were hard to describe.[71]

Howorth's first major sortie was a Defense Department–sponsored whirlwind tour of defense installations for representatives of women's organizations, with transportation provided by the U.S. Air Force, from 7 to 12 May 1951. She joined women from the American Legion Auxiliary, the National Council of Negro Women, the YWCA, the American Farm Bureau, B'nai B'rith, and a wide variety of women's service and patriotic groups in visits, some overnight, to Bolling and Parkland air bases, Forts Lee and Benning, Paris Island, and the Great Lakes Training Station. With a keen eye turned to facilities and the welfare of women service personnel, Howorth reported a satisfactory integration of women with men in U.S. Army training, but she did not like the use of women exclusively for clerical positions in the Marines.[72]

The AAUW board had determined in 1950 that the second vice president should be responsible for administrative aspects of the association and maintain close contacts with the general director with respect to personnel, staff, and headquarters arrangements. The assignment fit in well with Howorth's earlier preoccupation with administration at the headquarters. She welcomed another opportunity to do what she could to draw more members into policymaking, and she encouraged frank discussion of AAUW policies and the qualifications of national officers on her visit to branches.

She continued to meet with the Committee on the Status of Women in an ex-officio manner. At its meeting soon after the election of Dwight D. Eisenhower as president in 1952, she reminded members that the AAUW should forward a revised roster of women qualified for officeholding to the new president and to the Women's Division of the Republican National Committee. With India Edwards replaced by Bertha Adkins as head of the women's division of the party in power, AAUW leaders had reason to begin a new round of lobbying for the appointment of women to federal offices.[73]

Howorth performed her duties during 1952 under a personal burden. Her mother, already in declining health, developed cancer and was confined to a nursing home in Ruleville, a small town near Cleveland. Until her death in July 1952 Somerville remained interested in public affairs and an avid reader.[74] She lived to know that in 1951 the Jackson AAUW branch established the Somerville-Howorth International Study Grant, through which a woman from a war-torn country could pursue graduate research in the United States,[75] and she knew of Howorth's promotion from assistant general counsel of the War Claims Commission to deputy general counsel in June 1952. She died before the final promotion in 1953, when Howorth became the general counsel of the commission, making her the first woman ever to be named a general counsel of an executive-department commission. Both advancements came at the intercession of India Edwards with President Truman's appointment advisers.[76] As general counsel, Howorth was responsible for the direction of the Claims Service, the Legislative Section, and the Appeals and Hearing Section, most of whose functions she planned and executed.[77] She described the work as demanding. It entailed long hours because claimants wanted quick settlements; internal pressures were heavy, and preparations of budget requests were tedious. A commission colleague later spoke of Judge Howorth as a "very capable lawyer," often "very set in her opinions . . . domineering [but] usually right."[78]

The move to the top spot came shortly after the inauguration of Dwight D. Eisenhower as president. Thus, Howorth worked as general counsel on borrowed time. In December 1953 the death of Dan Cleary precipitated a shake-up of the commission. "Hungry Republicans," as Howorth called them, waited in line for commission appointments even though by law the agency was to end its work in March 1955. Washington-wise, she understood the transition. She wrote to Georgia Lusk that "our Republican friends can scarcely control their impatience. . . . No one can blame them since it is entirely natural to want to reach for the presents hanging on the tree, once you know they are going to be yours." Eisenhower named three new commissioners, who in turn replaced Howorth. Entitled by law to a commensurate position, she "settled" for a three-month stint as a consultant, but with accrued leave she vacated her office in mid-January 1954. For the first time in nineteen years she was off the government rolls and no longer a presence at the White House. But that aspect of her public life had been limited. "My invitations during the Eisenhower years were very scanty," she admitted.[79]

Howorth was not happy about leaving. She wrote India Edwards that "the Republicans finally worked around to the War Claims Commission . . . [and] I don't pretend I'd have quit voluntarily." She said frankly, "I left because I was thrown out." Howorth knew that the commission's budget could not continue to absorb another employee at her level, and she did not wish to "stir up a big fight." However, she advised the two Democratic commissioners, Georgia Lusk and Myron Weiner, to contest their dismissal on grounds that the president could not fire members of an independent agency. Lusk chose to return to New Mexico, and Weiner's contest eventually was sustained by the U.S. Supreme Court, but by then the War Claims Commission had been dismantled and its jurisdiction transferred to the State Department.[80]

At last Howorth was free to enjoy a vacation. She combined business and pleasure and left in February 1954 for a month's trip to West Germany, England, Spain, and Portugal. As one of three lawyers, guests of the West German Federal Republic, she was to study "legal affairs," but her greater interest was to meet with members of the German Federation of Business and Professional Women and the German Association of University Women. She was particularly interested in learning how professional and academic women had fared under the Nazi regime, and upon her return she reported that the underground resistance to the Nazis had been spearheaded by university women, the IFBPW, the YWCA, and other professional women's groups. In London she attended a meeting of the IFUW and was the guest of honor at a dinner given by the British Federation.[81] She left London for Madrid to visit the newly formed Spanish Association for University Women. A pleasure jaunt into Portugal rounded out her foreign travel in 1954. After she returned home, Howorth drew the line at an invitation from U.S. promoters of the Korean-American Foundation, who sought to involve the AAUW in its fund-raising program because too little was known about its operations.[82]

Next, Howorth embarked on rapid-fire visits to AAUW branches in the Southwest and the Southeast, including the newly organized branch in Cleveland, Mississippi. In fact, by the time she gave another annual report to the AAUW board in 1955, she had attended an IFUW meeting in Paris and continued to travel to branches scattered from New York to the Dakotas. In concluding her last report as an AAUW executive officer, Howorth warned: "The AAUW must forever be on guard against mediocrity." She continued, "There must be an unremitting search for dynamic, creative minds as members and chairmen of our committees." She described her own associations during eight continuous years on the national board as "stimulating, interesting, and enlivening."[83]

Upon leaving her AAUW office, Howorth prepared a "Job Description" emphasizing that an AAUW second vice president should have expertise in financial oversight of the headquarters operation. Functioning with an annual budget of $350,000 and a staff of more than fifty employees and maintaining a fellowship endowment fund exceeding $1 million, the AAUW had become big business by the 1950s.[84] Howorth's legal knowledge served the organization well on several occasions. She gave legal advice regarding litigation when local branches sued seceding members to recover property in St. Louis, Baltimore, and Washington. The Washington case had come about after 1949, when the national board was compelled to purchase its headquarters property from the dissident members who opposed integration. In the St. Louis branch, the small majority that defied the national AAUW policy of branch integration won a circuit-court decision that permitted retention of branch assets, while the minority retained its AAUW affiliation and open membership. Castigating those members who resisted black membership, the *St. Louis Post Dispatch* deemed it "strange that following on the heels of the 1954 Supreme Court decision . . . a group whose binding interest is graduation from college [would] pursue a practice that colleges are giving up." Not surprising, Howorth retained a copy of the editorial.[85]

In 1955 Howorth became chair of an AAUW Building Commission, charged with studying the problem of facilities, for the association that had outgrown its quarters on I Street in Washington, first occupied in 1922. She donned rubber hip boots to examine the Foggy Bottom locale on Virginia Avenue, overlooking the Potomac River, that the AAUW had purchased for its new Educational Center. Meeting over a period of three years, the commission oversaw almost every detail of construction and furnishing until the handsome new headquarters opened.[86] It was one of Howorth's treasured memories of service to the AAUW. Later, when the AAUW voted in convention to establish a new complex at still another location, some members feared that Howorth's feelings would be hurt, but she understood the move and "never gave it a thought." At a later time, Howorth drew up the legal document that placed AAUW Educational Foundation funds in an irrevocable trust, safe from any transfer a future board might consider. She was anxious to protect the fellowships that Margaret Rossiter has called "a kind of female Guggenheim."[87]

One last assignment came when Howorth joined seven other AAUW members in 1956 to serve on a Survey Committee, chaired by Hallie Farmer and appointed in anticipation of the association's seventy-fifth anniversary. Its duty was to assess social and economic expectations for the following quarter-century and, President Susan Riley hoped, "the whole matter of staff relationships and functions," apparently still a concern to the national president in 1955. Riley suggested to Farmer that the committee concern itself with AAUW's need to reaffirm itself as an educational organization, the gap between effort and effect in the association's work in the field of national legislation, the cessation of its accreditation of institutions, its slowing growth in membership, and its need for more respectful public notice.[88]

Farmer, then completing her tenure at Alabama College, stated that the committee "floundered a good deal . . . and finally came a day when

Lucy Howorth said, 'Now it looks to me like this' and we all reached for our pencils." Members traveled throughout the country to examine services of the AAUW and determine how they could be reorganized.[89] The final report did not address any of Riley's concerns. Instead it pointed to a need to analyze the AAUW travel program, its publications and program materials, the lack of understanding of AAUW activities by local branches, the scholarship programs of branches and state divisions, and the distinction between policy formation and action responsibilities of elected national officers and the professional staff.[90] Much of the report reflected concerns that Howorth had long held.

As an aside to the committee's work, Howorth offered some projections of her own, entitled "Dateline 1980," about what lay ahead in women's education and employment. Likely she based her notions on her vast reading, particularly of government bulletins, and conferences she and Margaret Hickey attended, such as the October 1955 Columbia University–sponsored conference of the National Manpower Council (NMC). Apparently Howorth attended only one of the sixteen meetings of the NMC, but she followed its recommendations and studied its publications on womanpower. Considerable discussion at the 1955 meeting on the payment of unemployment compensation during and after pregnancy piqued Howorth's interest, and thus she rebutted comments that the payment of benefits during pregnancy would result in a higher birthrate among women in lower economic levels. "That," she countered, "is on par with the chatter as to tenants using bath tubs for coal bins." Her view that pregnancy constituted a medical disability and was not a "natural physiological process" had formed in her mind when women veterans had sought hospitalization for pregnancy while she was on the VA Board of Appeals. "The old belief, that childbearing was a personal and intimate family matter," she wrote, "presently conflicts with economic factors and the public concern in maintenance of the birth rate and maternal health." Consequently she petitioned the executive secretary of the NMC to provide "fresh air and sunshine" on the matter in studies following the Columbia conference.[91]

Howorth based her own projections of what lay ahead in 1980 on the premise that "the AAUW does not function in a vacuum" and hence should "think of what the social structure will be like." She predicted that there would be a 20 percent increase in graduates of women's colleges, a decline in the number of women's colleges, and a predominance of coeducational colleges. Elementary and secondary education increasingly would be provided in private schools. More married women would be drawn into paid jobs outside the home by increased mechanization and the money economy. Living forty years beyond forecasts made in 1956, Howorth saw them become actuality.[92]

Although Howorth was forced into retirement from government at age fifty-eight, she enjoyed the tributes paid her in the press and by friends. Augusta Marshall wrote, "It's more than absurd that your intelligence and experience should be subtracted from the country, it's disgusting." Molly Dewson wrote from Maine, "Your efforts and life and achievements came up to my expectations." Howorth told a Washington feature writer, "With all due modesty, but without an excess of it, I've done very well in my profession. I enjoy meeting people and working with them. I've had a wonderful life doing both."[93]

At one point, when Howorth declined the leadership of another of her organizations, Susan Riley wrote, "You have your personal life, your professional life, and your AAUW life, and that's lives enough for any woman."[94] Retirement after nearly two decades of government work in Washington and easing out of eight years in AAUW leadership would leave Howorth more time for a personal life that, she would have anyone know, had always been rich with friendships, travel, a devoted husband, and numerous social functions. In the years ahead all the pleasures of a private life would multiply, but women's organizations and activities for the public good would still bring her honors and satisfaction. And for a brief interim she would even work in Washington again.

8

"Just being Cleveland folks"
Retirement after 1957

HOWORTH DID NOT return to Mississippi immediately after she left government service in 1954. There was a brief stint at "lawyering" and a short period on the federal payroll before her resettlement in Cleveland. Even so, in retirement she would be consumed by the same interests that had always engaged her: the Mississippi branches of all her organizations, satisfying years with Joe, family, and friends, and abundant time to read and to pursue her interest in history. She admitted that political types such as herself found it hard to give up the center of attention, but reading helped her through it.[1] To a great extent, retirement to Cleveland and then advancing age relegated Howorth to the sidelines of women's activism, but she still found avenues to promote the status of women and retained a lively interest in the world around her.

In 1952, two years before she retired, Howorth's cousin James Somerville left the foreign service and opened a law practice in Washington. He had earlier worked in the Department of Commerce in foreign trade, and thus the firm of James Somerville Associates did business as foreign-trade consultants for corporations, securing information about projects and bids and doing related work. The firm did no lobbying or claims work. Howorth had gained admission to the Federal Bar of the District of Columbia in 1950 and joined the firm in the summer of 1954 to "look after legal matters and general Washington know how." The work did not interest her, and she left the firm in 1956.[2]

Still living in Washington, Howorth was anxious for short-term employment in the federal government, which would give her higher retirement benefits. Hence her interest was piqued in July 1955 when she read about the creation by Congress and President Dwight Eisenhower of a Commission on Government Security. The chairman was Loyd Wright, a Californian and president of the American Bar Association, and the vice chairman was Mississippi Senator John C. Stennis. Howorth approached Stennis about employment by the commission, and his recommendation to Wright of her "excellent background and qualification" carried weight, as did the support from Susan Riley of the AAUW, a member of the Advisory Committee of the Foreign Operations Administration, and one of the ten members of the commission. Riley assured Stennis that both of them would "profit from having another member on the staff whom we know personally." Thus, Howorth received a position in the legal-research arm of the commission's professional staff after an extensive but routine scrutiny by the FBI. Senators Stennis and his Mississippi colleague James O. Eastland gave assurances of her competence and unquestioned loyalty. One woman interviewed considered her "a very straightforward, blunt person . . . loyal and discreet"; another described her as "a woman with a great deal of common sense and honor . . . whose associates are above reproach." A Jackson, Mississippi, male lawyer responded that Howorth "possessed more judicial temperament than any woman he had ever known." Once she was past the routine scrutiny, Howorth's appointment was cleared "in two minutes flat."[3]

Howorth was always frank in admitting that she wanted the job to "push" her over the twenty-year mark for early retirement at age sixty-two. She knew that that was "not highly noble," but she gained added status with Wright when Stennis asked her to act as his representative on the commission.[4] The commission began its work in summer 1956 with lukewarm interest from the Eisenhower administration and too late to offset the worst of the anti-Communist hue and cry provoked by the McCarthy hearings. In June 1957 the commission issued an 807-page volume that stated its mission as to study and report on laws, executive orders, practices, and programs intended for the protection of national security. Senator Stennis and no doubt Lucy Howorth, in view of her earlier defense of women harassed by the McCarthy committee, believed that the "greatest single recommendation made by the Commission's report was the right to confront an accuser." She agreed with the commission's basic finding that a security program was imperative even though she believed that "such a program is a limitation on the free ranging of the mind."[5]

Howorth never addressed the commission's actual contribution to the creation of a positive image of Eisenhower's national security program, though she attributed the lack of attention its finding received to its work's being "too late." By the time the report appeared, national attention was focused upon issues other than vigilance against Communism. "We are all sailing off to the moon now, or wrestling with the specter of the depression," she wrote Susan Riley. She enjoyed, as she said, "being paid to read a great deal of material I had wanted to read but lacked time": Supreme Court decisions on security and treason matters, Whittaker Chambers's *Witness*, the Alger Hiss papers, congressional testimony, hearings on passport cases, and the like. For the final report, she wrote the legal basis for the sections on port security, passports, immigration, international organizations, and civil air transport. While she was happy to have the work, she later admitted that most special commissions "serve at best to deflect heat from officials," implying that the Commission on Government Security had done that for Eisenhower. No fan of the Republican president, she was likewise critical of his secretary of state, John Foster Dulles, citing him as "the heaviest footed person in that job since William Jennings Bryan and perhaps I am being hard on William Jennings."[6]

With the commission's work completed and Joe's Pentagon duty to end in September 1957, giving him a twenty-year retirement status as well, Howorth returned to Mississippi in July.[7] She convinced Joe that they should settle in Cleveland, where there would be lectures and concerts centered around Delta State University. After he joined her, they dabbled in a joint law practice, but neither was enthusiastic about it. Joe's work with the U.S. Army had been in legislative preparation and had not involved much law. He was "out of familiarity with decisions," and Lucy, "being very rusty," found that circuit-court trials absorbed too much of her time and energy. She longed to travel and pursue other interests. But when her brother Abram was ill for two years, she and Joe took over his practice.[8]

Howorth began renovation of the white frame house adjacent to the home of Keith Frazier Somerville, her brother Bob's widow, left to her by her mother. That, of course, was another strong reason to make Cleveland their permanent home. Howorth never regretted leaving Washington, convinced that it was wise to leave behind what was over. Her mother had written Ellen Woodward in 1938, "I cannot believe that anyone really wants to live permanently up there. . . . I tell Lucy the home folks are the real people." And Molly Dewson had written Howorth of her own desire to leave Washington,[9] but what seems to have most prompted Howorth's decision was her pique at being introduced after 1954 as "Mrs. Howorth WAS . . ." "I must get out of here," she thought, "and go someplace where I can BE." Other women Democrats felt a letdown when their work ended. Although never close to Emily Newell Blair, Howorth would have agreed with her statement in 1937 that "few experiences are more trying to the ego than that of becoming a has-been." Later, when her dear friend Ellen Woodward suffered serious bouts of depression in the 1960s, Howorth was convinced that Woodward should have left a Washington virtually empty of the women of the New Deal and returned to Mississippi. And Howorth knew, as Augusta Marshall wrote regarding the Washington career, "As [we] used to say of Randolph-Macon, you squeezed the lemon dry." Neither Lucy nor Joe missed Washington. They were "as happy if not happier just being Cleveland folks."[10]

Although Cleveland was a college town and known as one of the social hubs of the Mississippi Delta in the late 1950s, with a population of about seven thousand, it was hardly Washington. Howorth's sister-in-law Keith Somerville observed that many townswomen found little to do in Cleveland, "but not Lucy." Somerville recorded in her autobiography that "Lucy, back from her long full years in Washington, has joined every organization in town, thrown herself avidly into them and seems happy doing them." In time, Howorth became a regular at meetings of the AAUW, the Cleveland Woman's Club, the BPW, the Daughters of the American Colonists, the Daughters of the American Revolution, and the United Daughters of the Confederacy. She even became an honorary member of Delta Kappa Gamma, the honor society for teachers. Most often yearbooks listed her as parliamentarian, world-affairs chair, a member of the by-laws committee, or recipient of a "Woman of Achievement" award. Her sister Eleanor's membership in patriotic societies probably prompted Howorth to join, but unlike their mother, she never expressed sentiments for the Lost Cause. Howorth, however, did enjoy the explorations into history that were the usual program subjects of many of the groups. In addition to local groups, Howorth revived her work with the Mississippi YWCA and became a member of the state board of directors in 1958 and the state member of the national Public Affairs Committee in 1959. In accepting a lifetime, but absentee, membership in the Washington Soroptimist Club, she assuaged the fears of members who worried that she "was sitting on the front porch fanning and sipping a cold drink most of the day!"[11]

The Howorths returned to Mississippi at a time when racial animosity was at fever pitch. On the first day in her new home Howorth received an anonymous telephone call from someone angry about a statement she had made to the AAUW in Little Rock that public schools must be preserved "no matter what happens." More disturbing to her were threatening calls to her sister. Lucy and Joe had always held liberal views regarding race, but they had exercised caution and restraint, being careful not to join causes that would place them in the company of controversial individuals. For example, in the 1940s, upon the advice of Sue Shelton White, Lucy had chosen not to join the Southern Conference on Human Welfare. She viewed it as "a weapon widely used by die hards and demagogues to discredit all who would work toward change and solutions of pressing problems."[12] Nor had she made any effort while in Washington to become involved with Virginia Durr and the small band of southern liberals aligned against the poll tax. She admired Durr and later found her autobiography absorbing but avoided causes that she deemed unsuitable for a federal employee in her position.[13]

Pure and simple, the Howorths were reluctant to join the civil rights movement in Mississippi. Neither before nor after the Washington years could they afford to jeopardize their law practice. "We had to make a living," she once said, and in her reminiscences with Constance Myers in 1975 she stated her conviction that "you can't do more than one crusade in a lifetime." Moreover, by the time she and Joe returned to Cleveland, "we were tired."[14] Although they did not openly advocate civil rights for blacks, they contributed to the campaigns of the black candidates Reuben Anderson in his race for the Mississippi Supreme Court and Mike Espy in his quest for a seat in Congress. After Espy's victory in 1986 Lucy wrote a friend, "I am impressed with Espy though I would like a half hour with him, then I tell myself I am past 90 and should let others run the world— including Mississippi." Few people knew that she often made contributions to Amzie Moore, a prominent black civil rights figure in Cleveland, and to the National Association for the Advancement of Colored People.[15]

When Linda Coleman, a young black lawyer, was elected to the Mississippi legislature in 1991, Howorth invited her for a visit to offer encouragement and the generous advice that she was always ready to dispense. Of former Mississippi senator James Eastland, an archopponent of civil rights legislation who was living in retirement in nearby Doddsville,

Howorth thought the "less said about Jim the better." As for Mississippi politics in general, Joe and Lucy both eschewed openly joining forces with candidates from their new base in Cleveland because of the bitterness over civil rights, and they spurned an invitation to join the anti-integrationist White Citizens' Council. Unknown segregationists who resented the Howorths' liberal tendencies threw garbage on their lawn and rocks at their windows, and they received "dirty phone calls."[16]

One opportunity to advance interracial progress came through Lucy Howorth's role on the Cleveland Public Library Commission and through the town's library, long a beneficiary of women's organizations. Howorth represented the AAUW on a Cleveland Chamber of Commerce committee to develop a "little bitty" library into a countywide system. Her library work brought her into contact with LePoint Smith, the new library director, whom Howorth described as "a genius for administration" and to whom she offered sage advice for the smooth integration of the library.[17] When Pauline Tompkins, general director of the AAUW, asked Howorth to marshal support in Cleveland for compliance with the provisions of the public-accommodations title of the civil rights bill in 1964, Howorth declined. She reasoned that she needed to preserve her influence in the community to maintain library service for blacks. "Libraries," she wrote, should "serve all citizens, many of whom have never experienced a library and some of whom have never loved a book."[18]

Howorth did not have the affiliation with a religious denomination that motivated many women of conscience to join the civil rights movement. In fact, she had little interest in formal religion because she believed that churchmen had been dilatory in advancing women's rights, a viewpoint that she may have gained from her mother's early encounter with church elders. "Oh, they just burn me up," she told Constance Myers, in speaking of the rejection of women leaders by males in many southern churches. After Anne Scott described opposition in North Carolina to the ERA, Howorth retorted, "I would not be surprised if some of these religious zealots do not revive the argument as to whether or not women have souls." Never shy about the subject, Howorth was certain that organized religion throughout the ages had "sat on" women to "push them back."[19]

Lucy Howorth consciously chose not to "take on" racial injustice as a major cause even though she considered herself to be "liberal on race" because the one major cause for her was the all-encompassing matter of women's rights.[20] Living in Cleveland did not isolate her from the national women's movement. She maintained ties with the stalwarts, particularly Margaret Hickey, now a senior editor of the *Ladies' Home Journal.* Late in 1961 Hickey wrote to arrange time together when Howorth would be in Washington early the next year. "We might manage to have a dialogue about the world we want," Hickey hoped. She had just been appointed to President John F. Kennedy's President's Commission on the Status of Women (PCSW). In December 1961 Kennedy established the official body to examine and make recommendations on a number of federal procedures and legislation that concerned women, particularly employment, social insurance and earnings, labor laws, child care, and legal treatment. Hickey was to chair the Federal Employment Policies and Practices Committee, one of seven commission task forces.[21]

The two old friends must have discussed the new commission during their dinner in Washington in early March 1962, for Howorth received an appointment to join Hickey's fourteen-member committee, with its first meetings slated for 3 and 9 April in Washington. Members heard depositions on employment practices and discussed the scope of their activities. "Your presence meant so much to me today in so many ways," Hickey wrote Howorth after the first meeting. "I cherish our conversations," she added, anticipating Howorth's reactions to the start of the work.[22]

After a meeting of PCSW commissioners at the Hyde Park home of the commission honorary president, Eleanor Roosevelt, Hickey could report to her committee members that the PCSW had adopted the Federal Employment Policies and Practices Committee resolution on equity for women in the military. The presence on Hickey's committee of John Macy, chairman of the Civil Service Commission, added weight to the committee's request that a woman employee with a nondependent husband receive the same governmental contribution toward health insurance as a male employee with a family. By the time the Federal Employment Policies and Practices Committee met again in September 1962 it had accomplished several goals, but it had not yet dealt with presidential appointment of women to federal positions. At the September session the committee heard from a panel of six winners of the Federal Women's Award, among them three scientists.[23]

After years of observing a president's reluctance to appoint women to important policy jobs, Howorth believed from the start that John F.

Kennedy's own appointment practices were subject to severe criticism. He had named no woman to his cabinet, and he had made fewer Senate-confirmed appointments of women to executive and judicial posts than either Truman or Eisenhower. Furthermore, he had given no attention to the roster of women his aides inherited from his predecessors; more to the point, he had failed to consult Democratic women leaders. In a letter to Sarah Hughes, Howorth estimated that about 75 percent of the president's appointments of women were "social . . . nothing in the power structure." Howorth was certain that the president's motivation in creating the PCSW was "to take the heat off" his failure to recognize political women.[24]

Speaking to the student body at the Mississippi State College for Women in October 1962, Howorth reported the PCSW finding that of the more than half-million women in civil service jobs, 79 percent were in the lowest five of eighteen grades. In grades thirteen and above there were twenty-five men to one woman, a ratio of 98 percent. The Federal Employment Policies and Practices Committee scored a major success when Attorney General Robert F. Kennedy asked for a review of an 1870 statute that gave the head of a governmental department the right to request that men be employed in high-level jobs. In June 1962 the statute was rescinded, ending a practice by which 94 percent of job requests had resulted in positions for men.[25]

Although not a member of Hickey's task force, Evelyn Harrison, a deputy director in the Civil Service Commission, assisted the committee, especially in assessing and reporting statistics for the final report. Writing on "facts, not fancy" about "Women in the Federal Service," she dispelled erroneous assumptions that women workers took excessive sick leave, left their jobs more frequently than men, had limited career aspirations, were not considered good training risks, and preferred men to women supervisors. She concluded that the "general composition of the Federal work force is a result primarily of lack of job opportunities for women"; furthermore, the negative attitudes of men about the capabilities of women for higher positions were "widespread."[26]

Thus, Howorth was alert to what the task force would propose. After Margaret Hickey sent committee members a draft of her report based upon meetings held thus far, Howorth replied that the "tone of the report as a whole seems smug." She believed that the committee had "acted on the premise that more was to be gained by being suave than by being aggressive." The report would be subject to censure for "its present rosy atmosphere.... We all know that women do not get the breaks." Hickey agreed that "this is the area where the Federal government has fallen down." Howorth found Hickey's second draft of the committee report in June 1963 to be a harder-hitting statement, but she still advised against any phrasing that might be construed as "a bit of whitewash that weakens the tone." But on the whole she found the report to be "excellent" and was "pleased to be associated with it."[27]

On 11 October 1963, Eleanor Roosevelt's birthday, President Kennedy accepted the report of his PCSW in the presence of a large number of commission members and representatives of the seven committees or task forces. Howorth was present but does not appear in the historic photograph because at the last minute she stepped to the second row and pushed forward a woman government employee who was in line for a promotion. Eight weeks later, after Kennedy's assassination, Howorth was glad that she had made the effort to be at the presentation and in the presence of "the wonderfully alert and friendly President who had so much to do, and unknowingly so little time to get it started."[28]

The segment of the final PCSW report prepared by Hickey's committee bore heavily the imprint of the chair and her mainstay, Lucy Howorth, as well as that of the influential John Macy. Yet again, a primary recommendation was that a roster of qualified women be submitted to the chief executive, and the task force advised him to appoint an interdepartmental committee on women's employment.[29] Kennedy's untimely death in November left PCSW implementation to Lyndon B. Johnson. Howorth was never again involved in any official deliberations on advancing women's status in federal employment, but at least she had the satisfaction of knowing that President Johnson tapped Margaret Hickey to carry out PCSW recommendations. Howorth continued to believe that Hickey had been a far more positive force on the PCSW than Esther Peterson, the anti-ERA chief of the Women's Bureau, who had been Kennedy's choice to direct the PCSW.[30]

Both Hickey and Howorth were disappointed that the PCSW report, *American Women,* avoided the subject of the ERA, but they agreed that the issue would fragment the commission's work. Endorsement of the ERA by the national AAUW in 1971 was immensely satisfying to Howorth, and release of the amendment by Congress to state legislatures in 1972 gave her new hope for victory. However, she feared its opposition by "employers who see a cheap source of labor going down the drain," and she was dismayed that proponents had "let themselves be taken over by crackpots, sexpots, etc." She found the arguments against the ERA as spurious as ever: "It's going to unsex you; it's going to break up the home, and so forth. . . . It's just exasperating to have to go over and over the same old ground."[31] And once again she saw the ERA meet defeat when the requisite number of states failed to ratify.

Howorth was merely an observer of the second wave of feminism in the 1960s and 1970s, but she wrote to Duke University historian Anne Firor Scott that it had "renewed my faith that all is not lost." She did not become involved with the National Organization of Women, but she thought it "has followed a fairly sound policy."[32] She did, however, consider its endorsement of gay rights "a political mistake." "If we are going to win political rights for women, we can't go picking up everybody that is wronged."[33] She had known lesbian and gay couples, "always easy to discern," but their liaisons "never played any part in my judgment of the abilities of the women or the men." Yet, she considered the "common practice" of historians in recent years to interpret associations of two women as sexual relationships "a great disservice." Howorth most assuredly never renounced her feminism, but she was concerned that some of the modern leaders were too blatantly anti-men. She never was "against men," and told Mississippi AAUW members in 1983 that "every door that opened for me in sixty-five years was opened by men."[34] It was odd that she did not add that in most cases it had been a women's group that had pressed upon the men the appointment she received.

The truth may be that the women's movement of the late 1960s and 1970s left Howorth somewhat behind the times, as did counterculture movements. She found "those awful hippies" appalling when she saw women walking behind men in "squaw-like fashion." She lamented, "If that didn't disgust me after all that most of my friends had done for thirty or forty years trying to get women respected as persons. . . . I was really very discouraged then."[35] She remained constant in her belief that no organization had done as much as the AAUW to bring about equity for women, and it was to that body that she devoted her remaining energies after 1956. She continued to attend national conventions and served on the boards of the *AAUW Journal* and the Educational Foundation board and also chaired the by-laws committee of the latter. Still, she intended to scale down her AAUW work at the national level. "If you really mean to be an interested observer instead of participant in national AAUW, it's a great loss, that's all I can say," her friend Augusta Marshall wrote. Pauline Tompkins, AAUW general director, wrote of Howorth's "truly extraordinary contributions," which had left the association and the Educational Foundation "far richer."[36]

Lucy Howorth's wisdom, a New Mexico leader wrote, was the "characteristic I valued the most and thus stood up the best thru the changing years." Knowing of Howorth's role in opening the AAUW to black graduates in 1949, AAUW leaders in southern states wrote to her of their own efforts to integrate local branches. Scholars writing on women's organizations during the racial conflict of the 1950s and 1960s have faulted the AAUW for its reluctance to tackle racial issues head on and its failure to endorse the 1954 Supreme Court decision on school desegregation. Susan Lynn writes that after the AAUW convention that admitted blacks to membership, "the AAUW never made civil rights a major priority." One Little Rock member expressed to Howorth her wish that the national office "would see fit to give some recognition to humble local branches which try to carry out the ideals handed down from there."[37]

Some branches whose members joined the AAUW for the social relationships it offered wished to use the AAUW name and remain within the state division without affiliating with the national AAUW, which made it possible for them to dodge accepting black members. Even though such groups were instructed that the tactic was not permissible, resistance to the national policy persisted. Howorth, knowing there would be problems for the AAUW nationally and locally, advised the national office to "aid the moderates and calm the radicals and with good will on all sides work out a resolution." In view of the failure or reluctance of the national AAUW leadership to act decisively on the 1954 Supreme Court decision, Howorth's advice seemed to offer the only sensible recourse. AAUW historian Susan Levine concluded in 1995, "The issue of race remained unsettled in AAUW as it did in other liberal organizations." It could well be that it was Howorth's disarming advice to Mississippi branches that helped alleviate some of the local AAUW friction over the integration of both local branches and the public schools, but as with so many of her actions on social issues, it is impossible to know how much credit she deserved for the betterment of race relations in Mississippi.[38] And certainly in her lifetime there were few black members in branches in the state.

When Pauline Tompkins wrote Howorth that AAUW members could enlist as a group to support civil rights measures before Congress, Howorth replied that most members of the Cleveland branch were "unprepared for what is happening." The majority of its members, public-school teachers and college faculty, could not assert themselves without reprisal. Even in her own speech at the Mississippi State College for Women in October 1962 she did not touch upon civil rights in deference to her sponsors, whom she did not want to "get into any difficulty." As for the citizenry in Mississippi, "the Snopeses are very much in control." Resentment of the public-accommodations measure of 1964 was so strong in many southern AAUW groups that the southeastern regional vice president appealed to Tompkins not to make "moves of the nature" suggested by the AAUW, that is, in favor of compliance. Howorth attempted to mediate the matter when she spoke in 1966 to the Mobile meeting of the Southeast Central Region: "Today we are faced with the new trend in civil rights legislation . . . we must cooperate and accept it intelligently or fall by the wayside."[39]

Howorth did not always agree with national AAUW policy. She told Arkansas AAUW members in 1958, "Education is the greatest concern of university women and we should continue to grow and expand our influence." In 1974, when she spoke to the state conference in Vicksburg, Mississippi, she warned that the national association was trying to "spread itself a little thin" by "running after fads and fancies that loom across the horizon." She would have been more helpful had she specified those activities that she considered to be outside the scope of the AAUW's mission. She said that the AAUW must remember that its basic purpose "is education broadly," but she did not say what she meant by that. However, in looking toward the fiftieth anniversary of the Mississippi Division in 1977, she was certain that the AAUW had "contributed to a better social structure" in the state. In the 1980s, when the national AAUW was beset by financial deficits and declining membership, Frances Concordia, a former national treasurer with whom Howorth had worked well, wrote to ask Howorth to contact the national president to say that she was "disappointed that educated women are not able to handle financial affairs better than they did."[40] Howorth stayed out of the muddle.

Cora Norman, who received national recognition for her leadership in the Mississippi Division, credits Howorth with introducing her to AAUW procedures at the Chicago convention in the late 1960s. For Norman, who served as Mississippi Division president from 1974 to 1976 and was elected vice president for development of the Educational Foundation in 1985, Howorth was the "foremost role model" and her "first feminist." Norman has noted that Howorth became "more a mentor than an activist at the state level."[41] She never held a major office in the state division after retirement and served only as the chair of the International Relations Committee in 1961, but she was a commanding presence from the time she returned to Mississippi until well past the age of ninety.

In 1973 Norman began a national drive to establish an Educational Foundation fellowship named for Howorth. Launched with the largest initial amount ever for a fund of its kind, the drive developed momentum as "We Love Lucy" buttons carried the message across the nation about her more than sixty years' affiliation with the AAUW. That affiliation had begun in New York City in 1918 when Howorth entered a door whose sign read "University Women's Club." She had joined as a member-at-large in 1923, before Mississippi had an AAUW organization, and then she had joined the Jackson branch in 1928, a year after the state division was formed.[42]

Within three years contributions reached the figure required to meet the national AAUW stipulation for completion of a fellowship. The drive "has given new vitality to the Mississippi Division of AAUW," a state officer wrote in 1976. National officers were present for the honors bestowed upon Howorth as the Lucy Somerville Howorth Fellowship Endowment was finalized with the sum of eighty thousand dollars at the Mississippi Division conference at Tupelo in 1983. In the book of letters presented to her that day was a letter from her Monteagle Assembly neighbor and longtime friend Andrew Lytle in which he had written, "Where Lucy is, darkness is not."[43] The event was the culmination for Lucy of long eventful years with the organization that above all others had meant the most to her.

Howorth always enjoyed the study of history and its uses and never failed to draw upon its lessons in her talks. Anne Firor Scott once wrote to her, "A good legal training is also useful for historical reconstruction." Able after retirement to pursue the past at leisure, Howorth concentrated upon women's history, particularly that of Mississippi women of achievement. In speaking to the Jackson BPW in 1943 on the response of women to calls for wartime service, she had lamented the "reluctance" of many nonsoutherners to admit that southern women had "any ability or intelligence" or had made "any contribution toward a solution of public problems." Forty years later she was still "amazed" at the lack of knowledge among "apparently informed women" about recent issues. She was upset at the time because a widely read Mississippi woman columnist did not know who Ellen Woodward was. Even Eleanor Roosevelt would be unknown "unless historians keep writing and shouting."[44]

Thus, Howorth set about to rectify matters. In 1975 she presented her paper "Recollections of Mississippi Women in Public Life" to members of the Mississippi Historical Society, emphasizing women who had served in the state legislature before and during her own tenure and women in the legal profession. A favorite was Bessie Young, the first woman graduate of the University of Mississippi Law School (1915), who as a lawyer in the Treasury Department had had "hair raising" experiences with rumrunners off Long Island in the 1920s. Howorth spoke also of Helen Carloss, a Yazoo City native who went to Washington in 1918 and became a clerk in the Income Tax Division of the Internal Revenue Service and entered the George Washington University law school, receiving her degree in 1923. In 1930 she became an assistant to the U.S. attorney general, and she later won the admiration of U.S. Supreme Court Chief Justice Harlan Stone, who called her arguments as a Department of Justice tax attorney "an intellectual treat." Nor did Howorth omit Burnita Shelton Matthews of Hazlehurst, the George Washington University law school graduate, who in 1949 became the first woman to be named a federal district court judge.[45] Howorth had known all three jurists during the Washington years.[46] Two years later, in 1977, Howorth gave the eulogy on Ellen Woodward at ceremonies in Jackson when Woodward's portrait was added to the Mississippi State Hall of Fame.[47]

In retirement Howorth enjoyed a personal friendship with a number of authors, particularly Karen Morello and Anne Firor Scott. From 1981 to 1987 Howorth maintained a lively exchange with Morello, who published several articles and a book, *The Invisible Bar: The Woman Lawyer in America, 1638 to the Present*, describing their achievements despite myriad forms of discrimination. Morello's work to grant visibility to long-forgotten and little-known women of the bar engaged Howorth's cooperation. "So far I haven't been able to name a woman lawyer you don't know something about," Morello wrote in 1981 after the two had met in New York City. Howorth took particular delight in Morello's account of her success and that of other women who had been denied admission to Columbia University before 1927.[48]

Even more lasting was Howorth's association with Anne Scott. The two first met soon after Scott discovered the Somerville-Howorth Collection at the Schlesinger Library and began research on her classic work, *The Southern Lady: From Pedestal to Politics, 1830–1930,* first published in 1970. A correspondence of more than forty years' duration and a few personal contacts in Mississippi followed their initial conversation at the AAUW headquarters, in Washington, during a snowstorm in 1958. Assigned to write entries on Belle Kearney, the Mississippi suffragist and temperance advocate, and Nellie Nugent Somerville for *Notable American Women,* Scott enlisted Howorth's aid. Long letters followed in which Howorth wrote of her personal knowledge of the two, both of whom had entered the Mississippi legislature in 1924. After Howorth read *The Southern Lady* "with delight and admiration," she took steps to see that it circulated among her friends.[49]

"You are an ever-present inspiration to me," Scott wrote Howorth, but the influence was mutual.[50] It is likely that Scott's initial inquiries about Nellie Nugent Somerville prompted Howorth to undertake publication of the wartime letters of William L. Nugent, her maternal grandfather, to his young wife, Eleanor Smith Nugent, who died in 1866, when Nellie was three years old. Coedited by Howorth and Delta State University professor William M. Cash, *My Dear Nellie* was published in 1977.[51]

Howorth always knew that contentions surrounded her mother's causes. "I was very aware as a child of controversy," she said in 1984. "If anybody said anything snippy about my mother, I would have none of it."[52] Thus, years later few historians, if any, openly confronted Howorth with the fact that Nellie Somerville's influence declined precipitately in her later years as she became a social reactionary and personally cantankerous. Somerville had been critical of the New Deal but had taken pride in Howorth's appointment in Washington. There is no record, however, that she ever visited her daughter while she was there. Her son Bob's sudden death in 1946 was a terrible blow to Somerville. Unfortunately, Lucy's work was especially demanding just then, and she could not be away from Washington for long.

By the 1940s Nellie Somerville had defended the poll tax and segregation, opposed President Truman's civil rights, and bolted the Democratic Party in 1948 for the States Rights Party.[53] She had even turned against jury service for women, convinced that women were not intelligent enough to serve. Because she was bored in Cleveland, her children advised Somerville to take a hotel room in Greenville during the coldest months, but with the death of many of her Greenville friends, she decided to make Memphis her second home after she became involved with an Independent Methodist Church there. She had left her own church when the northern and southern Methodist congregations united in an action to heal old disputes over race.[54] Nellie Somerville was uncompromising on her principles. She erased from her family tree the branch of her family who owned a tavern.[55] She kept stacks of silver dollars on hand at Monteagle to offer to any bare-legged young woman for the purchase of hose. She wanted Monteagle to remain decent, she said.[56] One Monteagle resident observed that Somerville did not "suffer fools gladly," and another recalled that "when she spoke people listened."[57] Once told that people were afraid of her, she retorted, "I find that very convenient."[58] Nellie Somerville's unrelenting arguments, her stolid opposition to inevitably changing social customs, and her fearsome demeanor alienated many of Cleveland's citizens and made life difficult for members of her family.[59]

Whether Howorth, away in Washington, was aware of her mother's hostility to most of the world around her or chose to dismiss her mother's recalcitrance by remembering the many positive aspects of her life is not clear. Whatever the reason, Howorth lapsed into nothing less than a canonization of her mother. In long hours of conversation with historians Howorth gave no indication of the changes that marked her mother's aging years, when she became alienated from both people and the principles for which she once stood. "It's accurate, but I guess it's impossible to capture the life," Howorth said unenthusiastically when shown the entry Dorothy Shawhan had written on Somerville for *American National Biography*. And she said little about Anne Scott's honest sketch of her mother for *Notable American Women*, which explored contrasting elements within Somerville's makeup.[60]

Yet Nellie Somerville could be unassuming. "I never sought office. My rule was to accept only when no one else was both able and willing to serve. If other competent women were available then I had no call to take time from home and family duties. I have sometimes said that my holding various offices was due to lack of material."[61] This apologia from her older, conservative self is not convincing in light of the new ground she broke for women in her time and place in history, nor does it ring true in light of the direction in which she guided Lucy. However difficult Nellie Somerville became in her latter years, it did not diminish the fact that she was a major liberalizing force in Mississippi for forty years. Several persons whom the FBI questioned in 1933 about Howorth's family background lauded her mother, one stating that "she made a very decided mark for herself as a campaigner for a better type of citizenship."[62] In 1981 she became the fourth woman to be named to the Mississippi Hall of Fame in ceremonies at the Old Capitol that drew a proud Lucy and thirty-five descendants. In 1983 Anne Scott remarked about the remarkable Somerville mother-daughter team that "together they ought to upset everybody's stereotypes of Mississippi."[63]

By that time Howorth knew that her mother would be a major subject in the resurgence of scholarship on the woman's suffrage movement that came in the wake of a new wave of feminism. A renewed interest in the women in the New Deal made Howorth aware that she too was a potential candidate for a biography, and she was gratified to see that historians such as Susan Ware and Leila Rupp had written of her in their books. She was "just plain glad" that books were coming out showing "we did not play dead 1920–1960."[64] When Constance Myers expressed appreciation for the time granted her over a period of three days in 1975 at Monteagle, Tennessee, the eighty-year-old Howorth replied, "That is no particular gift at my stage in life."[65] She told another historian, "I lose no sleep as to whether or not anything is written about me." She "never did expect to be up front in history," but she was "amazed" at the short memory of the public, "with so many really great women being unknown in the records of today's women." Hence, Howorth renewed efforts to forward additional material to the Schlesinger Library and spent countless hours in interviews with historians, who recorded recollections of her mother's life, her own, and those of women of her century. She also devoted time to sorting through her possessions and distributing personal mementoes and photographs to friends for whom they would have meaning. "We do not get up each day thinking it may be our last. . . . We do know if items are to get into the hands of someone who will appreciate them, we'd better see to it ourselves."[66]

"Never daughten youth," she advised one of the academicians who visited her. Throughout her working years she had spoken to collegiates at Randolph-Macon. When the college instituted a women's studies program and named for Howorth that section of the library housing works on women's studies, she sent more than one hundred books. That was in 1972, but as early as 1929 she had written that the college should have a collection of the biographies of women.[67] In addition to podium appearances on college campuses, she enjoyed meeting with classes to discuss the history of the women's movement and engage in exchanges with students. Graduate students at Delta State University produced theses based on interview sessions at the Howorth home.[68] She visited classes at Delta State and at the University of Mississippi. Uncertain about how students would react to an octogenarian dressed in fashions long out of style, including her signature beret, professors found that she stimulated student discussions. Often on the university campus at Oxford, she was a guest of her AAUW friend Katherine Rea, dean of women, and, later, of Joanne Varner Hawks, head of the Sarah Isom Center for Women's Studies. Howorth became a campus favorite. She advised a class in women's history, "Put some iron in your spine and remember life can be fascinating, and it can be fun and you can get something done if you just keep your mind on it."[69]

Partial to Delta State, the Howorths were generous in their financial support.[70] In 1974 they endowed the Nellie Nugent Somerville Lectures in Government and Public Affairs, which brought to campus distinguished public figures, beginning with Congresswoman Edith Green of Oregon and later including an eminent leadership group that included Senators Mark Hatfield of Oregon and Nancy Kassebaum of Kansas and also future First Lady Hillary Clinton. Howorth herself was a frequent speaker on campus, challenging the student body in an Honors Day speech in 1985 to assist in building "a unified community from a great diversity of people." She admitted her discouragement at the lack of openness in students' approach to racial issues. "I see little of young white college students but what I see tells me they are back in 1910," she wrote a friend, but, she added, "occasionally one turns up who seems to face reality and the necessity for change."[71]

One final gift to Delta State came in a stipulation in her will that the new university archives receive a handsome sum for an ongoing exhibit and a lecture series focusing upon the accomplishments of women. Howorth also devoted time and allocated money to the University of Mississippi. Dean of Women Rea was elated in 1958 when she saw Howorth "in a huddle" with Alpha Omicron Pi members, for she had wanted the college women to know the celebrated alumna. Howorth saw in a university organization plan that would eliminate programs in which high numbers of women were enrolled an effort "to knock out anything that would put any real sense in the heads of women students." She promoted a resolution of the Mississippi AAUW to support retention of the newly established but endangered Isom Center for Women's Studies. She spent the summer of 1983 "beating the drums to save the Isom,"[72] but in the end the actions of Chancellor Porter Fortune proved to be the saving grace.

Over the years the three institutions that held Lucy's strongest affections heaped honors upon her. In 1940 she became an alumna initiate of Phi Beta Kappa at Randolph-Macon, and in 1976 the Delta State chapter of the leadership honorary Omicron Delta Kappa elected her to membership, as did the scholastic honorary Phi Kappa Phi at the University of Mississippi in 1985.[73] Among the honorary membership approved by the national board of Phi Kappa Phi that year was another nominee of the University of Mississippi, the writer Eudora Welty.

Numerous honors came to Howorth, by now past the age of eighty. In 1975 she was named Mississippi Woman of the Year by a consortium of six major women's organizations in the state.[74] In 1981 Randolph-Macon selected her as one of three women to receive the first Alumnae Achievement Award. Three universities in her home state honored her: the University of Mississippi named her to the Alumni Hall of Fame in 1984; the Mississippi State University President's Commission on Women named her Outstanding Mississippi Woman in 1985, and the Mississippi University for Women presented its Medal of Excellence in 1990 to five women leaders in the legal profession in the state, among whom Howorth was the oldest. Recognition by institutions of higher learning, in state and out, gave her immense satisfaction, for she remained a constant learner, leading one writer to observe, "Education is more than addendum to the volume of her 91 years, it's more like the thesis statement of each chapter of her life."[75]

The most prestigious of all honors that came to Lucy Howorth in her retirement was a Lifetime Achievement Award presented in 1983 at a celebration of the fortieth anniversary of the Arthur and Elizabeth Schlesinger Library at Radcliffe College. Upon learning that she was to be a recipient, she confessed, "I'm not making any pretense—I'm excited," adding, "I'm not too much of a modest person in life—but I'm overcome by this." She was pleased that two of the nine recipients were Mississippians; the other was Eudora Welty. The award was granted with the citation, "Leadership in voluntary associations and the profession of law, you have brought humor, empathy and skill with a story of a life devoted to advancing the opportunities open to women. Participant in federal, state, and local government, tireless in your support of needed change, you have by your example helped to shape an expanded role for American women in the twentieth century."[76]

Before leaving for Cambridge, Howorth told a reporter, "I'm going to talk about women's organizations over the years because you wouldn't be where you are today if it were not for them."[77] In a mosaic of her life experiences, Howorth spoke of her long work with women's organizations from the New York City days to the 1960s, when she served on the task force of the PCSW. As a tribute to organizational work, she said, "We do not always appreciate that what is accomplished in the United States is accomplished through organizations. Organizations open doors for women. Advances for women do not happen by accident. Nothing happens by accident." Departing from her prepared remarks, she challenged the statement of the previous honoree, Dr. Helen Brooke Taussig, who had said that "laws do not change things." Howorth cited the Civil Rights Act of 1960, which protected the black woman's right to vote, one of many laws that had guaranteed rights to women. Witty, somewhat acerbic, controlled, and strong in voice, Howorth "stole the show," Anne Scott heard when she returned to Cambridge several months later.[78]

Later in 1983 Howorth boasted, "I, in my stormy days, could shake up an audience."[79] She had not gone to Cambridge to create a sensation, nor had she done so. Yet the limited remarks she made there are among the most telling of her deep appreciation for what united women had done to advance her career. The Radcliffe program was easily the ultimate event in Lucy Howorth's nearly six decades at public podiums.

9

"Nothing like living a long time"
The Last Years

"THERE'S NOTHING like living a long time; try to see that you do," Judge Lucy advised a young historian who interviewed her in 1983.[1] Already she had lived almost thirty years since her retirement from government work. Fourteen more years would follow, filled less with the advocacies that had been her lifeblood and more with the pleasures of life as a private citizen among old acquaintances. Correspondence and travels during the last three decades of her life, which centered around old friends and favorite haunts at home and abroad, were offset by the sadness that came with the illness and loss of her husband in 1980.

The University of Mississippi remained a focus of Lucy Howorth's attention. In 1986 she attended a reunion at the university of the small group of remaining staff members of the *Mississippian*, and she witnessed a revival of interest in the Marionettes, the drama group through which she had known William Faulkner. Earlier, in 1950, when Faulkner had balked at attending the dinner at Stockholm where he would receive the Nobel Prize, Howorth had been first in the chain of contacts to try to persuade him to go. Muna Lee, a graduate of the University of Mississippi who had been a favorite poet of the reluctant author and at the time an officer in the cultural arm of the Department of State, learned from Howorth just which Oxford residents would be most likely to persuade Faulkner to relent, which he did in the end.[2] Howorth later wrote an article based on her reminiscences of Faulkner for the *Delta Review*, and she was one of the old circle often visited by scholars writing on the Oxonian. "These Faulkner people really dig," she chortled, "however, such visits keep life from growing dull." Carvel Collins, in his introduction to Ben Wasson's biography of Faulkner, *Count No 'Count*, recorded that Howorth had supplied "significant information."[3]

Howorth devoted many days to her correspondence with friends of long standing. Polly Graham had first come to the Delta in the 1920s, when Nellie Nugent Somerville had supervised the work of the YWCA. When Polly left Mississippi, she went to Manila, the capital of the Philippines, to work for the YWCA. There she married Will Babcock, a businessman, and they barely made it back to the United states before the Japanese attack in 1941. She and Howorth saw each other occasionally in Washington and in New York. When her husband Will died, Polly married Henry Feustal and moved to Florida. In 1968 Polly returned to Mississippi for a celebration of the fiftieth anniversary of the Jackson YWCA, and she returned again in 1983, when she and her husband visited Cleveland, after which Polly wrote Howorth, "Thanks for your tips about books for China."[4] Books were always Howorth's passion, and Polly was one of many friends who received reading tips from Howorth.

Of all her hometown friends, it was Augusta Stacy Marshall with whom Howorth had the most sustained contacts. They had seen one another briefly when Howorth's travels out of Washington took her near Gus's homes in the Midwest. "You are truly irreplaceable in my life," Gus wrote after a visit with Howorth in Washington. There were long lapses in personal visits, but in 1965 Howorth spent time with Marshall, who was then living near a daughter in California. "I was so proud to show off what the South and your parentage and Randolph-Macon and your career and your marriage could do for a woman," Marshall wrote after Howorth's return. Later she quipped, "We Southern girls make cute old ladies."[5]

Over the years Marshall had written news of their Randolph-Macon faculty and the Alpha Omicron Pi sorority sisters. It had been an unusual group. Stella Perry, a national founder (Barnard, 1898), to whom Howorth remained close, later suggested why an independent spirit such as Howorth would have had a lifelong devotion to a social sorority. "We were very simple, not one wealthy, and not one valuing very highly the show-window superficialities of life."[6] On Howorth's ninetieth birthday in 1985 a representative from Alpha Omicron Pi presented a silver tray to her at her Cleveland home. The birthday was memorable because a syndicated column of the journalist Rheta Grimsley Johnson prompted friends from Maine to California to write to Howorth enclosing copies of the piece from local newspapers.[7]

After returning to Cleveland in 1957, Howorth continued to exchange personal and professional news and comments with her closest friends in

AAUW and BPW leadership circles. Susan Riley, "one of the most gifted and loveliest women I have ever known" returned to her home in Clinton, Mississippi, in 1965.[8] Within a year she was stricken by anemia and arthritis, and her death in 1973 denied Howorth the time she had counted on having with a friend whose paths had so often crossed her own.

More than any other of her feminist friends from the Washington days, Margaret Hickey kept Howorth current on developments in women's advancement. Public-affairs editor of the *Ladies' Home Journal* after 1946, Hickey had numerous contacts, which were widened by her follow-up work with the PCSW. Mutual affection kept the correspondence alive. "Lucy beloved friend," Hickey wrote before the inauguration of President Lyndon B. Johnson in 1965, "let's hope for more opportunities for women in the Great Society." Semiretired in Tucson after 1971 and widowed in 1973, but still involved with national voluntary associations, Hickey wrote of work as chair of the Voluntary Foreign Aid Committee of the State Department's Agency for International Development. Her travels to keep the *Ladies' Home Journal* current on concerns of women worldwide made Hickey long for "one of our old visits."[9] They enjoyed such visits in 1975 and 1977, when Hickey joined Lucy and Joe at their summer place at Monteagle, Tennessee.

"How I wish we could talk over the outlook now with a new New Deal promised by a gifted politician," Hickey wrote after the election of Jimmy Carter in 1976. Howorth shared her views on Carter. Before the election she had written that she hoped Carter "might start the clean up Washington needs," adding, "I'm tired of that [Richard] Nixon gang. I never could stand Nixon from the first time he hit Washington." She had written a relative in 1968, "I never liked the 'old Nixon' and I mistrust the 'new Nixon.'"[10] Not likely to have much good to say of a Republican president, Howorth later spoke of Ronald Reagan as given only to "little pleasantries . . . which is infuriating. . . . I do not have the feeling that he deals with women as people." She commented to friends of other disappointments on the national scene. Of North Carolina's archconservative senator Jesse Helms, she said she hoped "he could be ditched."[11]

As two aging feminists, Hickey and Howorth wrote of their experiences with women's studies programs, Howorth writing of the program at the University of Mississippi and Hickey of her "residual career" on college campuses. Both wished to set the record straight on women's achievements in the 1930s and 1940s. Hickey agreed with Howorth that it was futile "to answer the overall false and misleading impact of the new comers," and like Howorth, she hoped that historians would be encouraged "to use the vast accumulation of papers and commentaries for more definitive research." Neither liked what they perceived as radical in the current women's movement. "I am just incensed at the [Bella] Abzug militant segment of the current phase," Hickey wrote in 1979. Later she longed for a talk on the "strange and frightening regression in human rights" she believed to be a manifestation of the defeat of the ERA. Hickey styled herself and Howorth as "two veterans" who had survived the "so-called woman's movements 1945–1960" and recounted contributions each had made. "We both know," Hickey wrote, "what a treasure-house we have in library books, particularly those well-written ones from the Thirties and Forties when women's leadership made possible the human rights progress which we all enjoy." At the time of their last communication, in 1987, when Hickey was eighty-five and Howorth was ninety-two, reveries were consoling when further activity was not possible. Nonetheless, Howorth remained aware of women's issues. In 1987 she wrote Elizabeth Boyer, of the Women's Equity Committee, "You may be sure I pitch in when an occasion presents itself and I try to stiffen the backs of those younger women who more or less take things for granted and sometimes need a rude awakening."[12]

The Monteagle Sunday School Assembly, Howorth's haven since childhood, became a central focus in the retirement years. During some of their Washington years Lucy and Joe had not been able to squeeze in a summer sojourn there at all. After their return to Cleveland, they often spent a languorous two or three summer months at Katydid Cottage. Joe fished and taught children's art classes, while Lucy busied herself with the programs and administration of Monteagle operations and entertained old friends and historians such as Constance Ashton Myers, who came for a lengthy, three-day interview in 1975.

If it was said that the family matriarch, Nellie Somerville, "did not suffer fools gladly," the same was true of Lucy when the management of Monteagle became lax and financial disaster threatened the assembly. In 1959 she was elected treasurer of the Monteagle board at a time of a reorganization, which seemed to occur every twenty years. It was "the time for this generation," she wrote a friend that year. Five years later she was the first woman president of the assembly. The summer of 1964 was "strenuous," and so she declined reelection.[13] Nonetheless, in subsequent years, after serving as president again, she was named a life member of the board of trustees and honorary president for the remainder of her life. In 1984 the Monteagle executive committee made her the recipient of its Distinguished Service Award. "Your leadership and guidance has brought the Assembly through some very difficult years," wrote the board secretary. "A number of the villagers credit [Howorth] with keeping the retreat itself briskly alive," wrote a chronicler of Monteagle. Her legal expertise and financial acumen and no-nonsense administration helped to restore the caliber of programs and decorum that longtime permanent and summer residents expected. She professed to enjoy it all—"even the rows and fighting." "Being a lawyer," she said, "I guess those things come easier to me than they do to some other people."[14]

Howorth attributed the difficulties that Monteagle experienced in the 1960s and 1970s to the presence of many more automobiles, the changing youth culture, the preference for indoor television over outdoor recreational and educational programs, more house parties, and the diminishing desire of families to allocate summer weeks to what was basically a retreat that reflected a social order of the past. The "place reeks with sentimentality," she knew.[15] Monteagle, she wrote another resident, "cannot be put on paper."[16]

Monteagle counted among its residents the writers Andrew Lytle and Peter Taylor, and both knew the Howorths well. A sanctuary for the elite among the white professional and business classes across the South, Monteagle afforded cottage owners a privileged existence. "We try not to be snobby about this thing, but of course we are," she admitted. Howorth took pleasure in exercising her leadership and parliamentary skills among such a group after she left government work and her law practice. Her statement to a favorite great-nephew that "everything I have done has turned out to be helpful later" summed up her habit of applying old experiences to the new.[17]

Lucy found much solace at Monteagle after Joe's death and again after her sister Eleanor died. Joe was not well during the fall of 1979, and in February 1980 he was diagnosed and hospitalized with terminal lung cancer. When Lucy, who visited him every day until the end, wrote Augusta Marshall of Joe's illness, she was struck by Lucy's comment that she and

Joe "had had more than their share of the good." Sadly, Marshall told Lucy of her own diagnosis of ovarian cancer. Marshall died in March 1980, and Joe died in May; he was eighty-three. The couple had celebrated their fiftieth anniversary two years earlier. "The long road has come to an end," Howorth wrote Margaret Hickey, adding "I think I am alright, except weary."[18]

In 1975 Howorth talked to Constance Myers about her marriage. Her union with Joe had made her a "sweeter" person, although she doubted the word could be "applied" to her. "I am pretty mean," she admitted. She believed that some single women "come out [with] a rasping quality," and Joe had saved her from that. "I certainly would not change the course of my life," she said. She attributed her happiness to Joe's initial decision that the marriage was to be a "freeing experience" for her. She had always referred to him in an almost reverential tone, and she continued to do so for the remainder of her life. Margaret Mahoney, a Monteagle friend, described the Howorths as "an unusual twosome sharing so much and still maintaining [their] individuality."[19] More than twenty years earlier Anne Scott had told Howorth, "It always cheers me on to see someone who has managed to pull off the marriage & career business successfully."[20]

Katydid Cottage, a Somerville second home since Nellie had purchased it in 1893, symbolized "family" for Howorth.[21] Forty-seven of Nellie's descendants and their spouses from seven generations gathered at Monteagle for a reunion over the Fourth of July 1986, one hundred years after Myra Cox Smith had visited Monteagle and returned to recommend the place to Nellie.[22] Howorth and Eleanor were the senior members of the scattered Somervilles, but Eleanor was unable to attend the reunion. Nor was Ashton Somerville Ingram there; one of her brother Bob's two daughters, who were extremely close to Howorth, Ashton had died of cancer at her home in Maine. But her sister, Keith Dockery McLean, who lived in Cleveland, became a mainstay for Howorth. She and the other nieces saw to it that Howorth enjoyed yet a few more summers at Katydid.

During the last decade of Howorth's life summer retreats to Tennessee became less frequent. She found the place "hopping" in 1988, with "lots of fights on management issues," which she avoided as "too emotional for someone in the ninth decade." She left the cottage in June to attend an "exciting and stimulating but tiring" AAUW national convention in Washington.[23] In October Eleanor, who was ninety-six, died of a virulent kidney infection, leaving Howorth "in rather a state," although she reacted with characteristic stoicism. She spent the Friday of Eleanor's death on the telephone notifying kin and making arrangements. The next day Dorothy Shawhan found her sitting in her living room alone, reading a book by former secretary of state Dean Acheson. Howorth remarked that she and her sister had been as different as they could possibly be but that Eleanor had always done anything in the world she could to help her. "If she thought I needed a party, she gave a party. If she thought I needed new clothes, she'd spot some. Now I'm the only one left." Eleanor had been the first woman to earn a physics degree at Randolph-Macon and had returned to Cleveland to marry Audley Shands. Widowed in 1934, she had remained a respected civic leader and clubwoman all of her life.[24] Her death left Lucy as the last survivor of her immediate family, one that had directed public affairs in Cleveland for over a century.

Unable to be at Monteagle without someone with her all of the time, Howorth did not return after 1989. "We miss seeing you," Peter Taylor wrote in 1993. Bob and Eleanor's daughters would go for short stays, but Lucy's absence was noticeable. "We will always miss you on the mountain,—politically as well as socially," one resident wrote.[25]

Her inability to be at Monteagle in her latter years did not mean that Howorth was homebound. She had found a travel mate in LePoint Smith as early as 1963, when she wanted to go to New York. "I love it," Lucy said, but Joe did not, and so he arranged for Smith, Lucy's new friend at the Bolivar County library, to accompany her. Lucy returned each year for the theater and concerts until 1969, when the Howorths assumed her brother Abe's law practice during his illness. In 1970 Smith and Howorth toured England, Scotland, and Ireland; in 1971 they went to the Orient; and in 1972 they were in Portugal and Spain. The next trip was to France. "You've been hopping," Constance Myers remarked during the interview in 1975. "Well, why not," Howorth retorted. "Where will I hear from Lucy next?" Augusta wrote after Howorth returned to France in 1977.[26]

The removal of two cataracts early in 1978 meant there would be no summer trip other than a four-month residence at Monteagle. The surgery left her able to see with her "former facility," and she no longer had difficulty in reading. The following years of Joe's deteriorating health and death left Lucy with no desire to leave home, but she and Smith later resumed their travels, returning to London in 1983 and again in 1985.

Howorth had once written, "I have always had a feeling of coming home there, having spent so much time with English history, literature, and law."[27] Passage on the *Queen Elizabeth II* in 1985 had the added bonus of placing the two Clevelanders with Margaret "Sissy" Boeth, an old friend from their hometown, who at one time had been a foreign correspondent for *Time* magazine. It was in 1985 that Howorth told a local reporter that her current ambition was "to beat the life expectancy tables." When at home she spent much of the day sitting and reading in a straight-backed chair in her sunroom. She refused to be photographed sitting in a rocking chair: at age ninety she insisted, "Rockers are for used-up old people."[28]

Removal of a cancerous breast in 1986 did not preclude a summer trip to Alaska. The most serious effect of the operation appeared to be a problem with her balance, for Howorth was large-busted for a woman of her short stature. Asked how she would cope with the loss of one breast, she said, "I'll just tie some buckshot up there and go on." "It's your iron will that counts," Margaret Mahoney wrote after hearing of Howorth's operation and subsequent travel.[29]

Cancer struck again in 1987 in the form of skin lesions, but prior to an extensive operation in Jackson in July to remove the facial growth, Howorth and Smith sailed in June for a tour of England and Italy and returned on the Concorde. Two months at Monteagle later that summer helped relieve the weariness that Howorth admitted had overcome her even before the trip to Europe. She was, after all, ninety-two years old, and she would not again make a transoceanic trip. Still able to travel within the United States, she was in Lynchburg, Virginia, in March 1988 to speak at the inauguration of Linda Koch Latimer, the first woman president of Randolph-Macon. It pleased Howorth when she first learned of the appointment that "those old Methodist trustees finally gave in." The last visit to the campus afforded a parting opportunity to extol her education there. "What Randolph-Macon produced was a sense of *how to live* and a sense you are a person." Her charge to the new college head was "to make certain" that the school "never deviates from teaching and believing that women first, last, and all the time are people. They aren't just housewives; they aren't just hand maidens. They are people."[30]

Reconstructive surgery in May 1988 to repair scars left by the previous facial surgery did not prevent Howorth from attending the national AAUW convention in Washington, a metropolis whose politics still excited her and where a few old friends remained. In 1992 Dan Cleary's widow, Gertrude, wrote, "Isn't it great we lived long enough to see the Democrats in the White House?" but nothing is on record to indicate what Howorth thought of President Bill Clinton. However, she had thoroughly enjoyed entertaining Hillary Clinton when she delivered the Nellie Nugent Somerville lecture at Delta State University in 1991. The last journeys were relaxing trips with LePoint Smith aboard the *Mississippi Queen* in 1990 and 1992, each "one week on the great river." Howorth had always loved the Mississippi River. It had held a power over her much like that described years earlier by David Cohn, who wrote, "The Mississippi, to some extent, made each of us a world citizen. . . . It therefore fostered an urbanity rare in a small, isolated town . . . gave it an unwonted sympathy for alien men and women and alien concepts, redeemed it from many of the aspects of landlocked provincialism."[31]

Never to travel again after reaching the age of ninety-seven, Howorth had one last great occasion in life, the celebration of her hundredth birthday in 1995. Once again Rheta Grimsley Johnson produced a column that heralded the career of this daughter of Nellie Somerville who "didn't fall far from the tree." The Cleveland Country Club was the site of a party attended by a large outpouring of the town's citizens, while official greetings arrived from Randolph-Macon, Delta State, the University of Mississippi, and national officers of all the women's organizations that Howorth had served.[32] Because her centennial birthday preceded by only weeks the seventy-fifth anniversary of the ratification by the Tennessee legislature of the Nineteenth Amendment, guaranteeing women the right to vote, an event Howorth had witnessed, newswriters nationwide used the occasion to explore the women's progress toward equality.[33]

In an essay entitled "Old Wives' Tales" (1981) Anne Firor Scott commented again on her discovery of Nellie Nugent Somerville, defining her long life as "a laboratory experiment" on the strong corollary between a commitment to service and hard work and the nature of aging. Similarly, the sociologist Lydia Bronte described Howorth at age ninety-three as an "explorer" who had "had career patterns with a continuous central track and many branches off to one side or another." Bronte often studied the daughters of first-generation suffragists, who grew to maturity assuming that women were entitled to equality with men and confident in the choices they made. Of the twenty-one individuals with whom Bronte cast

Howorth "not one . . . believed that being a wife, mother, and housewife was enough to fill a normal adult woman's life."[34] In still another book on aging Howorth explained her longevity simply, "My formula for a long life wasn't premeditated. I never made it an ambition to be a hundred, but when I got within sight of it, well, I thought it would really be a distinction."[35]

Lucy Howorth faced the losses and handicaps of old age without complaining. She called Arch Dalrymple, an old Monteagle friend, one evening during one of her last summers there. "I have fallen and I think my arm is broken," she told him. "Would you mind taking me to the emergency room?" He took her immediately, but with no one on duty to x-ray her arm until morning, Howorth lay throughout the night fully dressed with a broken arm. Early in life, after going with her mother to visit an elderly relative who complained throughout the entire visit, she had resolved never to do that.[36] While her body was failing, her mind was still engaged. "If you see me slipping, give me a jolt," she said. On Valentine's Day 1995, dressed in a red sweater, she sat watching on television the trial of O. J. Simpson, a professional football legend accused of murdering his wife, and drinking her customary five o'clock bourbon and water from a peanut butter glass. Asked if she and Joe had celebrated Valentine's Day, she answered, "We celebrated every day." As for the Simpson trial, as a lawyer she was interested in the legal maneuvering, but she could not penetrate the surface of the made-for-TV show to get to the real story, which she said was "trashy anyway."[37]

By 1995 Howorth was frail and almost completely confined to home, where she used a walker to move from her bedroom to the sunroom, where she spent most of the day reading or visiting with frequent callers. She was able to remain at home because a roomer, Frances Hood, a realtor's secretary, occupied the spare bedroom at night; during the day Howorth was in the care of cooks and housekeepers. She matter-of-factly prepared for death, sorting through papers for the Schlesinger Library with LePoint Smith, putting her will and other legal affairs in order, and having a good friend and neighbor supervise the painting of her house. "I don't want the nieces to have to jump in and do that." She enjoyed visits from fundraisers as well: "I don't mind their trying to shake me down."[38]

Until the end she was keenly interested in the lives of her caretakers and neighbors. When James Eaton, the son of Ergie Lee Smith, a longtime cook and housekeeper, was disabled by an automobile accident in Chicago, Howorth called him every day until he agreed to come home. After Eaton's return in 1992 he liked to sit at the dining-room table for conversation with Howorth. She loaned him books, introduced him to the work of Eudora Welty, and filled him in on the dynamics of the local community. He described her accounts as "Delta tidbits from somebody who knew everybody's business."[39] As Mrs. Smith aged, she and Dollie Forrest developed a "tag-team" arrangement to care for Howorth during her last seven years. When Smith became too ill to work, Howorth continued to pay her. Forrest, a Jehovah's Witness, and Howorth discussed the "Good Book," as Howorth called it. "I learned a lot from her business wise and so many other things," Forrest wrote. "I never saw her sad. She always was cheerful and upbeat."[40] In addition to attentive caretakers, Howorth's daily contact with LePoint Smith and Keith McLean gave further assurance that assistance was near if needed.

That need came early in the morning of 23 August 1997. Howorth's restlessness and discomfort led her sitter to telephone LePoint Smith and Dollie Forrest shortly after midnight. They arrived to find Howorth having difficulty breathing; congestive heart failure brought death soon. Two days later, following graveside services at the Greenville City Cemetery conducted by a Presbyterian minister, Lucy was interred adjacent to her mother and Joe.[41]

Lucy Somerville Howorth, at age 102, was the last survivor of the twenty-eight "Women in the New Deal" who are the subjects of Susan Ware's well-known study.[42] Some held more prestigious positions during the Roosevelt years, but few lasted through the Truman era, and only Howorth and Clara Beyer, associate director of the Division of Labor Standards from 1934 to 1958, continued to hold a presidential appointment into the Eisenhower administration.[43] And Howorth returned to Washington for a brief assignment during the Kennedy years. Howorth's vigorous activity spanning six decades to advance opportunities for women to hold public office and attain policymaking positions, not only in government but also in higher education, should hold greater importance for historians than her longevity as a federal officeholder.

While in her early twenties, in New York City, Howorth was moved by the plight of working women, particularly young girls. Had she remained in the circle of activist women who led her into liberal causes, even toward the social and political left, her feminism might have been directed at a social class to which she did not belong. But returning to Mississippi in 1920 and then moving as an attorney to Jackson in 1928, she developed an interest in advancing opportunities for the white, middle-class business and professional women that she came to know through the organizations she joined in Jackson.

Successful herself at the game of politics, her move from Mississippi to Washington opened new avenues for what became her one major cause: to promote women to positions of influence in government. She based her crusades upon her own experiences and those of the educated women she knew, and by choice she limited her major stirrings to her own social and professional class. She had concerns for the non-college-educated business and professional women she knew through years of work with the BPW, but as time went by, she concentrated her efforts to promote women through the AAUW. From at least 1943 and extending into her retirement years in her hometown of Cleveland the AAUW was the organization that gained the most from her vitality. Nancy Cott, who has written with authority on the course of modern feminism, has indicated that many professional women, giving in to the demands of their careers, never joined feminist causes. "Although declared feminists often were women pursuing professions . . . that did not mean that professional women generally were feminists."[44] If that is true, Lucy Howorth did not fit the common mold.

Yet, as restricted to her own circles as Howorth's advocacy for women may have been, her life as an activist was full and vibrant. She exuded an infectious spirit of optimism: "Oh, I can't stand the way people say, 'Oh, I'm not happy.' Get your mind on something else and do it and then if you do it right, happiness will come."[45] She never laid claim to having changed the course of women's history herself, but she fervently believed that women's organizations had. And but for her conscientious documentation of every arena she entered, historians would know less about the women's movement from at least 1930 through 1960. Withal, the richest of Lucy Somerville Howorth's legacies is the understanding she has given of the "glory in being a feminist."

Appendix
Recorded Speeches of Lucy Somerville Howorth

1922

"Intellectual Integrity and College Education." Commencement Address, University of Mississippi, Oxford.

1924

"Laws about Lawyers." Mississippi State Bar Association, Jackson.

1932

"The Mechanics of Voting." WJDX radio broadcast, Jackson.

1935

"Observations on Law and Politics." N.p.
"In Behalf of State Legislators." National Association of Women Lawyers, Los Angeles.
"The Consent of the Governed." Randolph-Macon Woman's College Alumnae, Lynchburg, VA.
"A Business Woman Sees Washington, the City." Monteagle Sunday School Assembly, Monteagle, TN.

1936

"Remarks in Memory of Susan B. Anthony." National Woman's Party, Washington, DC.
"Federal Benefits to Veterans." Women's National Democratic Club, Washington, DC.

1937

"The Place of State Legislators." Federal Bar Association, Washington, DC.
"The Trained Woman's Responsibility for Leadership." Business and Professional Women's Club, Staunton, VA.

1938

"International Contracts." Business and Professional Women's Club, Baltimore, MD.

"Forward with the Federation." Business and Professional Women's Club, Reading, PA.

"Program Planning: My Business and Yours." Business and Professional Women's Club, New York City.

1939

"My Business and Yours." Business and Professional Women's Club, Lynchburg, VA.

"Women's Contributions to Social and Economic Change." Zonta Club, Washington, DC.

"Business Women in Europe." Credit Women's Breakfast Club, Washington, DC.

"Women's Contribution to the Zonta Club." Zonta Club, Washington, DC.

"Business Women in a Democracy." North Carolina Business and Professional Women's Clubs, Raleigh.

1940

"Making Democracy Work." Business and Professional Women's Club, Bristol, TN.

"Living and Working in Peace Building Years." Business and Professional Women's Club, n.p.

1941

"Responsibility of the Exceptional Woman to the Average Woman." Quota Club, Washington, DC.

"Strengthen Democracy for Defense." Business and Professional Women's Club, Jackson, MS.

1942

"The Guardians of Our Culture." Randolph-Macon Woman's College Alumnae, New York City.

1943

"United for Victory." Business and Professional Women's Club, Jackson, MS.

1944

"Women's Responsibility in World Affairs." White House Conference on Women in Post-War Policy Making, Washington, DC.

1945

"Education for What?" Randolph-Macon Woman's College Alumnae, Washington, DC.

1946

"Roads to Unity." Assembly of Daughters of Rebecca, Washington, DC.
"Effective Citizenship." American Association of University Women, Burlington, NC.

1947

"A Program of Action." South Carolina White House Conference, Columbia.
"To Make Peace Grow." Business and Professional Women's Club, Chadron, NE.

1948

"All Dressed Up." Winthrop College Alumnae, Rock Hill, SC.
"From a One-Horse Surrey to the Atomic Age." Randolph-Macon Woman's College, Lynchburg, VA.

1949

"Task Force '49." Multi-Party Committee of Women, Washington, DC.
"Practical Education: Our Big Job." American Association of University Women, Oxford, MS.
"A Review of the Record." Phi Delta Delta legal fraternity, Bedford Springs, PA.
"The Future Belongs to Those Who Grow." Hannah More Academy, Reisterstown, MD.

1950

"Assignment in Human Freedom." American Association of University Women, Buffalo, NY.
"Southern Women and the Atomic Age." Alabama College, Montevallo.

1951

"Acceptance of Chair of Assembly of Women's Organizations." Washington, DC.
"Main Street: The Place to Begin." American Association of University Women, Huntingdon, VA.
"Forever the Assistant to the Assistant." National Association of Deans of Women, Chicago.

1952

"Less Aspirin and More Action." American Association of University Women, Elmira-Corning, NY.

1953

"Now We See Darkly." American Association of University Women, Kensington, MD.

1954

"University Women at Home and Abroad." Radio broadcast, St. Joseph, MO.
"Public Service." Cottey College, Nevada, MO.
"The Road Ahead." American Association of University Women, St. Joseph, MO.

1955

"Precedent or Space Ships." Phi Delta Delta legal fraternity, Georgetown University, Washington, DC.

1959

"The Earth Where We Live." Young Women's Christian Association, Memphis, TN.
"Through a Glass Darkly." Mississippi College, Clinton.

1962

"Room at the Top." Mississippi State College for Women, Columbus.

1975

"Reflections of Mississippi Women in Public Life Whom I Have Known." Mississippi Historical Society, Jackson.

1977

"Eulogy on Ellen S. Woodward." Mississippi Hall of Fame, Old Capitol, Jackson.

1983

"On a Lifetime Achievement Award." Radcliffe College, Cambridge, MA.
"The Future Will Not Wait." American Association of University Women, Mobile, AL.
Address on Completion of Howorth Endowment. American Association of University Women, Tupelo, MS.

1985

"Honors Day Address." Delta State University, Cleveland, MS.

1988

Remarks as a Distinguished Alumna. President's Inauguration, Randolph-Macon Woman's College, Lynchburg, VA.

Notes

The following abbreviations appear frequently in the notes:

AAUW	American Association of University Women
AES	Arthur and Elizabeth Schlesinger Library, Radcliffe Institute for Advanced Study, Cambridge, MA
CELSW	Committee on the Economic and Legal Status of Women, AAUW
DSU	Delta State University, Cleveland, MS
FDRL	Franklin D. Roosevelt Library, Hyde Park, NY
LSH	Lucy Somerville Howorth
LSHC	Lucy Somerville Howorth Collection, Capps Archives
RMWC	Randolph-Macon Woman's College, Lynchburg, VA
SHC	Nellie Nugent Somerville—Lucy Somerville Howorth Collection
WD-DNC	Papers of Women's Division, Democratic National Committee
YWCA	Young Women's Christian Association

Preface

1. Anne Firor Scott, *The Southern Lady: From Pedestal to Politics, 1830–1930*, Twenty-fifth Anniversary Edition (Charlottesville: University Press of Virginia, 1995), 252–54.

2. Lucy Somerville Howorth (hereafter LSH), quoted in University of Mississippi, *Ole Miss Women's Council for Philanthropy* (Oxford, 1998).

3. LSH, quoted in *Jackson (MS) Clarion-Ledger*, 28 November 1986.

4. LSH to Martha Swain, 10 February 1984, in authors' possession.

Chapter 1

1. LSH, "Women Meet at the White House to Claim a Role in Postwar Foreign Policy Making, 1944," in *Major Problems in American Women's History*, ed. Mary Beth Norton and Ruth M. Alexander (Boston: Houghton Mifflin, 2003).

2. LSH, quoted in Cora Norman, "Judge Lucy Howorth: A Woman Ahead of Her Time" (speech, Pleadies Club, Jackson, MS, 20 March 2002), copy in authors' possession.

3. LSH, interview by Dorothy Shawhan, 29 September 1991; all interviews of LSH by Shawhan were conducted in Cleveland, MS, and notes for all are in the authors' possession.

4. Ibid., 12 January 1990.

5. LSH, typescript, 1963, box 1, Nellie Nugent Somerville—Lucy Somerville Howorth Collection (hereafter SHC), Arthur and Elizabeth Schlesinger Library, Radcliffe Institute for Advanced Study, Cambridge, MA (hereafter AES). The voluminous collection is arranged in a series of thirteen boxes, five less well organized cartons, and some unprocessed material.

6. LSH, "Mrs. John Pratt Nugent (1801–1873)," box 1, SHC, AES.

7. Quoted in Leila J. Rupp and Verta Taylor, *Survival in the Doldrums: The American Women's Rights Movement, 1945 to the 1960s* (New York: Oxford University Press, 1987), 109.

8. LSH to Elbert Hilliard, 27 August 1981, Lucy Somerville Howorth Collection, Capps Archives (hereafter LSHC), Delta State University, Cleveland, MS (hereafter DSU). Files that remained in the Howorth home at Lucy's death are in this collection.

9. Hannah Boyle, "Anne (Nancy) Hardeman Lewis," in "The Records of the Lewis-Hardeman-Nugent Families," by Anne Nugent Edmonds, typescript (1927–28), in Somerville family papers in possession of Dorothy Martin, Alexandria, VA.

10. Quoted in Coralee Nugent Lobdall, "Richard James Nugent," in *History of Bolivar County, Mississippi*, comp. Florence Warfield Sillers (Jackson: Hederman Brothers, 1948; reprint, Spartanburg, SC: Reprint Publishers, 1976), 490.

11. Bishop Charles B. Galloway, *Colonel William L. Nugent* (n.p., n.d.) box 1, SHC, AES.

12. S. Myra Smith, "A diary of religious meditations," 15 November 1860, box 2, SHC, AES.

13. William M. Cash and LSH, eds., *My Dear Nellie: The Civil War Letters of William L. Nugent to Eleanor Smith Nugent* (Jackson: University Press of Mississippi, 1977).

14. Ibid., 143.

15. LSH, interview by Shawhan, 22 April 1987.

16. Mrs. W. R. Trigg, "In Memory of Mrs. Myra Smith," in *Papers of the Washington County Historical Society,* ed. William D. McCain and Charlotte Capers (Jackson: Mississippi Historical Society, 1954), 165; Nell Thomas, *This Is Our Story, This Is Our Song* (Greenville, MS: First United Methodist Church, 1954), 260; Marjorie Spruill Wheeler, *New Women of the New South: The Leaders of the Woman Suffrage Movement in the Southern States* (New York: Oxford University Press, 1993), 108 (Somerville quotation). Myra Smith's autobiography and diary are in box 2, SHC, AES.

17. LSH to Shawhan, 10 January 1993, in Shawhan's possession.

18. LSH, interview by Constance Myers, 20, 23, 25 June 1975, Monteagle, TN, transcript in Southern Oral History Collection, University of North Carolina, Chapel Hill, 20–22. The transcription of this extensive interview is more than two hundred pages long.

19. "Nellie Nugent Somerville Was State's First Woman Representative," *Greenville (MS) Delta Democrat-Times,* 31 December 1943; Anne Firor Scott, "Nellie Nugent Somerville," in *Notable American Women: The Modern Period,* ed. Barbara Sicherman and Carol Hurd Green (Cambridge, MA: Harvard University Press, 1980), 654–56.

20. Eleanor Somerville Shands, interview by Shawhan, 5 July 1985, Cleveland, MS.

21. LSH, interview by Allen Dennis, 16 January 1973, Cleveland, MS, transcript in LSHC, DSU.

22. Keith Frazier Somerville, "Random Thoughts," typescript in Capps Archives, DSU.

23. Nellie Nugent Somerville, speech, in Marion Barnwell, *A Place Called Mississippi: Collected Narratives* (Jackson: University Press of Mississippi, 1997), 171–74.

24. Rebecca Hood-Adams, "Nellie Nugent Somerville, 1 Woman, 1 Vote," *Jackson (MS) Clarion-Ledger,* 7 March 1989; John Patrick McDowell, *The Social Gospel in the South: The Woman's Home Mission Movement in the Methodist Episcopal Church South, 1886–1939* (Baton Rouge: Louisiana State University Press, 1982), 118, 134–35.

25. LSH, interview by Myers, 10.

26. Couprey Shands, interview by Shawhan, 26 October 1996, Jackson, MS. On Somerville and suffrage, see Wheeler, *New Women of the New South.*

27. For details on the Civic Improvement Club, see Mary Louise Merideth, "The Mississippi Woman's Rights Movement, 1889–1923: The Leadership of Nellie Nugent Somerville and Greenville in Suffrage Reform" (master's thesis, DSU, 1974).

28. LSH, interview by Marjorie Spruill Wheeler, 15 March 1983, Cleveland, MS, transcript in Mississippi Oral History Collection, University of Southern Mississippi, Hattiesburg.

29. David L. Cohn, *The Mississippi Delta and the World: The Memoirs of David L. Cohn,* ed. James C. Cobb (Baton Rouge: Louisiana State University Press, 1995), 3; James C. Cobb, *The Most Southern Place on Earth: The Mississippi Delta and the Roots of Regional Identity* (New York: Oxford University Press, 1992), 141; Bertram Wyatt-Brown, *The House of Percy: Honor, Melancholy, and Imagination in a Southern Family* (New York: Oxford University Press, 1994), 174; William Alexander Percy, *Lanterns on the Levee: Recollections of a Planter's Son* (New York: Knopf, 1941), 129.

30. Robert Somerville's original diaries, DSU, copies in carton 2, SHC, AES; C. H. West and W. E. Elam, "Memories of Deceased Members, Robert Somerville," box 1, SHC, AES. West was chief engineer of the Mississippi Levee District from 1898 to 1910, and Elam held that position from 1946 to 1951. The journals and diaries of the engineering trips of William Starling, chief engineer of the Board of Mississippi Levee Commissioners from 1884 to 1898, frequently mention trips with Somerville. Special Collections, Mitchell Memorial Library, Mississippi State University, Starkville; LSH, interview by Myers, 125.

31. Cobb, *Most Southern Place,* 95; Wyatt-Brown, *House of Percy,* 174, 180; Eleanor Somerville Shands interview.

32. Eleanor Somerville Shands interview.

33. *Cleveland (MS) Bolivar Commercial,* 18 March 1986.

34. LSH, interview by Shawhan, 12 January 1990.

35. LSH, "Note to Accompany Membership Cards," box 4, SHC, AES.

36. Frank C. Waldrop, ed., *Mountain Voices: The Centennial History of the Monteagle Sunday School Assembly* (Nashville, TN: Parthenon, 1982), 346.

37. LSH, interview by Shawhan, 12 August 1989.

38. LSH, interview by Edith Provost, 1975, Monteagle, TN, transcript of tape in carton 2, SHC, AES.

39. Ibid.

40. Ibid.; LSH, interview by Shawhan, 25 January 1990. Correspondence with Kate Zerfoss from later years is in LSHC, DSU.

41. LSH, interview by Shawhan, 31 August 1991.

42. Phyllis Ten Elslof, "Education at Root of Mississippian's Achievement," *Jackson (MS) Clarion-Ledger,* 28 December 1986; LSH, interview by Shawhan, 22 February 1991.

43. LSH to Francis E. Hall, 17 December 1975, LSHC, DSU; LSH, interviews by Shawhan, 22 April, 24 December 1987, 17 November 1990; Jane Whiteside Elliott, "Profile: Lucy Somerville Howorth; One of Mississippi's Finest," *Delta Scene* 1 (Winter 1973): 18.

44. LSH, interview by Shawhan, 17 November 1990.

45. Ibid., 5 June 1993.

46. Ibid., 17 November 1990.

47. LSH to Carvel Collins, 5 May 1964, carton 3, SHC, AES.

48. LSH to Hall; LSH, interview by Shawhan, 20 November 1989.

49. LePoint Smith, interview by Shawhan, 30 November 1999, Cleveland, MS.

50. Sixty years of letters from Augusta Stacy Marshall to LSH are in unprocessed material, SHC, AES.

51. LSH, interviews by Shawhan, 4 September 1990, 18 January 1991.

52. Ibid., 3 September 1996.

53. LSH, interview by Myers, 58–60.

54. Nellie Nugent Somerville Papers, box 2, SHC, AES.

55. LSH, "Note to Accompany Membership Cards."

56. Dorothy Shawhan, "Lucy Howorth Saw Community Beginning to Spark and Lit a Match," *Cleveland (MS) Bolivar Commercial,* 4 July 1986.

57. LSH, interview by Shawhan, 13 March 1984; Eleanor Somerville Shands interview.

Chapter 2

1. LSH, speech, Radcliffe College, 1983, box 9, SHC, AES.

2. Amy Thompson McCandless, *The Past in the Present: Women's Higher Education in the Twentieth Century American South* (Tuscaloosa: University of Alabama Press, 1999), 32. The other women's college was Goucher, then the Women's College of Baltimore.

3. Roberta D. Cornelius, *The History of Randolph-Macon Woman's College* (Chapel Hill: University of North Carolina Press, 1951), 145.

4. McCandless, *Past in the Present,* 61.

5. Ibid., 56; LSH, quoted in *Randolph-Macon Alumnae Bulletin* 86 (Fall 1973): 30; Pearl Buck, *My Several Worlds: A Personal Record* (New York: Day, 1954), 90–91.

6. LSH, "We Remember Class Parties," *Randolph-Macon Alumnae Bulletin* 36 (September 1943): 51–55; LSH to William Safire, printed in Safire, *On Language* (New York: Basic Books, 1980), 117–18. Lucy took her challenge to the class from the Old Testament Hebrew warrior Gideon, who drove his men to victory.

7. LSH, interview by Dorothy Shawhan, 4 September 1993; all interviews of LSH by

Shawhan were conducted in Cleveland, MS, and notes for all are in the authors' possession. LSH, "The Bill Faulkner I Knew," *Delta Review* 2 (July–August 1965): 38, editor's note.

8. Cornelius, *History,* 187–88.

9. *Sun Dial,* 1 October 1915, 7 April 1916.

10. *Helianthus,* 1914, 84; 1915, 99, 103.

11. LSH, interview by Constance Myers, 20, 23, 25 June 1975, Monteagle, TN, transcript in Southern Oral History Collection, University of North Carolina, Chapel Hill, 20–21.

12. Ibid., 16.

13. Ibid., 22.

14. Ibid., 27; "Equal Suffrage League," *Sun Dial,* 10 December 1915.

15. LSH, interview by Myers, 17.

16. Ibid., 16; Robert Booth Fowler, "Carrie Chapman Catt, Strategist," in *One Woman, One Vote: Rediscovering the Woman Suffrage Movement,* ed. Marjorie Spruill Wheeler (Troutdale, OR: New Sage, 1995), 307. See also Eleanor Flexner, *Century of Struggle* (New York: Athenaeum, 1973).

17. LSH, interview by Shawhan, 29 May 1986.

18. LSH, interview by Ruth Campbell, *Faces,* Mississippi ETV, 2 January 1986.

19. Arguments in box 4, SHC, AES; LSH, interview by Shawhan, 29 May 1987.

20. *Sun Dial,* 7 April 1916.

21. LSH, interview by Shawhan, 9 September 1990; grade reports, box 4, SHC, AES.

22. Crooks's letter, dated 10 May 1917, is in box 4, SHC, AES.

23. LSH, interview by Myers, 62–63.

24. *Helianthus,* 1914, 80; LSH to Mrs. Grace Yankey, 31 July 1943, box 12, SHC, AES. Yankey was Buck's sister and, under the pseudonym Cornelia Spencer, wrote a biography of Buck entitled *The Exile's Daughter* (New York: Coward-McCann, 1944).

25. LSH to Yankey.

26. *Helianthus,* 1916, 70.

27. LSH, interview by Myers, 79.

28. LSH, "Application for Employment," Papers of Women's Division, Democratic National Committee (hereafter WD-DNC), Franklin D. Roosevelt Library, Hyde Park, NY (hereafter FDRL).

29. LSH, interview by Myers, 65; J. T. Peake to LSH, 7 September 1917, SHC, AES; *Cleveland (MS) Bolivar Commercial,* 20 November 1985.

30. LSH, interview by Myers, 66.

31. LSH, "Autobiographical Sketch," box 4, SHC, AES; LSH, interview by Shawhan, 24 December 1986.

32. LSH, printed card, box 3, SHC, AES; Ida Clyde Clarke, *American Women and the World War* (New York: Appleton, 1918), 25, 298. See also Emily Newell Blair, *The Woman's Committee, United States Council of National Defense: An Interpretative Report, April 21, 1917 to February 27, 1919* (Washington, DC: Government Printing Office, 1920).

33. LSH, interview by Myers, 67; Clarke, *American Women and the War,* 299.

34. McCandless, *Past in the Present,* 35; LSH to Carvel Collins, 5 May 1964, carton 3,

SHC, AES. In her letter to Collins Howorth contrasted her life in New York with her life at the University of Mississippi.

35. LSH, interview by Shawhan, 2 December 1988.

36. LSH, interview by Myers, 78.

37. Ibid., 78, 60, 74.

38. Ibid., 75, 76; "Record of Lucy Somerville Howorth," WD-DNC, FDRL.

39. LSH, interview by Myers, 69; Columbia grade reports, box 4, SHC, AES.

40. LSH, interview by Shawhan, 18 June 1984. See also Hollinger F. Barnard, ed., *Outside the Magic Circle: The Autobiography of Virginia Foster Durr* (Tuscaloosa: University of Alabama Press, 1985), 56–58. Rather than leave Wellesley because a black student was placed at her dining table, Durr chose to remain.

41. Keith Somerville Dockery McLean, interview by Shawhan, 30 July 1986, Cleveland, MS; Allied Bureau discharge certificate, 31 December 1918, box 4, SHC, AES.

42. LSH, interview by Myers, 70. For a discussion of the evangelical and social-gospel aspects of the YWCA, see Frances Helen Mains and Grace Loucks Elliott, *From Deep Roots: The Story of the YWCA's Religious Dimensions* (New York: National Board of the Young Women's Christian Association of the USA, 1974).

43. Anna V. Rice, *A History of the World's Young Women's Christian Association* (New York: Woman's Press, 1947), 108. See also Mary S. Sims, *The Natural History of a Social Institution—the YWCA* (New York: Woman's Press, 1936).

44. Elizabeth Wilson, *Fifty Years of Association Work among Young Women* (New York: YWCA, 1916), 289–91.

45. Mary Frederickson, "Citizens for Democracy: The Industrial Programs of the YWCA," in *Sisterhood and Solidarity: Workers' Education for Women, 1914–1984*, ed. Joyce Kornbluh and Mary Frederickson (Philadelphia: Temple University Press, 1984), 77.

46. Nina Mjagkij and Margaret Spratt, eds., *Men and Women Adrift: The YMCA and the YWCA in the City* (New York: New York University Press, 1997), 7–8; Marion W. Roydhouse, "Bridging Chasms: Community and the Southern YWCA," in *Visible Women: New Essays on American Activism*, ed. Nancy A. Hewitt and Suzanne Lebsock (Urbana: University of Illinois Press, 1993), 272–73.

47. LSH, interview by Myers, 71. Federal Bureau of Investigation agents, seeking to verify Howorth's YWCA employment, reported in 1956 that records for 1919–20 were incomplete and no reference to her work could be located. Thus, there is a blank here in official records about her very interesting experiences during these years. Federal Bureau of Investigation, Lucy Somerville Howorth file, FBI 77-HQ-7131, 10 February 1956.

48. Glenda Riley, *Inventing the American Woman: An Inclusive History*, vol. 2 (Wheeling, IL: Harlan Davidson, 1995), 21.

49. LSH, interview by Myers, 72; LSH, interview by Shawhan, 6 February 1992; LSH, speech at RMWC, March 1988, in *Randolph-Macon Alumnae Bulletin* 81 (June 1988): 16.

50. LSH to Shawhan, 12 February 1992, in authors' possession; LSH, interview by Shawhan, 6 February 1992; Richard Roberts, *Florence Simms: A Biography* (New York: Woman's Press, 1926), 212–15; Marion O. Robinson, *Eight Women of the YWCA* (New York:

National Board of the Young Women's Christian Association of the USA, 1966), 96–99. Howorth and several friends underwrote the Simms biography.

51. LSH, interview by Myers, 190; Lucy Randolph Mason to LSH, 10 September 1936, box 5, SHC, AES.

52. LSH, interview by Myers, 168–69; LSH, "Note Accompanying [an] Olive Van Horn Article," box 4, SHC, AES.

53. LSH, "Note to Accompany Margaret Wells Wood Correspondence and Article," box 5, SHC, AES; LSH, interview by Shawhan, 20 November 1989; "Record of Lucy Somerville Howorth"; John A. Salmond, *Miss Lucy of the CIO: The Life and Times of Lucy Randolph Mason, 1892–1959* (Athens: University of Georgia Press, 1988), 15–20.

54. LSH to Martha Swain, 18 August 1980, in authors' possession; LSH, interview by Swain, 19 June 1984, Cleveland, MS, tape in LSHC, DSU; Roydhouse, "Bridging Chasms," 221.

55. Ruth Chivvis and Lucy Somerville, eds., *A Handbook for Delegates: National Industrial Conference* (New York: National Board of the Young Women's Christian Association of the USA, 1919), copy in New York Public Library.

56. Augusta Stacy to LSH, 5 October 1919, unprocessed, SHC, AES; LSH, interview by Shawhan, 20, 21 November 1989; LSH, interview by Myers, 73, 192; LSH, "Note to Accompany Bulletin No. 8," box 7, SHC, AES.

57. LSH, interview by Shawhan, 29 December 1989. See also Adrienne Lash Jones, "Struggle among Saints: African-American Women and the YWCA, 1870–1920," in Mjagkij and Spratt, *Men and Women Adrift,* 167–87.

58. LSH, interview by Myers, 192, 73, 170.

59. Memorandum, "LSH and the BPW Clubs," February 1988, LSHC, DSU; Geline Bowman, *History of the National Federation of Business and Professional Women's Clubs, 1919–1944* (New York: NFBPW, 1944), 16; Nancy Cott, "Across the Great Divide: Women in Politics before and after 1920," in Wheeler, *One Woman, One Vote,* 363.

60. LSH, interview by Myers, 192; LSH to Collins, 27 May 1964, carton 3, SHC, AES.

61. LSH, "Note on James Somerville," box 5, SHC, AES.

62. LSH, interview by Shawhan, 22 November 1985.

63. LSH, interview by Myers, 80; Karen Berger Morello, *The Invisible Bar: The Woman Lawyer in America, 1638 to the Present* (New York: Random House, 1986), 96; Penina M. Glazer and Miriam Slater, *Unequal Colleagues: The Entrance of Women into the Professions, 1890–1940* (New Brunswick, NJ: Rutgers University Press, 1986), 226; Virginia G. Drachman, *Sisters in Law: Women Lawyers in Modern American History* (Cambridge, MA: Harvard University Press, 1998), 143 (Stone quotation); Cynthia Fuchs Epstein, *Women in Law* (New York: Basic Books, 1981), 51.

64. James A. Cabaniss, *A History of the University of Mississippi* (University: University of Mississippi, 1949), 102.

65. Mrs. William W. Rossiter to LSH, 6 August 1920, and Mildred Corbett to LSH, 11 June 1920, both in carton 3, SHC, AES.

66. LSH to Mabel Hood, 23 July 1920, ibid.

67. LSH, interview by Marjorie Spruill Wheeler, 15 March 1983, Cleveland, MS, transcript in Mississippi Oral History Collection, University of Southern Mississippi, Hattiesburg.

68. LSH to Olive Van Horn and Corbett to LSH, both 8 September 1920, both in carton 3, SHC, AES.

69. LSH, "Note to Accompany Letters," box 5, SHC, AES.

70. LSH to Vassar Bishop, 9 March 1939, ibid.; LSH, interview by Shawhan, 21 December 1984. By 1930 the percentage of women lawyers had increased to only 2.1 percent. Epstein, *Women in Law*, 4.

71. Michael De L. Landon, *For the Honor and Dignity of the Profession: A History of the Mississippi State Bar, 1906–1976* (Jackson: University Press of Mississippi, 1979), 43; David L. Cohn, *The Mississippi Delta and the World: The Memoirs of David L. Cohn*, ed. James C. Cobb (Baton Rouge: Louisiana State University Press, 1995), 55.

72. LSH, interview by Myers, 55, 84–85; *Boston Globe*, 31 October 1983.

73. LSH, interview by Shawhan, 4 September 1984.

74. David. G. Sansing, *The University of Mississippi: A Sesquicentennial History* (Jackson: University Press of Mississippi, 1999), 178–79; Cabaniss, *History of the University*, 147–48; LSH, interview by Shawhan, 28 February 1988; "Former judge recalls colorful past," *Cleveland (MS) Bolivar Commercial*, 9 December 1981.

75. Sansing, *University of Mississippi*, 203. For an account of the Marionettes, see Joseph Blotner, *Faulkner: A Biography* (New York: Random House, 1974), 283–84; and LSH comments on a panel on Faulkner in *University of Mississippi Studies in English* 15 (1978): 188–90. Sansing describes Wasson's and Howorth's friendships with Faulkner as "lasting," although Howorth has said she did not see him after 1922.

76. LSH, interview by Shawhan, 17 November 1986; Ben Wasson, *Count No 'Count: Flashbacks to Faulkner* (Jackson: University Press of Mississippi, 1983), 50, 52; Elizabeth Spencer, *Landscapes of the Heart: A Memoir* (New York: Random House, 1997), 206.

77. LSH to Collins, 5 May 1964.

78. LSH, interview by Shawhan, 4 April 1985.

79. LSH, "The Bill Faulkner I Knew," 38–39.

80. LSH to Swain, 5 December 1984, in authors' possession; LSH, interview by Joanne Varner Hawks, 11 April 1979, Oxford, MS, videotape in AAUW, Mississippi Division Papers, Special Collections, Williams Library, University of Mississippi, Oxford, transcript in authors' possession.

81. LSH, interview by Myers, 87.

82. LSH, interview by Shawhan, 4 April 1985.

83. Ibid.

84. Ibid.

85. LSH, interview by Myers, 158; Beverly Blair Cook, "Florence Ellinwood Allen," in *Notable American Women: The Modern Period*, ed. Barbara Sicherman and Carol Hurd Green (Cambridge, MA: Harvard University Press, 1980), 12–13.

86. LSH to Van Horn, 8 January 1923, box 12, SHC, AES; LSH to Mary van Kleeck, 7, 25 April 1923, and van Kleeck to LSH, 11 April 1923, all in Mary van Kleeck Papers, Sophia

Smith Collection, Smith College, Northampton, MA; LSH, interview by Myers, 158; Eleanor Flexner, "Daisy Florence Simms," in *Notable American Women, 1607–1971,* ed. Edward T. James (Cambridge, MA: Harvard University Press, 1971), 293.

87. University of Mississippi Law School grade reports, box 4, SHC, AES; Parham Williams (dean) to LSH, 23 February 1983, carton 5, SHC, AES.

88. LSH, interview by Myers, 88.

89. LSH, commencement speech, 29 May 1922, box 12, SHC, AES. The speech appeared in the *Mississippian,* 19 March 1963.

90. Ibid.

91. LSH, interview by Myers, 88.

92. Eleanor Somerville Shands, interview by Shawhan, 5 July 1985, Cleveland, MS; LSH, interview by Shawhan, 4 September 1994.

93. LSH, interview by Myers, 92; Bill Minor, "Lucy Howorth: Rare State Legislator," in *Eyes on Mississippi: A Fifty-Year Chronicle of Change* (Jackson: Prichard Morris Books, 2001), 301.

94. Simms to LSH, 4 August 1923, box 12, SHC, AES.

Chapter 3

1. LSH, interview by Constance Myers, 20, 23, 25 June 1975, Monteagle, TN, transcript in Southern Oral History Collection, University of North Carolina, Chapel Hill, 94; Joe E. Hairston, "Practicing Law: Lucy Somerville Howorth, in Court and Elsewhere, 1922–1934" (seminar paper, Department of Anthropology, University of Mississippi, 1992), copy in authors' possession; Bertram Wyatt-Brown, *The House of Percy: Honor, Melancholy, and Imagination in a Southern Family* (New York: Oxford University Press, 1994), 188–89.

2. *Greenville (MS) Delta Democrat-Times,* 12, 20 June 1922; LSH, interview by Dorothy Shawhan, 31 March 1990; all interviews of LSH by Shawhan were conducted in Cleveland, MS, and notes for all are in the authors' possession.

3. LSH, interview by Myers, 95; *Cleveland (MS) Bolivar Commercial,* 7 February 1923; Anabel Power, "The Lady from Hinds," *To Dragma* (Alpha Omicron Pi) 27 (May 1932): 12.

4. Ethel M. Ferrell to LSH, 23 October 1922, and LSH, 1958 note, both in box 4, SHC, AES; Lydia Bronte, *The Longevity Factor: The New Reality of Long Careers and How It Can Lead to Richer Lives* (New York: HarperCollins, 1993), 268; hat story in LSH, speech at RMWC, March 1988, reprinted in *Randolph-Macon Alumnae Bulletin* 81 (June 1988).

5. LSH, 1958 note.

6. LSH to Minnie Brewer, 21 June 1923, box 12, SHC, AES; Hairston, "Practicing Law."

7. LSH, interview by Myers, 107; LSH, interview by Shawhan, 30 January 1986; Fannie Belle Cutler to LSH, 1 November 1922, box 12, SHC, AES; LSH "Note To Accompany Papers Relating to Mississippi YWCA," box 4, SHC, AES.

8. LSH, interview by Shawhan, 30 January 1986.

9. Mollie Heath Conn to LSH, 26 June 1935, box 12, SHC, AES; Polly Babcock to "Ruth, Mollie, et al.," 29 December 1967, and LSH, note on Polly Graham, both in LSHC, DSU.

10. On Mound Bayou, see Janet Sharp Hermann, *The Pursuit of a Dream* (New York: Oxford University Press, 1981).

11. LSH, interview by Shawhan, 20 October 1987.

12. LSH to Mrs. Walter Clark, 2 December 1922, box 12, SHC, AES; "Another Blot on Mississippi's Fair Name," *Woman Voter*, 8 February 1924. The doctor was convicted and sent to the state penitentiary, but he was later pardoned by Governor Lee Russell.

13. Dorothy Shawhan, "Women behind the *Woman Voter*," *Journal of Mississippi History* 49 (May 1987): 115–28.

14. LSH, interview by Shawhan, 22 November 1985. Howorth thought her activities and Brewer's were important and thus saved mutual correspondence through 1934. Box 2, SHC, AES.

15. LSH, "Recommendations of the Chairman and Vice-Chairman of the Department of Uniform Laws" [1923], box 12, SHC, AES; *Woman Voter*, 22 November 1922, 23 March 1923. Other members of the committee were Bessie Scarborough, of Poplarville, and Mrs. W. G. Plummer, of Jackson. The letterhead stationery clearly named Howorth as a League of Women Voters committee chair, though she later downplayed her role in the League.

16. *Woman Voter*, 27 April 1923. See Michael De L. Landon, "The Origins of the Mississippi Law Journal," *Mississippi Law Journal* 50 (March 1979): 3.

17. Claudia Brewer Strite to Vinton Price, 11 March 1980, and Dorothy Shawhan, "Two Women Voters from a Mississippi Network" (paper presented at the annual meeting of the Southern Historical Association, New Orleans, 1987), both in authors' possession.

18. LSH to "Miss Annie," 18 May 1923, box 12, SHC, AES; LSH to Martha Swain, 18 August 1980, authors' possession.

19. LSH, interview by Shawhan, 9 November 1984.

20. Quoted in Brewer to LSH, 12 December 1923, box 12, SHC, AES.

21. LSH, interview by Myers, 99–100; LSH to Nannie Sue Rice, 22 April 1923, box 12, SHC, AES.

22. LSH, interview by Marjorie Spruill Wheeler, 15 March 1983, Cleveland, MS, transcript in Mississippi Oral History Collection, University of Southern Mississippi, Hattiesburg.

23. Vivian Cook to Burnita Shelton Matthews, 20 February 1923, National Woman's Party Papers, Texas Woman's University, Denton, microfilm reel 123; *Woman Voter*, 23 February 1923; *Clarksdale (MS) Daily Register*, 20 February 1923; *Memphis Commercial Appeal*, 4 March 1923. For a larger context, see Martha Swain, "Organized Women in Mississippi: The Clash over Legal Disabilities in the 1920s," *Southern Studies* 23 (Spring 1984): 91–102.

24. Jim Money Brewer to LSH, 12 March 1923, box 12, SHC, AES.

25. LSH, interview by Shawhan, 22 November 1985; LSH to Swain, 18 August 1980; Christine A. Lunardini, *From Equal Suffrage to Equal Rights: Alice Paul and the National Women's Party, 1910–1928* (New York: New York University Press, 1986), 138.

26. "Flooding Memories," *Jackson (MS) Clarion-Ledger*, 12 May 1991; *Ladies' Home Journal*, May 1952, 129.

27. Minnie Brewer to LSH, [June 1923?], box 12, SHC, AES.

28. LSH to Minnie Brewer, 4 June, 2 August 1923, ibid.

29. Ibid., 21 May 1923.

30. Ibid., 5 July 1923; Emy Lou Gillespie to Shawhan, 19 February 1986, in authors' possession. Gillespie was a high-school English teacher who taught the writer Eudora Welty in her senior year.

31. LSH to Blanche Montgomery Ralston, 10 August 1923, box 12, SHC, AES; LSH to Swain, 18 August 1980, in authors' possession; Albert D. Kirwan, *Revolt of the Rednecks: Mississippi Politics, 1876–1925* (New York: Harper & Row, 1951), 304–5. See also Vinton Price, "Women, Politics, and the Press: The Mississippi *Woman Voter,*" *Southern Studies* 19 (Winter 1980): 365–72.

32. Somerville's opponents were J. E. Chisholm, William T. Wynn, Sam V. Anderson, and Harry Hulen.

33. Anne Firor Scott, "Nellie Nugent Somerville," in *Notable American Women: The Modern Period,* ed. Barbara Sicherman and Carol Hurd Green (Cambridge, MA: Harvard University Press, 1980), 655. On the sheriff election, see Wyatt-Brown, *House of Percy,* 235–36.

34. LSH to Minnie Brewer, 21 July 1923, box 12, SHC, AES.

35. Ibid., 2, 11 August 1923.

36. LSH, interview by Shawhan, 7 November 1992; *Woman Voter,* 17 August 1923.

37. *Woman's Press,* 10 July 1923, copy in box 9, SHC, AES. In Mississippi, divisions within counties from which supervisors were elected were known as "beats."

38. Minnie Brewer to LSH, 20 August 1923; Rush H. Knox to Earl Brewer, 23 August 1923; Minnie Brewer to LSH, 8 September 1923; and LSH to Knox, 11 September 1923, all in box 12, SHC, AES.

39. LSH material on the National Association of Women Lawyers, 1937–55, box 6, SHC, AES.

40. LSH to Minnie Brewer, 28 September, 14 October 1923, box 12, SHC, AES; *Woman Voter,* 12 November 1923.

41. Dorothy Shawhan, "Lucy Saw a Community Beginning to Spark and Lit a Match," *Cleveland (MS) Bolivar Commercial,* 4 July 1986.

42. Linton Weeks, *Cleveland: A Centennial History, 1886–1996* (Cleveland, MS: City of Cleveland, 1986), 111–19; Jack Winton Gunn and Gladys C. Castle, *A Pictorial History of Delta State University* (Jackson: University Press of Mississippi, 1980), 3–12.

43. *Woman Voter,* 15 February 1924; LSH, interview by Shawhan, 9 November 1984.

44. *Woman Voter,* 15 February 1924.

45. LSH to Minnie Brewer, 26 June 1934, and LSH to Strite, 11 May 1939, both in carton 3, SHC, AES; Earl Brewer to LSH, box 5, SHC, AES. For more on Minnie Brewer, see Dorothy Shawhan, "Minnie Brewer (1878–1978): The Life and Times of a Feminist Flapper," in *Mississippi Women: Their Histories, Their Lives,* ed. Martha Swain, Elizabeth Anne Payne, and Marjorie Julian Spruill (Athens: University of Georgia Press, 2003).

46. LSH, interview by Myers, 112.

47. News clipping, 2 July 1924, box 2, SHC, AES; Anne Firor Scott, *Making the Invisible Woman Visible* (Urbana: University of Illinois Press, 1984), 235.

48. Delegate designation, 16 June 1924, box 6, SHC, AES.

49. LSH, "Note to Accompany Invitations," ibid.

50. LSH to Nellie Nugent Somerville, 2 September 1924, ibid.

51. LSH, "Laws about Lawyers," box 9, SHC, AES; Michael De L. Landon, *For the Honor and Dignity of the Profession: A History of the Mississippi State Bar, 1906–1976* (Jackson: University Press of Mississippi, 1979), 54.

52. LSH to Bill R. Baker, 23 February 1971, carton 2, SHC, AES; "Women as Bar Examiners," *Equal Rights* (National Woman's Party), 27 December 1924, 263. Years later Howorth's picture was on the cover of the *Bar Examiner*, journal of the National Conference of Bar Examiners, for August 1996.

53. LSH, note and pamphlet, "Instructions to Applicants and Rules and Regulations of the Mississippi State Board of Law Examiners, 1927," box 4, SHC, AES; *Northeast Mississippi Daily Journal* (Tupelo), *View Magazine*, 5 April 1985.

54. LSH, interview by Shawhan, 8 October 1986.

55. *Official and Statistical Register of the State of Mississippi, 1924–1928* (New York: J. J. Little, 1928), 285; Scott, "Nellie Nugent Somerville," 655.

56. LSH, interview by Myers, 95; LSH, interview by Shawhan, 4 October 1992.

57. LSH, interview by Myers, 96.

58. LSH, quoted in Elizabeth L. Riley, "Women and the Law: Beginnings," *Mississippi Lawyer* 31 (January–February 1985): 9.

59. *Jackson Daily News*, 28 August 1927. Commissioners are now called U.S. magistrates.

60. Tennessee Williams, *Cat on a Hot Tin Roof* (New York: Signet, 1955), 65; Margaret Allen Green, "Reminiscences of the River," in *History of Bolivar County, Mississippi*, comp. Florence Warfield Sillers (Jackson: Hederman Brothers, 1948; reprint, Spartanburg, SC: Reprint Publishers, 1976), 188–93.

61. Pete Daniel, *Deep'n As It Comes: The 1927 Mississippi River Flood* (New York: Oxford University Press, 1977), 126.

62. Marie M. Hemphill, *Fevers, Floods, and Faith: A History of Sunflower County, Mississippi, 1844–1976* (Indianola, MS: Marie Hemphill, 1980), 637.

63. Daniel, *Deep'n As It Comes*, 9–10.

64. Robert W. Harrison, *Levee Districts and Levee Building in Mississippi: A Study of State and Local Efforts to Control Mississippi River Floods* (Cleveland, MS: Delta Council and Mississippi Agricultural Experiment Station, 1951), 1, 5; *Laws of the State of Mississippi . . . January, February and March, A.D. 1846* (Jackson: C. M. Price & G. R. Fall, State Printers, 1846), 172–78.

65. Marquis Childs, *Mighty Mississippi: Biography of a River* (New York: Tichnor & Fields, 1982), 183.

66. LSH, "The Flood," interview by Shawhan, 21 June 1986, Cleveland, MS, tape in LSHC, DSU.

67. Ibid.; William Alexander Percy, *Lanterns on the Levee: Recollections of a Planter's Son* (New York: Knopf, 1941), 247.

68. LSH, "The Flood"; Percy, *Lanterns on the Levee*, 249.

69. LSH, "The Mississippi Flood of 1927," *Woman's Press*, June 1927, copy in box 9, SHC, AES.

70. Ibid., 1, 4; Percy, *Lanterns on the Levee*, 250–51.

71. *The Mississippi Valley Flood Disaster of 1927*, official report of relief operations (Washington, DC: American National Red Cross, 1929), 4.

72. LSH, "The Flood"; Frederick Simpich, "The Great Mississippi Flood of 1927," *National Geographic Magazine* 52 (September 1927): 266.

73. LSH, "The Flood"; LSH, "Mississippi Flood of 1927," 8.

74. LSH, "The Flood."

75. Percy, *Lanterns on the Levee*, 256; LSH to Blanche McKeown, n.d., carton 3, SHC, AES. In her letter to McKeown, Howorth took issue with the account by Noel Workman, "Forty Years Ago the Rampaging River Brought the Cry . . . De Levee Done Broke," *Delta Review* 4 (March–April 1967): 22–27, 53–55.

76. Two major studies deal with the friction between the two Percys: John M. Barry, *Rising Tide: The Great Mississippi Flood and How It Changed America* (New York: Simon & Schuster, 1994), 309–10; and Wyatt-Brown, *House of Percy*, 241–44. Both authors confirm Nellie's criticism that the Red Cross played politics.

77. LSH, "The Flood."

78. Hairston, "Practicing Law," 19.

79. LSH, as quoted in a review of *Count No 'Count*, by Ben Wasson, *Greenville (MS) Delta Democrat-Times*, 24 April 1983.

80. Daniel, *Deep'n As It Comes*, 101, 114.

81. LSH, "The Flood."

82. Ibid.; Hairston, "Practicing Law," 17; Percy, *Lanterns on the Levee*, 274.

83. LSH, "The Flood"; *Greenville (MS) Delta Democrat-Times*, 12 July 1927. An article in the 8 July 1927 *Delta Democrat-Times*, "Women Played Prominent Part in Relief Work," made no mention of the Somervilles' distribution program but did cite WCTU work.

84. LSH, "The Flood."

85. Joseph Howorth, interview by Jane Whiteside Elliott, 2 February 1975, Cleveland, MS, transcript in Capps Archives, DSU.

Chapter 4

1. Obituary for Joseph M. Howorth, *Cleveland (MS) Bolivar Commercial*, 19 May 1980.

2. LSH, interview by Dorothy Shawhan, 8 February 1985; all interviews of LSH by Shawhan were conducted in Cleveland, MS, and notes for all are in the authors' possession.

3. Virginia G. Drachman, *Sisters in Law: Women Lawyers in Modern American History* (Cambridge, MA: Harvard University Press, 1998), 245.

4. *Northeast Mississippi Daily Journal* (Tupelo), *View Magazine*, 20 March, 5 April 1985; U.S. Congress, *Congressional Record*, 83rd Cong., 2nd sess., 1954, vol. 100, appendix, pt. 1, 399.

5. LSH, interview by Constance Myers, 20, 23, 25 June 1975, Monteagle, TN, transcript in Southern Oral History Collection, University of North Carolina, Chapel Hill, 109.

6. Dick Boeth to LSH, 15 July 1980, LSHC, DSU. Boeth was a reporter for *Time* who

married a Cleveland native and friend of Lucy Howorth's, Sissy Green. His article "Behind the Magnolia Curtain: A Yankee in Mississippi," *Atlantic Monthly,* August 1963, caused a stir in Bolivar County.

7. Joseph Howorth Journal, LSHC, DSU.
8. Ibid.
9. LSH, interview by Myers, 11.
10. LePoint Smith, interview by Shawhan, 1 June 1989, Cleveland, MS.
11. Couprey Shands, interview by Shawhan, 26 October 1996, Jackson, MS.
12. Drachman, *Sisters in Law,* 246.
13. LSH, interview by Myers, 104.
14. Couprey Shands interview.
15. Ibid.; Smith, interview by Shawhan, 2 February 1997.
16. LSH, interview by Myers, 108.
17. LSH, interview by Jane Whiteside Elliott, 28 January 1975, Cleveland, MS, transcript in LSHC, DSU; LSH, "Note to Accompany Membership Cards," box 4, SHC, AES.
18. LSH, campaign card, box 4, SHC, AES.
19. LSH, note on NCCCW, ibid.
20. Linda K. Schott, *Reconstructing Women's Thoughts: The Women's International League for Peace and Freedom before World War II* (Stanford, CA: Stanford University Press, 1997), 89–90; Judy Barrett Litoff and David C. Smith, eds., *What Kind of World Do We Want? American Women Plan for Peace* (Wilmington, DE: Scholarly Resources, 2000), 4–5.
21. *Jackson Daily News,* 18 November 1928.
22. Ibid., 17 November 1928.
23. LSH, interview by Myers, 167.
24. *Jackson Daily News,* 15 November 1928; *Clarksdale (MS) Daily Press Register,* 16 November 1928.
25. Linda Schott, "Middle-of-the-Road Activists: Carrie Chapman Catt and the National Committee on the Cause and Cure of War," *Peace and Change: A Journal of Peace Research* 21 (January 1996): 1–21; Susan Zeiger, "Finding a Cure for War: Women's Politics and the Peace Movement in the 1920s," *Journal of Social History* 24 (Fall 1990): 69–86.
26. LSH, "Note on the Mississippi Legislative Session, 1932–34," carton 2, SHC, AES.
27. Joseph Howorth, interview by Jane Whiteside Elliott, 2 February 1975, Cleveland, MS, transcript in Capps Archives, DSU.
28. LSH, interview by Elliott.
29. LSH, quoted in *Congressional Record,* 83rd Cong., 2nd sess., 1954, vol. 100, appendix, pt. 1, 399.
30. LSH, interview by Shawhan, 17 October 1987.
31. Quoted in Joe E. Hairston, "Practicing Law: Lucy Somerville Howorth, in Court and Elsewhere, 1922–1934" (seminar paper, University of Mississippi, 1992), copy in authors' possession.
32. LSH, interview by Myers, 110.
33. Ibid.; LSH to Robert Somerville, 27 May 1931, carton 3, SHC, AES.

34. LSH, interview by Myers, 133.

35. Elliott, "Lucy Somerville Howorth: Legislative Career, 1932–1935" (master's thesis, DSU, 1975), 20; *Jackson (MS) Clarion-Ledger,* 2 July 1931.

36. *Jackson (MS) Clarion-Ledger,* 28 June 1931.

37. LSH, interview by Elliott.

38. Elliott, "Lucy Somerville Howorth," 23.

39. LSH, interview by Myers, 133; LSH, interview by Allen Dennis, 16 January 1973, Cleveland, MS, transcript in LSHC, DSU.

40. LSH, interview by Myers, 42; *Greenville (MS) Daily Democrat-Times,* 4, 30 June 1927.

41. LSH, interview by Myers, 134.

42. Broadcast transcripts, carton 2, SHC, AES.

43. LSH, interview by Elliott.

44. Ibid.; unidentified newspaper article, carton 3, SHC, AES.

45. LSH, interview by Elliott.

46. *Jackson (MS) Clarion-Ledger,* 28 June 1931. On Nugent, see William C. Harris, *The Day of the Carpetbaggers: Republican Reconstruction in Mississippi* (Baton Rouge: Louisiana State University Press, 1979), 448.

47. Joseph Howorth interview; LSH, interview by Elliott; LSH, interview by Joanne Varner Hawks, 11 April 1979, Oxford, MS, videotape in AAUW, Mississippi Division Papers, Special Collections, Williams Library, University of Mississippi, Oxford, transcript in authors' possession.

48. Couprey Shands interview.

49. LSH, interview by Elliott.

50. Ibid.

51. Ibid.

52. The tally was Posey, 5,471; Capers, 5,396; Howorth, 4,931; Chadwick, 4,572; and Key, 4,314. *Jackson Daily News,* 6 August 1931.

53. LSH, interview by Elliott, 30 January 1975.

54. The vote was: Capers, 6322; Howorth, 5673; Chadwick, 5426; and Key, 4974. *Jackson Daily News,* 31 August 1931.

55. LSH, memorandum, carton 2, SHC, AES; LSH, interview by Joe Hairston, 20 November 1991, Cleveland, MS, transcript in AAUW, Mississippi Division Papers.

Chapter 5

1. Many Mississippi women legislators succeeded dead husbands and served no longer than the unexpired term. See Joanne V. Hawks, M. Carolyn Ellis, and J. Bryan Morris, "Women in the Mississippi Legislature (1924–1981)," *Journal of Mississippi History* 43 (November 1981): 266–93.

2. *Literary Digest* 120 (19 July 1935): 13.

3. *Jackson Daily News,* 17 January 1932.

4. Hawks, Ellis, and Morris, "Women in the Mississippi Legislature," 270, 274. Fugler

suffered a debilitating stroke near the end of the 1934 session, and Topp chose not to seek reelection.

5. LSH, "A Representative of the People," *Randolph-Macon Alumnae Bulletin* 28 (April 1935): 5; Nancy Finerty, "Lucy Howorth: 'The Little Lady from Mississippi,'" *Ole Miss Magazine,* January 1983, 11; Jane Whiteside Elliott, "Lucy Somerville Howorth: Legislative Career, 1932–1935" (master's thesis, DSU, 1975), 37–40. Elliott provides a detailed account of Howorth's course of action based upon extensive interviews.

6. J. Oliver Emmerich, "Collapse and Recovery," in *A History of Mississippi,* ed. Richard A. McLemore, vol. 2 (Jackson: University & College Press of Mississippi, 1973), 97–98; William Winter, "Governor Mike Conner and the Sales Tax, 1932," in *Mississippi Heroes,* ed. Dean Faulkner Wells and Hunter Cole (Jackson: University Press of Mississippi, 1980), 161.

7. LSH, interview by Chester Morgan, 30 May 1984, Cleveland, MS, transcript in Mississippi Oral History Collection, University of Southern Mississippi, Hattiesburg.

8. Quoted in Winter, "Governor Mike Conner," 170; Bill Minor, "Lucy Howorth: Rare State Legislator," in *Eyes on Mississippi: A Fifty-Year Chronicle of Change* (Jackson: Prichard Morris Books, 2001), 301.

9. Winter, "Governor Mike Conner," 171; *Jackson (MS) Clarion-Ledger,* 26 February 1932.

10. LSH, "Notes on the Mississippi Legislature, 1932–34," carton 3, SHC, AES; LSH to Sara Lou Sartin, 6 February 1933, box 12, SHC, AES.

11. *Jackson (MS) Clarion-Ledger,* 25 February, 9 April 1932; LSH, interview by Morgan.

12. Mississippi House of Representatives, *Journal of the House of Representatives of the State of Mississippi . . . 1932* (Jackson: Hederman Brothers, 1932), 697 (19 April 1932) (hereafter *House Journal*); *Jackson Daily News,* 19 April 1932; Winter, "Governor Mike Conner," 174.

13. LSH, interview by Morgan. A staple of New Deal literature is the article entitled "One-Fourth of a State Sold for Taxes" in *Literary Digest* 113 (7 May 1932): 10. Topp was named chair of the Committee on Eleemosynary Institutions, and Fugler chaired the Joint Library Committee.

14. *House Journal,* 837–38 (13 May 1932); *Jackson (MS) Clarion-Ledger,* 4 May 1932.

15. Elliott, "Lucy Somerville Howorth," 44–45.

16. *House Journal,* 155 (26 January 1932), 341 (1 March 1932).

17. LSH, interview by Morgan; *Jackson (MS) Clarion-Ledger,* 1 March 1932.

18. *Jackson Daily News,* 12 February 1932; *Jackson (MS) Clarion-Ledger,* 13 February 1932; *House Journal,* 126 (10 May 1932).

19. On the Mississippi poll tax, see V. O. Key, *Southern Politics in State and Nation* (New York: Knopf, 1950), 580–81.

20. The sponsor of the jury-service bill was Hooker M. Coen, of Hazlehurst.

21. *House Journal,* 505 (22 March 1932), 834 (3 May 1932), 1140 (18 May 1932).

22. Ibid., 868 (5 May 1932).

23. Ibid., 413 (11 March 1932), 672 (15 April 1932); *Jackson Daily News,* 17 April 1932; LSH, interview by Morgan.

24. *Jackson Daily News,* 7 September 1930; LSH, "Note to Accompany Bilbo Letters," box 4, SHC, AES.

25. Frank Wallace, "A History of the Conner Administration" (master's thesis, Mississippi State University, 1959), 54–55; *House Journal,* 275–76, 279, 287 (18 February 1932); Elliott, "Lucy Somerville Howorth," 62; LSH to Pearl Guyton, 9 November 1933, box 12, SHC, AES; *Jackson (MS) Clarion-Ledger,* 28 December 1986.

26. Martha H. Swain, *Ellen S. Woodward: New Deal Advocate for Women* (Jackson: University Press of Mississippi, 1995), 9–11, 25–26.

27. *Jackson (MS) Clarion Ledger,* 19 May 1932.

28. Elliott, "Lucy Somerville Howorth," 66–67; Courtney Borden, writing for the *Jackson Daily News,* 1 July 1932. Howorth provided an insight into the intricacies of the Mississippi delegation's disputations in Chicago in a detailed, lengthy letter to the historian T. Harry Williams, 30 January 1970, carton 3, SHC, AES.

29. Pat Harrison to LSH, 6 July 1932; Richard F. Roper to LSH, 29 September 1932; and Franklin D. Roosevelt to LSH, 27 August 1932, all in carton 5, SHC, AES.

30. Mary W. Dewson to LSH, 24 October 1932, and LSH to Dewson, 19 November 1932, both in ibid.; LSH, "The National Democratic Convention," *Mississippi Business Woman* 1 (1932): 1; radio script, carton 2, SHC, AES.

31. LSH to Dewson, 19 November 1932, and LSH to Roosevelt, 7 February 1933, both in carton 5, SHC, AES; Dewson to LSH, 28 November 1938, carton 3, SHC, AES; Bess Furman, *Washington By-Line: The Personal History of a Newspaperwoman* (New York: Knopf, 1949), 227.

32. Dewson to LSH, 2 May 1933, carton 3, SHC, AES.

33. LSH to Harrison, 30 January, 22 February 1933; Harrison to LSH, 6 February 1933; and LSH to Whittington, 25 February 1933, all in carton 5, SHC, AES.

34. Federal Bureau of Investigation, Lucy Somerville Howorth file, 77-HQ-7131, 10 July 1933.

35. James B. Frazier to Cordell Hull, 28 February 1933, carton 5, SHC, AES.

36. Susan Ware, *Beyond Suffrage: Women in the New Deal* (Cambridge, MA: Harvard University Press, 1981), 52.

37. LSH to Harrison, 22 February 1933, and Harrison to LSH, 20 March 1933, both in carton 5, SHC, AES.

38. LSH to Homer Cummings, 23 April 1933, ibid.; Dewson to LSH, 4 December 1933, WD-DNC, FDRL.

39. Swain, *Ellen S. Woodward,* 41.

40. *Jackson (MS) Clarion-Ledger,* 17 January, 26 February 1934; WCTU pamphlets, carton 5, SHC, AES.

41. *Jackson (MS) Clarion-Ledger,* 30 March 1934.

42. Ibid., 16 February 1934.

43. Elliott, "Lucy Somerville Howorth," 75–80, quotation on 80. *Jackson Daily News,* 22 March 1934. LSH, interview by Dorothy Shawhan, 31 December 1984; all interviews of

LSH by Shawhan were conducted in Cleveland, MS, and notes for all are in the authors' possession. Michael Bogard, Mississippi Department of Geology, Jackson, telephone conversation with Martha Swain, 28 October 2003. Howorth stated her height and weight on her application for the VA job in 1934.

44. Elliott, "Lucy Somerville Howorth," 77.

45. Ibid., 70–72; *Jackson (MS) Clarion-Ledger,* 9, 14 March 1934; LSH, "Notes on the Mississippi Legislature, 1932–34"; LSH, interview by Morgan.

46. LSH, interview by Morgan; Roger D. Tate Jr., "Easing the Burden: The Era of the Great Depression in Mississippi" (PhD diss., University of Tennessee, 1978), 45.

47. LSH to Blanche Montgomery Ralston, 16 February 1934, LSH file on the Natchez Trace Association, Mississippi Department of Archives and History, Jackson.

48. *Jackson (MS) Clarion-Ledger,* 28 February, 13 March 1934; LSH to Swain, 31 February 1990, in authors' possession.

49. LSH to National Child Labor Committee, 28 August 1933, box 12, SHC, AES; Dewson to LSH, 29 January 1934, box 27, WD-DNC, Mississippi file, FDRL; Anne Firor Scott, "Nellie Nugent Somerville," in *Notable American Women: The Modern Period,* ed. Barbara Sicherman and Carol Hurd Green (Cambridge, MA: Harvard University Press, 1980), 655.

50. LSH to Dewson, 3 February 1934, WD-DNC, FDRL.

51. Ellen Woodward to Dewson, 20 February 1934, box 27, WD-DNC, FDRL; Ernest S. Jones to Woodward, 3 March 1934, copy in box 639, Eleanor Roosevelt Papers, FDRL.

52. LSH to Dewson, 3 February 1934, WD-DNC, FDRL.

53. LSH to Dewson, 10 March 1934, and Dewson to LSH, 14 March 1934, WD-DNC, Mississippi file, FDRL.

54. Dewson to LSH, 16 April 1934, and LSH to Dewson, 18 April 1934, both ibid.

55. LSH, interview by Constance Myers, 20, 23, 25 June 1975, Monteagle, TN, transcript in Southern Oral History Collection, University of North Carolina, Chapel Hill, 138; Bill Minor, "Let's not forget Lucy Howorth, a gem in the Legislature," *Jackson (MS) Clarion-Ledger,* 19 January 1984.

56. LSH, interview by Morgan; LSH, "Representative of the People"; Diane Casselberry Manuel, "Judge Lucy Howorth: Lawyer, feminist, organization woman," *Christian Science Monitor,* 14 February 1984.

57. Dewson to Ormond F. Lewis, 17 January 1934, and Dewson to LSH, 19 January 1934, both in WD-DNC, FDRL; Harrison to LSH, 27 January 1934, carton 3, SHC, AES.

58. Dewson to Missy LeHand, 5 January 1934; Dewson bound volume, "Patronage—1933 Women," Mary W. Dewson Papers; and Dewson to LSH, 7 March 1934, WD-DNC, all in FDRL. Dewson to LSH, 1 July 1934, box 12, SHC, AES.

59. Dewson to LSH, 16 April 1934, WD-DNC, FDRL.

60. Dewson to LSH, 26 April 1934, and LSH to Dewson, 3 May 1934, both ibid.

61. LSH to Eudora Ramsay Richardson, 15 June 1934, and LSH to Woodward, 4 June 1934, both in carton 3, SHC, AES.

62. John G. Pollard to LSH, 16 June 1934, ibid.; Nellie Nugent Somerville to a Memphis friend, 30 June 1934, box 1, SHC, AES.

63. Audley Shands to LSH, 29 October 1934, box 12, SHC, AES.

64. Greek Rice to LSH, 5 September 1935, ibid.

65. LSH to Horace Stansel, 12 November 1935, ibid. A pair is "an agreement between members of a legislative body on opposite sides of an issue that in case of the absence of one the other will also be absent or will refrain from voting" (Edward C. Smith and Arnold J. Zurcher, eds., *Dictionary of American Politics,* 2nd ed. [New York: Barnes & Noble, 1968), 273.

66. LSH to Rice, 14 December 1935, carton 3, SHC, AES; Rice to LSH, 19 December 1935, box 12, SHC, AES.

67. *Jackson (MS) Clarion-Ledger,* 1 May 1935.

68. Augusta Stacy Marshall to LSH, 11 July, 28 December 1934, unprocessed, SHC, AES.

Chapter 6

1. LSH to Martha Swain, 1 July 1987, in authors' possession.

2. Mary Agnes Brown, "New Dealer Feted," *Women Lawyers Journal* 21 (November 1934): 33.

3. "Administrative Authorization Order," 2 July 1934, in LSH Leave, Personnel Records folder, LSHC, DSU; LSH, "Washington Notes, 1934–58," box 4, SHC, AES; Mary W. Dewson to LSH, 7 March 1934, carton 3, SHC, AES.

4. Isabel K. Griffin, "Women You Hear About," *Democratic Digest* 8 (August 1934): 15; *Washington Post,* 13 July 1934. For Laura Brown's work among women, see Virginia Jeans Laas, ed., *Bridging Two Eras: The Autobiography of Emily Newell Blair, 1877–1951* (Columbia: University of Missouri Press, 1999), 209, 224.

5. LSH, interview by Joanne Varner Hawks, 11 April 1979, Oxford, MS, videotape in AAUW, Mississippi Division Papers, Special Collections, Williams Library, University of Mississippi, Oxford, transcript in authors' possession; Virginia G. Drachman, *Sisters in Law: Women Lawyers in Modern American History* (Cambridge, MA: Harvard University Press, 1998), 240.

6. LSH, speech, 1935, box 9, SHC, AES; LSH, interview by Marjorie Spruill Wheeler, 15 March 1983, Cleveland, MS, transcript in Mississippi Oral History Collection, University of Southern Mississippi, Hattiesburg.

7. LSH, interview by Constance Myers, 20, 23, 25 June 1975, Monteagle, TN, transcript in Southern Oral History Collection, University of North Carolina, Chapel Hill, 44.

8. Dewson to Ellen Woodward, 6 February 1935, box 27, WD-DNC, FDRL.

9. LSH, interview by Myers, 139, 195. See also Adalyn Davis, *The Women's National Democratic Club: The Place Where Democrats Meet* (Washington, DC: WNDC, 1991), 11; and Emily Newell Blair, "Why New Deal Washington Fascinates Women," *Liberty,* 8 December 1934, 15–17.

10. Dewson to LSH, 13 October 1936, box 6, SHC, AES; Dewson to LSH, 12 December 1936, and LSH to Dewson, 12 December 1936, both in box 7, SHC, AES; Dewson to May Thompson Evans, 8 March 1937, box 7, Mary W. Dewson Papers, FDRL.

11. Augusta Stacy Marshall to LSH, 19 October 1935, unprocessed, SHC, AES. LSH, in-

terview by Dorothy Shawhan, 21 November 1986; all interviews of LSH by Shawhan were conducted in Cleveland, MS, and notes for all are in the authors' possession. James M. Goode, *Best Addresses* (Washington, DC: Smithsonian Institution Press, 1988), 307–13. Joe's work was for his own pleasure and for that of their friends. Lucy never pretended that Joe's paintings were of gallery quality. "Joe painted fast," she once said. LSH, interview by Shawhan, 21 November 1986.

12. David Brinkley, *Washington Goes to War: The Extraordinary Story of the Transformation of a City and a Nation* (New York: Knopf, 1988), 12.

13. Sue Shelton White to LSH, 24 July 1933, carton 3, SHC, AES; LSH, quoted in "Recollections of Sue Shelton White," Sue Shelton White Papers, AES.

14. Fannie Dixon Welch to LSH, 21 October 1935; Florence Armstrong to LSH, 18 May 1939; and Marshall White to LSH, 15 May 1943, all in box 5, SHC, AES. Sue White burned most of her papers, but Howorth and Armstrong collected the remaining papers for deposit in AES. LSH to Swain, 17 October 1977, in authors' possession.

15. Eudora Ramsey Richardson to LSH, 27 April, 12 June, 15 December 1936, box 5, SHC, AES.

16. Harley R. Shands to Joseph Howorth, 14 January, 4 March 1941, ibid.; LSH, telephone conversation with Swain, 6 March 1991.

17. Emily Newell Blair to LSH, 23 February 1939, box 5, SHC, AES; LSH to Swain, 18 May 1986, in authors' possession. Howorth initially deposited the papers of Ella Harrison, a Missouri suffragist sent to Mississippi in 1895 and 1896, followed by those of her mother. The Harrison papers were given in 1940 to augment the records of the National American Woman Suffrage Association.

18. Carrie Chapman Catt to LSH, 16 February 1940, box 7, SHC, AES; LSH to Alena Ribble, 6 December 1957, carton 3, SHC, AES; *New York Times,* 26 November 1940.

19. R. E. McNeill to LSH, 8 June 1937, box 5, SHC, AES; LSH, interview by Hawks. For Howorth's numerous club associations, see box 5, SHC, AES.

20. Virginia Timmons to LSH, 12 June 1957, box 5, SHC, AES (an account of the Howorth's Soroptimist Club committee work).

21. Memorandum, "LSH and the BPW Clubs," February 1988, LSHC, DSU; Geline Bowman, *History of the National Federation of Business and Professional Women's Clubs, 1919–1944* (New York: NFBPW, 1944), 16; *Jackson Daily News,* 10 August 1934.

22. Memorandum, "LSH and the BPW Clubs"; Bowman, *History of the National Federation,* 74; Somerville, quoted in Susan Ware, *Beyond Suffrage: Women in the New Deal* (Cambridge, MA: Harvard University Press, 1981), 169n46.

23. Memorandum, "LSH and the BPW Clubs"; "Meet Three New Committee Chairmen," *Independent Woman* 16 (October 1937): 314–15; *Washington Post,* 9 May 1939. See Howorth's year-end report, "Program Coordinator," in *Independent Woman* 18 (August 1939): 233–35.

24. LSH to Nellie Nugent Somerville, 6 June 1939, SHC, AES, microfilm series, Women in Politics, reel 4; Marshall to LSH, 17 May 1939, unprocessed, SHC, AES.

25. Phyllis A. Deakin, *In Pride and With Pleasure* (London: International Federation of Business and Professional Women, 1970), 28.

26. Mary Alice Kimball, "Your Delegate Looks at Norway," *Independent Woman* 18 (September 1939): 303.

27. Lisa Sergio, *A Measure Fulfilled: The Life of Lena Madesin Phillips* (New York: Breese, 1972), 59.

28. Louise Franklin Bache to LSH, 20 July 1939; Dewson to LSH, 14 August 1939; and LSH, "Note on Proceedings, 5th Biennial Convention," all in box 8, SHC, AES.

29. See Martha H. Swain, *Ellen S. Woodward: New Deal Advocate for Women* (Jackson: University Press of Mississippi, 1995), 153–54; LSH to Swain, 26 January 1984, in authors' possession; and "Resolutions—Committee Reports—Recommendations," *Independent Women* 18 (August 1939): 232–33.

30. LSH, "To Accompany miscellaneous papers relating to the National Federation of Business & Professional Women's Club, the Jackson, Miss. and the District of Columbia Clubs," box 8, SHC, AES; "Here Are Your 1939–40 Committee Chairmen," *Independent Woman* 18 (October 1939): 328–29.

31. LSH to Dr. Minnie Maffett, 2 August 1941, box 8, SHC, AES.

32. Ibid., 29 May 1941. For more on Maffett's presidency, see Swain, *Ellen S. Woodward*, 153–43, 175.

33. LSH, "To Accompany miscellaneous papers relating to the National Federation of Business & Professional Women's Club. . . ."

34. LSH to Board of Directors, Mississippi BPW, 10 September 1940, box 8, SHC, AES; Dees Gurganes to LSH, 28 August 1947, and LSH to Gurganes, 8 September 1947, both in carton 4, SHC, AES.

35. Gillie A. Larew to LSH, 2 July 1946, box 13, SHC, AES.

36. Bowman, *History of the National Federation,* 87–88.

37. Memorandum, "LSH and the BPW Club."

38. LSH, " To Accompany miscellaneous papers relating to the National Federation of Business & Professional Women's Club . . ."; Leila J. Rupp and Verta Taylor, *Survival in the Doldrums: The American Women's Rights Movement, 1945 to the 1960s* (New York: Oxford University Press, 1987), 98.

39. Marguerite Rawalt to LSH, 28 August 1939, box 6, SHC, AES; Marguerite Rawalt, interview by Swain, 5 July 1987, Washington, DC; LSH, interview by Shawhan, 21 November 1986; Judith Patterson, *Be Somebody: A Biography of Marguerite Rawalt* (Austin, TX: Eakin, 1986), 86; Ronald Chester, *Unequal Access: Women Lawyers in a Changing America* (South Hadley, MA: Bergin & Garvey, 1945), 76–77.

40. Carroll Stewart to LSH, February 1943, box 12, SHC, AES; ibid., 5 July 1946, box 5, SHC, AES; LSH, "Washington Notes, 1934–58."

41. LSH, Application for Federal Employment folder, LSHC, DSU; LSH to Margaret Hickey, 28 January 1946, box 8, SHC, AES. Copies of legislation drafted by VA attorneys are in box 6, SHC, AES.

42. LSH, "Notes to Accompany AAUW News Release," 8 August 1943, and Kathryn McHale to Civil Service Commission, both in box 7, SHC, AES; Frances Valiant Speek to Sarah T. Hughes, 13 December 1943, American Association of University Women Papers, microfilm edition, Texas Woman's University, Denton (hereafter AAUW Papers), reel 118.

43. Committee on the Economic and Legal Status of Women (hereafter CELSW) to Speek; LSH to Speek, 19 January 1944; and "Should Women Be Drafted for the Armed Forces Report," 10 March 1944, all in AAUW Papers, reel 118.

44. Oveta Culp Hobby to LSH, 27 May 1944, and Mary Agnes Brown to LSH, 12 June 1944, both in box 5, SHC, AES.

45. Brown to LSH, 12 June 1944.

46. Hobby to LSH, 25 March 1942, and Brown to LSH, 20 September 1944, both in box 5, SHC, AES; LSH, interview by Swain, 19 June 1984, Cleveland, MS, tape in LSHC, DSU.

47. General Omar Bradley to LSH, 14 December 1945, and LSH, "Record of Red Cross/Veterans Administration, July 7, 1941–November 30, 1945," both in carton 5, SHC, AES; Nancy Finerty, "Lucy Howorth: 'The Little Lady from Mississippi,'" *Ole Miss Magazine,* January 1983, 11.

48. Dorothy Shands's letters from August 1943 to April 1945 are in box 5, SHC, AES.

49. LSH to McHale, 27 May 1944, copy in Eleanor Roosevelt Papers, FDRL; LSH, interview by Swain; Eleanor Roosevelt, "Women at the Peace Conference," *Reader's Digest* 14 (April 1944): 48–49.

50. Hickey to LSH, 5 October 1943, series 3, box 40, Margaret A. Hickey Papers, Western History Manuscript Collection, University of Missouri–St. Louis; LSH to McHale, 27 May 1944, and Hughes to McHale, 1 June 1944, both in AAUW Papers, reel 118. The first published work to describe the origins of the White House conference and to give Howorth's address its proper due is Judy Barrett Litoff and David C. Smith, eds., *What Kind of World Do We Want? American Women Plan for Peace* (Wilmington, DE: Scholarly Resources, 2000).

51. LSH, interview by Swain; List of observers, AAUW Papers, reel 122; *Washington Post,* 15 June 1944; *New York Times,* 15 June 1944.

52. LSH, "Women's Responsibility in World Affairs," *Journal of the American Association of University Women* (hereafter *AAUW Journal*) 37 (Summer 1944): 195–98, also in *American Women in a World at War: Contemporary Accounts from World War II,* ed. Judy Barrett Litoff and David C. Smith (Wilmington, DE: Scholarly Resources, 1997), 225–32. The statements of Woodward, Conkey, Schain, Thompson, and Perkins are in AAUW Papers, reel 122.

53. LSH, "Women's Responsibility," 197; "News and Notes," *AAUW Journal* 37 (Summer 1944): 247.

54. *Christian Science Monitor,* 14 June 1944; Margaret Chase Smith and Ruth Bryant Rohde, statements, AAUW Papers, reel 122.

55. LSH, interview by Swain.

56. *New York Times,* 15 June 1944; Malvina Lindsay to LSH, 9 July 1944, box 5, SHC, AES; Marshall to LSH, 2 June 1944, unprocessed, SHC, AES.

57. Herbert Lehman to Woodward, 26 June 1944, Ellen S. Woodward Papers 1139.2, box 5, Mississippi Department of Archives and History, Jackson.

58. Hickey to LSH, 14 November 1945, box 12, SHC, AES; Charl Williams to Edward R. Stettinius, 17 January 1945, and Background and Facts on Roster of Qualified Women, 22 January 1945, both in AAUW Papers, reel 122. Howorth is quoted on Hiss in the *Cleveland (MS) Bolivar Commercial,* 4 April 1973.

59. Williams to Continuation Committee, 11 December 1944, container 8, Charl O. Williams Papers, Library of Congress, Washington, DC.

60. *New York World Tribune,* 19 October 1933; *Washington Times-Herald,* 10 October 1944; *Independent Woman* 20 (March 1947): 87; LSH, keynote address, "A Plan of Action," box 9, SHC, AES.

61. LSH to Governor J. Strom Thurmond, 31 January 1947, box 13, SHC, AES; Mary E. Frayser to LSH, 7 February 1947, carton 5, SHC, AES; Nadine Cohodas, *Strom Thurmond and the Politics of Southern Change* (New York: Simon & Schuster, 1993), 97.

62. McHale to LSH, 14 June 1943, box 12, SHC, AES; Hughes to LSH, 21 December 1944, box 5, SHC, AES; "Questions for Consideration," 14 September 1944, AAUW Papers, reel 117.

63. Sarah T. Hughes, "Report of the Committee on Economic and Legal Status of Women (CELSW), 1941-1946," AAUW Papers, reel 118.

64. Minutes of the CELSW, 14 September 1944, ibid., reel 117.

65. *New York Herald Tribune,* 3 November 1940.

66. Esther Cole Franklin to Hickey, 11 April 1944, series 3, box 40, Hickey Papers.

67. Minutes, CELSW, 14 September 1944.

68. LSH, "The Wheel Spins Faster," *AAUW Journal* 38 (April 1945): 150-51.

69. Minutes, CELSW, 14 September 1945.

70. Ibid.

71. Ibid., 3 December 1946.

72. LSH, "Memo to Accompany Three Clippings," box 6, SHC, AES; Fleeson's article appeared in the *Washington Evening Star,* 4 October 1945.

73. Hughes to LSH, 18 July 1945, and Lindsay to LSH, 10 July 1945, both in box 5, SHC, AES; President's Appointments, 20 August 1945, Harry S. Truman Papers, President's Secretary's Files, Harry S. Truman Library, Independence, MO.

74. LSH, interview by Swain; Susan M. Hartmann, *The Home Front and Beyond: American Women in the 1940s* (Boston: Twayne, 1982), 148-49.

75. LSH, interview by Swain.

76. LSH, "Memo to Accompany Three Clippings."

77. Jewel Swofford to LSH, 21 February 1945, box 5, SHC, AES; Swofford to LSH, 21 June 1945, and LSH, "Note to Correspondence (1958)," both in box 6, SHC, AES; LSH, interview by Myers, 203.

78. Malvina Lindsay, "Setback for Women," *Washington Post,* undated clipping in Woodward Papers 1139.2, scrapbook.

79. LSH to Harriet Elliott, 5 June 1946, Harriet Elliott Papers, Walter Clinton Jackson Library, University of North Carolina, Greensboro.

80. LSH, "Recollections of Mississippi Women in Public Life Whom I Have Known," paper delivered at Mississippi Historical Society meeting, March 1975, copy in authors' possession.

81. LSH to Emily Hickman, 31 May 1946, copy in Elliott Papers; copy of letter drafted by LSH and Evans, 20 June 1946, in box 13, SHC, AES.

82. LSH, "Memo to Accompany Three Clippings"; LSH, interview by Myers, 145.

83. LSH to Dorothy Kenyon, 13 April 1954, and Kenyon to LSH, 13 April 1954, both in box 7, SHC, AES.

84. LSH to Mrs. Burnet Mahon, April 1951, copy in Dorothy Kenyon Papers, box 27, Sophia Smith Collection, Smith College, Northampton, MA; LSH, "Tribute to Emily Hickman," box 7, SHC, AES; Litoff and Smith, *What Kind of World Do We Want?* 22, 223, 236–37.

85. LSH, "To Accompany File of CWWA," box 7, SHC, AES.

86. LSH to Mrs. Arthur J. White, 17 January 1952, LSHC, DSU.

87. Gladys Tillett to Tom C. Clark, 30 November 1945; Tillett to Robert Hannegan, 30 November 1945; Tillett to LSH, 7 December 1945; and Hickman to Clark, 10 December 1945, all in Gladys Tillett Papers, Southern Historical Collection, University of North Carolina, Chapel Hill.

88. Clark to Truman, 13 February 1946, Truman Papers, Official File.

89. *Washington Evening Star,* 26 March 1946; LSH, "Memo to Accompany Items Relating to Appointment," and LSH to George E. Allen, 29 March 1946, both in box 6, SHC, AES.

90. Letters of support; Hickey to LSH, 21 March 1946; and Lindsay to Truman (copy), 3 April 1946, all in box 6, SHC, AES.

91. LSH, "Memo to Accompany Items," and LSH to Harley R. Shands, 5 April 1946, both in ibid.; LSH to Truman, 22 June 1946, Truman Papers, Official File; Clark to LSH, 8 July 1946, Tom C. Clark Papers, Truman Library.

92. Newspaper photograph, 27 June 1946, in box 6, SHC, AES.

93. File memorandum 15-A, 23 August 1946, Truman Papers.

Chapter 7

1. LSH, "From a One-Horse Surrey into the Atomic Age," address to RMWC alumnae, 5 June 1948, printed in *Randolph-Macon Alumnae Bulletin* 41 (June 1948): 2–10.

2. Doris Fleeson, in *Washington Evening Star,* 4 October 1945; Sarah T. Hughes to LSH, 8 October 1945, and Anna M. Kross to LSH, 11 December 1945, both in box 5, SHC, AES; William D. Hassett to LSH, 18 October 1945, Harry S. Truman Papers, Official File, Harry S. Truman Library, Independence, MO.

3. LSH to Gladys Tillett, 18 February 1945, box 5, SHC, AES; LSH, interview by Constance Myers, 20, 23, 25 June 1975, Monteagle, TN, transcript in Southern Oral History Collection, University of North Carolina, Chapel Hill, 156.

4. LSH to Martha Swain, 31 January 1990, in authors' possession.

5. India Edwards, *Pulling No Punches: Memoirs of a Woman in Politics* (New York: G. P. Putnam's Sons, 1977), passim.

6. Cynthia Harrison, *On Account of Sex: The Politics of Women's Issues, 1945–1968* (Berkeley and Los Angeles: University of California Press, 1988), 55, 58, 65; Doris Fleeson, "Equal Rights for Women," clipping in box 6, SHC, AES.

7. LSH, "Washington Notes, 1934–58," and LSH, "Notes to Accompany an Item from the *Congressional Record,*" 1954, both in box 4, SHC, AES; *Democratic Digest* 26 (Au-

gust–September 1949): 13; Tom C. Clark to LSH, 8 July 1946, Tom C. Clark Papers, Truman Library; Roger D. Hardaway, "Georgia Lee Lusk," in *Notable American Women: The Modern Period,* ed. Barbara Sicherman and Carol Hurd Green (Cambridge, MA: Harvard University Press, 1980), 434–35.

8. Mary W. Dewson to LSH, 21 August 1949, box 8, SHC, AES; Federal Bureau of Investigation, Lucy Somerville Howorth file, 77 HQ-77-7131, 6 February 1956.

9. *Democratic Digest* 26 (August–September 1949): 23; LSH, interview by Myers, 205.

10. *Washington Post,* 4 January 1949; *Christian Science Monitor,* 17 January 1949; JanAnn Sherman, *No Place for a Woman: A Life of Senator Margaret Chase Smith* (New Brunswick, NJ: Rutgers University Press, 2000), 90.

11. LSH, "Task Force '49," box 9, SHC, AES, printed in *Phi Delta Kappan* 27 (March 1949): 11–15; On the Multi-Party Committee of Women, see Emily Hickman's CWWA report for 1945–46 in *What Kind of World Do We Want? American Women Plan for Peace,* ed. Judy Barrett Litoff and David C. Smith (Wilmington, DE: Scholarly Resources, 2000), 234–35.

12. Kross to LSH, 24 March 1946, box 13, SHC, AES; Emma Dot Partridge to LSH, 3 February 1949, box 7, SHC, AES; Howorth's record of organization memberships, Federal Bureau of Investigation, Lucy Somerville Howorth file.

13. LSH to Hughes, 19 February 1949, and LSH to Maurice Tobin, 19 February 1949, both in box 6, SHC, AES; LSH to Harry S. Truman, 19 February 1949, Truman Papers, Official File; Dennis E. Bilger (Truman Library) to Swain, 23 October 2002, in authors' possession. There is a large file of endorsements in both the White House Central File, Truman Library, and the May Thompson Evans Papers, North Carolina State Archives, Raleigh.

14. For more on Matthews, see Kate Greene, "Torts over Tempo: The Life and Career of Judge Burnita Shelton Matthews," *Journal of Mississippi History* 56 (August 1994): 181–210; and Martha Swain, "Organized Women in Mississippi: The Clash over Legal Disabilities in the 1920s," *Southern Studies* 23 (Spring 1984): 91–102.

15. J. Howard McGrath to LSH, 24 October 1949, J. Howard McGrath Papers, Truman Library.

16. LSH, "Women Jurors," *AAUW Journal* 41 (February 1947): 61–62.

17. Minutes of the Committee on the Status of Women, 24 January 1948, AAUW Papers, reel 117; Melanie Rosborough to LSH, 4 February 1948, ibid., reel 118.

18. LSH, "From a One-Horse Surrey into the Atomic Age"; Augusta Stacy Marshall to LSH, 3 June 1948, unprocessed, SHC, AES; LSH, interview by Myers, 192; *Randolph-Macon Alumnae Bulletin* 34 (November 1940): 4.

19. LSH, "Committee on the Status of Women," *AAUW Journal* 43 (Fall 1949): 56–59.

20. Ibid., 56; Margaret Rossiter, *Women Scientists in America: Before Affirmative Action, 1940–1972* (Baltimore: Johns Hopkins University Press, 1995), 40.

21. For a full discussion of the dilemma, see Susan Levine, *Degrees of Equality: The American Association of University Women and the Challenge of Twentieth-Century Feminism* (Philadelphia: Temple University Press, 1995), 83–104, quotation on 86.

22. LSH to Marleen Hansen, 13 May 1988, in Hansen's possession, Columbus, MS.

Hansen was a leader in the Cleveland AAUW branch with whom Howorth corresponded after the Hansens moved to North Carolina.

23. LSH, "Southern Women and the Atomic Age," 3 December 1950, AAUW Papers, reel 122.

24. Levine, *Degrees of Equality,* 92.

25. Hilda Threlkeld to LSH, 27 April 1946, box 4, SHC, AES; LSH, "Forever the Assistant to the Assistant," 26 March 1951, AAUW Papers, reel 120; "AAUW Seeks Wider Employment of Women in Top College Posts," *Washington Daily News,* 27 March 1957; "AAUW's Resolution," *School and Society* 70 (24 December 1948): 427; LSH, interview by Myers, 174–75.

26. LSH, interview by Swain, 19 June 1984, tape in LSHC, DSU; LSH, statement, carton 3, SHC, AES.

27. Janice Leone, "Integrating the American Association of University Women, 1946–1949," *Historian* 51 (May 1989): 423–45.

28. LSH, interview by Dorothy Shawhan, 21 November 1986; all interviews of LSH by Shawhan were conducted in Cleveland, MS, and notes for all are in the authors' possession.

29. "Remembering a Leader Who Challenged Racism in AAUW," *AAUW in Action* 2 (Spring 2000): 1.

30. *Washington Times Herald,* 9 May 1948.

31. Levine, *Degrees of Equality,* 60; LSH, speech at RMWC, March 1988, in *Randolph-Macon Alumnae Bulletin* 81 (June 1988): 17.

32. LSH to Helen Bragdon, 26 January 1951, and Bragdon to LSH, 19 February 1951, both in AAUW Papers, reel 118. Bragdon served from 1950 to 1959.

33. LSH to Bragdon, 21 February 1951, AAUW Papers, reel 118.

34. Kathryn McHale to LSH, 23 April 1951, box 5, SHC, AES.

35. LSH to Anna Powell, 23 April 1948, box 4, SHC, AES.

36. Hughes to McHale, 5, 10 November 1942, AAUW Papers, reel 118; LSH, interview by Myers, 173; AAUW statement, box 1942, Sarah T. Hughes Papers, Willis Library, University of North Texas, Denton.

37. See the poll of 7 January 1944, AAUW Papers, reel 118.

38. Minutes of the CELSW, 3 December 1946, ibid., reel 117.

39. Minutes, Committee on the Status of Women, 3 December 1949, ibid.

40. Ibid., 2 December 1950.

41. LSH to James Forrestal, 11 October 1948; LSH to Louis Johnson, 7 October 1949; and LSH to George Marshall, 13 December 1950, all in AAUW Papers, reel 118; Minutes, Committee on the Status of Women, 3 December 1949, ibid., reel 117.

42. John Leon Collis to LSH, 15 November 1949, and LSH to Collis, 8 December 1948, both in ibid., reel 118; Margaret Hickey to LSH, 30 June 1950, box 4, SHC, AES.

43. LSH to George Marshall, 13 December 1950; AAUW press release, 16 October 1950; and Colonel Mary A. Halleran to LSH, 29 December 1950, all in AAUW Papers, reel 118; AAUW press release, 5 November 1948, quoted in Helen Laville, *Cold War Women: The International Activities of American Women's Organisations* (Manchester: Manchester University Press, 2002), 34.

44. LSH, "Note to Accompany Letters from Kathryn McHale," and McHale to LSH, 10 September 1951, both in box 5, SHC, AES; Levine, *Degrees of Equality*, 71–72.

45. McHale to LSH, 10 September 1951. See also Susan M. Hartmann, *The Home Front and Beyond: American Women in the 1940s* (Boston: Twayne, 1982), 156; and Levine, *Degrees of Equality*, 72. Levine's chapter 7 deals with the dilemma the AAUW faced during the period 1950–53. For an examination of the accusation against a number of women whom Senate investigators called "internationalists," see Landon R. Y. Storrs, "Red Scare Politics and the Suppression of Popular Front Feminism: The Loyalty Investigation of Mary Dublin Keyserling," *Journal of American History* 90 (September 2003): 518–21.

46. LSH, "Report of the Committee on the Status of Women to the National Board of Directors," 30 November 1950, AAUW Papers, reel 121.

47. Ibid.; Eleanor Dolan, draft report, 22 November 1953, AAUW Papers, reel 121; Minutes, Committee on the Status of Women, 2 December 1950, ibid., reel 117. Accounts of the first meeting in Washington vary as to the number of organizations represented.

48. Dolan, draft report; LSH, "Report of the Committee on the Status of Women," 30 November 1950.

49. *Women's Clearing House for National Security Bulletin*, March 1951, AAUW Papers, reel 121.

50. LSH, Report of the Status of Women Committee Chairman to the National Board of Directors, 2 April 1951, ibid.

51. LSH, statement upon accepting office, 19 July 1951, and *Assembly of Women's Organizations for National Security Bulletin*, June 1951, both in ibid.; *New York Times*, 19 July 1951.

52. *Washington Times-Herald*, 20 July 1951.

53. Laura McEnaney, *Civil Defense Begins at Home: Militarization Meets Everyday Life in the Fifties* (Princeton, NJ: Princeton University Press, 2000), quotation on 121; LSH, "Final Report of the Chairman of the Committee on the Status of Women, July 1951–February 1952," and *Assembly of Women's Organizations for National Security Bulletin*, March 1952, both in AAUW Papers, reel 121. For AAUW work, see Dorothy Stackhouse, "Assembly of Women's Organizations for National Security," *General Federation Clubwoman* 34 (January 1954): 26.

54. Pauline Mandigo to LSH and Marguerite Rawalt, 2 February 1953, box 7, SHC, AES; Marguerite Rawalt, comp., *History of the National Federation of Business and Professional Women's Clubs, Inc.*, vol. 2, *1944–1960* (Washington, DC: NFBPWC, 1960), 100–101.

55. LSH to Riley, 12 November 1951, carton 3, SHC, AES; LSH, "Progress in Cooperation," *American Soroptimist* 25 (January 1952): 15–16, 19; summary, Assembly of Women's Organizations for National Security annual meeting, AAUW Papers, reel 121.

56. Leila J. Rupp and Verta Taylor, *Survival in the Doldrums: The American Women's Rights Movement, 1945 to the 1960s* (New York: Oxford University Press, 1987), 79.

57. McEnaney, *Civil Defense Begins at Home*, 93, 110–11, 116; Althea Hottel to LSH, 19 May 1951, AAUW Papers, reel 49.

58. LSH, interview by Myers, 165–66.

59. Ibid., 163. David Levering Lewis, *W.E.B. DuBois: The Fight for Equality and the American Century, 1919–1963* (New York: Holt, 2000), 546–47.

60. "Suggested Questions for Voice of America Interview," 19 September 1954, box 7, SHC, AES.

61. See J. Stanley Lemons, *The Woman Citizen: Social Feminism in the 1920s* (Urbana: University of Illinois Press, 1973), 209–27.

62. Patricia Carol Walls, "Defining Their Liberties: Women's Organizations during the McCarthy Era" (PhD diss., University of Maryland, College Park, 1994), 25, 289.

63. Levine, *Degrees of Equality*, 69.

64. LSH, statement, 19 July 1951, carton 2, SHC, AES; LSH, "Note on Transcript of Assembly . . . ," box 7, SHC, AES. The description of the *Tribune* opposition in the transcript of the Assembly minutes for 6 October 1950 and the pamphlet are in carton 4, SHC, AES.

65. LSH, interview by Swain; LSH, "Tribute to Emily Hickman," box 7, SHC, AES.

66. See Storrs, "Red Scare Politics," 494–96. The quotation is from Joanne Meyerowitz, ed., *Not June Cleaver: Women and Gender in Postwar America, 1945–1960* (Philadelphia: Temple University Press, 1994), 8. Mary Dublin Keyserling, the subject of Storrs's article, like Woodward, was at one time a member of the U.S. delegation to an UNRRA conference.

67. *Jackson Daily News,* 24 April 1932. The 124-page FBI file on Howorth (77-HQ-7131), released to the authors under the Freedom of Information Act, is unpaginated. Deletions make difficult the identification of individuals interviewed, but internal evidence reveals that it was Susan Riley who provided the strong endorsement of Howorth.

68. LSH to Hottel, 12 March 1951, AAUW Papers, reel 118.

69. "Introducing New AAUW Board Members," *AAUW Journal* 44 (Summer 1951): 237–39.

70. Rosborough to LSH, 29 September 1950, carton 5, SHC, AES; LSH to Board of Directors, December 1951, AAUW Papers, reel 49; McHale to LSH, 17 April 1951, box 5, SHC, AES.

71. Board minutes, 30 October 1951; LSH, Report of Second Vice-President, June 1952; and LSH, memo to Bragdon in re telephone conversation, 27 January 1953, all in AAUW Papers, reel 49.

72. LSH to Board of Directors, December 1954, ibid. See Eleanor N. Shenehon, "American Baedeker," *Journal of Social Hygiene* 37 (November 1951): 358–59.

73. LSH, Report of Second Vice-President, June 1952; Minutes, Committee on the Status of Women, 11 November 1952, and LSH, memo to Bragdon in re telephone conversation, 27 January 1953, both in AAUW Papers, reel 49.

74. Obituary for Nellie Nugent Somerville, *Cleveland (MS) Bolivar News-Enterprise,* 31 July 1952.

75. *Jackson (MS) Clarion-Ledger,* 4 March 1951.

76. LSH, telephone message to India Edwards, 13 December 1949; Edwards to William Boyle, 21 June 1950; and Boyle to Edwards, 23 June 1950, all in India Edwards Papers, box 2, Truman Library; LSH, "Notes to Accompany Positions," box 4, SHC, AES.

77. LSH, "The War Claims Commission," *United Nations League of Lawyers Review* 1 (November 1950): 3–4; "Judge Lucy Somerville Howorth," *Randolph-Macon Alumnae Bulletin* 45 (April 1952): 35–36.

78. LSH to A. C. Davis, 6 January 1954, Personal File, LSHC, DSU; Federal Bureau of Investigation, Lucy Somerville Howorth file, 6 February 1956.

79. LSH, "Notes to Accompany Positions"; LSH to Georgia Lusk, 8 January 1954, LSHC, DSU; LSH, interview by Myers, 176.

80. LSH, "Notes to Accompany Positions"; LSH to Edwards, 2 February 1954, Edwards Papers; LSH to Benedict K. Zobrist, 16 March 1978, Howorth Papers, DSU; LSH, interview by Myers, 177–78.

81. LSH, Report of Second Vice-President, November 1953–June 1954, AAUW Papers, reel 49; "Mrs. Howorth in Germany," *AAUW Journal* 47 (March 1954): 188; "Three Lawyers Visit Germany," *Journal of the American Bar Association* 40 (September 1954): 738.

82. LSH, "Madrid and the Spanish University Women," *AAUW Journal* 47 (May 1954): 241; LSH to Riley and Bragdon, 22 July 1954, both in AAUW Papers, reel 49.

83. LSH, Report of Second Vice-President, 6 May 1955, AAUW Papers, reel 49.

84. LSH, "Job Description," 4 August 1954, ibid.

85. LSH, Report of Second Vice-President, November 1953–June 1954; "College Women Can Help," *St. Louis Post Dispatch,* 25 July 1954.

86. LSH, "Report of the Building Commission," 1 December 1956, box 13, SHC, AES; Henrietta M. Thompson, "AAUW Educational Center Completed in Washington," *Journal of Home Economics* 53 (April 1961): 298–99.

87. Levine, *Degrees of Equality,* 55; LSH, interview by Shawhan, 21 November 1986; Rossiter, *Women Scientists,* 355.

88. Riley to LSH, 2 February 1955, carton 3, SHC, AES; Riley to Hallie Farmer, 25 November 1955, copy in box 4, SHC, AES.

89. "State Presidents Discuss Issues of the Future," *AAUW Journal* 50 (October 1956): 20.

90. "Final Report of the Survey Committee to the Board of Directors," November 1957, box 4, SHC, AES.

91. LSH to Dr. Henry David, 2 November 1955, and conference program, both in carton 5, SHC, AES. On the NMC, see Susan M. Hartmann, "Women's Employment and the Domestic Ideal in the Early Cold War Years," in Meyerowitz, *Not June Cleaver,* 84–88.

92. LSH to Farmer, 2 April 1956, printed in *AAUW Journal* 49 (May 1956): 230–31.

93. Augusta Stacy Marshall to LSH, 1 January 1954, unprocessed, SHC, AES; Dewson to LSH, 13 November 1954, box 5, SHC, AES; *Washington Post,* 15 January 1954. According to Howorth, Malvina Lindsay "engineered" the complimentary article in the *Post* (LSH, interview by Swain, 5 March 1988, Oxford, MS, notes in authors' possession), and Mississippi Congressman Frank Smith inserted it in the *Congressional Record,* 83rd Cong., 2nd sess., 1954, vol. 100, appendix, pt. 1, 399.

94. Quoted in Rupp and Taylor, *Survival in the Doldrums,* 72.

Chapter 8

1. LSH, interview by Dorothy Shawhan, 12 November 1994; all interviews of LSH by Shawhan were conducted in Cleveland, MS, and notes for all are in the authors' possession.

2. LSH, "Notes on James Somerville," box 5A, SHC, AES; LSH, "Notes on Washington, 1934–1958," box 4, SHC, AES; LSH to Robert J. Farley, 24 January 1952, and LSH to Virginia Blood, 30 June 1954, both in box 5, SHC, AES.

3. Loyd Wright to John C. Stennis, 9 January 1956, and Susan Riley to Stennis, 21 March 1956, both in series 44, box 2, John C. Stennis Papers, Special Collections, Mitchell Memorial Library, Mississippi State University, Starkville; Riley to LSH, 28 February 1956, carton 3, SHC, AES. FBI agents in New Orleans, Memphis, Richmond, New York, St. Louis, Chicago, and Washington all made investigations and conducted interviews. Internal evidence strongly indicates that the two women who gave statements were Gillie Larew and Susan Riley. Federal Bureau of Investigation, Lucy Somerville Howorth file, 77-HQ-7131, 23, 25 January, 6, 10 February 1956.

4. LSH, interview by Constance Myers, 20, 23, 25 June 1975, Monteagle, TN, transcript in Southern Oral History Collection, University of North Carolina, Chapel Hill, 179; Stennis to Wright, 7 January 1957, series 44, box 2, Stennis Papers.

5. LSH to Mrs. Richard Borden, 16 October 1957, box 4, SHC, AES; *Report of the Commission on Government Security* (Washington, DC: Government Printing Office, 1957); John Stennis, "Comments of United States Senator John Stennis, Vice Chairman, Commission on Government Security, on the Final Report of That Commission," in series 44, box 2, Stennis Papers. For a discussion of the origin and limited impact of the commission, see Jeff Broadwater, *Eisenhower and the Anti-Communist Crusade* (Chapel Hill: University of North Carolina Press, 1992), 198–203.

6. LSH, "Notes on Washington, 1934–1958"; LSH to Martha Swain, 1 June 1987, in authors' possession; LSH to Riley, February 1958, carton 3, SHC, AES; LSH to Hallie Farmer, 14 January 1956, carton 4, SHC, AES. In sending a copy of the report to the Schlesinger Library, Howorth explained her commission role to Mrs. Richard Borden. LSH to Borden, 1 July 1957, box 4, SHC, AES.

7. LSH to Mrs. Saul Habas, 21 July 1957, box 35, AAUW, Mississippi Division Papers, Special Collections, Williams Library, University of Mississippi, Oxford.

8. LSH to Katherine Rea, 7 December 1958, ibid.; LSU, interview by Myers, 179–80.

9. Nellie Nugent Somerville to Ellen Woodward, 23 December 1938, box 1, Ellen Sullivan Woodward Papers, AES; Mary W. Dewson to LSH, 13 December 1954, box 5, SHC, AES.

10. LSH, interview by Shawhan, 21 November 1985; Augusta Stacy Marshall to LSH, 16 August 1958, unprocessed, SHC, AES; Virginia Jeans Laas, ed., *Bridging Two Eras: The Autobiography of Emily Newell Blair, 1877–1951* (Columbia: University of Missouri Press, 1999), 351; *Cleveland (MS) Bolivar Commercial*, 7 February 1963.

11. LSH to Catherine Creek, 16 August 1968, box 4, SHC, AES; Lilace Reid Barnes (YWCA) to LSH, 15 June 1959, carton 5, SHC, AES; Keith Frazier Somerville, "Random Thoughts," undated entry, typescript in Capps Archives, DSU. Numerous club programs and yearbooks from the 1960s into the 1990s are in LSHC, DSU.

12. LSH, interview by Shawhan, 21 November 1986; LSH, "Note to Accompany Invitation to SCHW Dinner," carton 5, SHC, AES.

13. LSH to Swain, 9 December 1986, in authors' possession.

14. LSH, interview by Myers, 181; LSH, interview by Shawhan, 30 May 1986.

15. LSH to Marleen Hansen, 27 August 1987, in Hansen's possession, Columbus, MS; Margaret Block, interview by Shawhan, 3 July 2001, Cleveland, MS. Block's mother was a housekeeper for Howorth.

16. LSH, interview by Myers, 16; LSH, interview by Shawhan, 21 May 1986; LePoint Smith, interview by Shawhan, 13 August 2001, Cleveland, MS; James Eaton, interview by authors, 12 August 2001, Cleveland, MS. Eaton is the son of Ergie Lee Smith. Neither Joe's nor Lucy's name appears among the list of subjects under scrutiny by the segregationist Mississippi Sovereignty Commission. (Hank Holmes to Swain, 20 July 1999, in authors' possession.)

17. LSH, interview by Myers, 199; Smith interview.

18. LSH to Pauline Tompkins, 7 June 1964, box 35, AAUW, Mississippi Division Papers; LSH, "Library Trustees: A Maxi or Mini Office," *Mississippi Library News* 34 (March 1986): 27.

19. LSH, interview by Myers, 40; LSH to Anne Firor Scott, 15 June 1981, LSHC, DSU; LSH, interview by Shawhan, 21 November 1986.

20. LSH, interview by Shawhan, 21 November 1986.

21. Margaret Hickey to LSH, 29 December 1961, carton 3, SHC, AES. A copy of the executive order is in the AAUW Papers, reel 121. "What kind of world do women want?" was the theme of a *New York Times*-sponsored conference for women leaders on 7 April 1943.

22. Hickey to LSH, 27 March, 5 April 1962, both in carton 3, SHC, AES.

23. Ibid., 26 June 1962; Margaret Rossiter, *Women Scientists in America: Before Affirmative Action, 1940–1972* (Baltimore: John Hopkins University Press, 1995), 294. Hickey's committee met a third and fourth time in January and May 1963.

24. LSH to Sarah T. Hughes, 27 November 1961, box 13, SHC, AES; LSH to Swain, 9 August 1984, in authors' possession; Cynthia E. Harrison, "A 'New Frontier' for Women: The Public Policy of the Kennedy Administration," *Journal of American History* 67 (December 1980): 635. See also Patricia G. Zelman, *Women, Work, and National Policy: The Kennedy–Johnson Years* (Ann Arbor: UMI Research Press, 1980), 25–26.

25. LSH, "Room at the Top" (speech), carton 2, SHC, AES; Evelyn Harrison, "The Quiet Revolution," *Civil Service Journal* 3 (October–December 1962), copy in carton 5, SHC, AES.

26. Evelyn Harrison, "Women in the Federal Service," *Civil Service Journal* 4 (October–December 1963), copy in carton 5, SHC, AES.

27. LSH to Hickey, 5 March 1963; Hickey to LSH, 15 March 1963; and LSH to Hickey, 14 June 1963, all in carton 3, SHC, AES. See also Rossiter, *Women Scientists,* 295.

28. LSH to Swain, 6 March 1983, 29 April 1985, in authors' possession; LSH to Esther Peterson, 6 December 1963, carton 5, SHC, AES. A copy of the *Report of the Committee on Federal Employment to the President's Commission on the Status of Women,* in *American Women: Report of the President's Commission on the Status of Women* (Washington, DC: Government Printing Office, 1963), is in AAUW Papers, reel 121.

29. *Report of the Committee on Federal Employment Policies and Practices*, 51–66, in *American Women*.

30. LSH to Hickey, 6 March 1963, carton 3, SHC, AES; LSH, interview by Joanne Varner Hawks, 11 April 1979, Oxford, MS, videotape in AAUW, Mississippi Division Papers, transcript in authors' possession.

31. LSH to Scott, 15 April 1963, LSHC, DSU; LSH, interview by Hawks.

32. LSH to Scott, 14 November 1970, LSHC, DSU; LSH, interview by Myers, 203.

33. LHS, interview by Marjorie Spruill Wheeler, 15 March 1983, Cleveland, MS, transcript in Oral History Collection, University of Southern Mississippi, Hattiesburg.

34. LSH to Swain, 7 January 1988, in authors' possession; LSH, speech to AAUW, 26 March 1983, tape recording, LSHC, DSU. Howorth was bothered by Susan Ware's interpretation of Molly Dewson's "partnership" with Polly Porter in *Partner and I: Molly Dewson, Feminism, and New Deal Politics* (New Haven, CT: Yale University Press, 1987).

35. Nancy Finerty, "Lucy Howorth: 'The Little Lady from Mississippi,'" *Ole Miss Magazine*, January 1983, 11.

36. Marshall to LSH, 26 April 1970, unprocessed, SHC, AES; Tompkins to LSH, 3 July 1963, box 25, AAUW, Mississippi Division Papers.

37. Adaline Gilstrap to LSH, 8 July 1962, unprocessed, SHC, AES; Eleanor Reid to LSH, 25 January 1959, box 25, AAUW, Mississippi Division Papers; Susan Lynn, *Progressive Women in Conservative Times: Racial Justice, Peace, and Feminism, 1945 to the 1960s* (New Brunswick, NJ: Rutgers University Press, 1992), 65.

38. Mary T. Giddings to Mrs. C. F. Carlton, 6 June 1968, box 25, AAUW, Mississippi Division Papers; Susan Levine, *Degrees of Equality: The American Association of University Women and the Challenge of Twentieth-Century Feminism* (Philadelphia: Temple University Press, 1995), 135 (LSH quotation), 132.

39. LSH to Tompkins, 24 December 1962, carton 5, SHC, AES; Katherine Vickery to Tompkins, 11 June 1964, in box 35, AAUW, Mississippi Division Papers; *Mobile Register*, 12 March 1963. The Snopeses are a family of degenerates that populate the novels of William Faulkner.

40. LSH, speech at Mississippi state conference, 6 April 1974, cassette recording in AAUW, Mississippi Division Papers; *Arkansas State Division Bulletin* 32 (November 1958): 1, 3; Frances Concordia to LSH, 25 April 1984, in Marleen Hansen's possession, Columbus, MS.

41. Cora Norman, quoted in Gayle Graham Yates, *Mississippi Mind: A Personal Cultural History of an American State* (Knoxville: University of Tennessee Press, 1990), 116; Cora Norman to Swain, 20 July 1995, in authors' possession.

42. "Women of Achievement Honored by AAUW," *Journal of the American Association of University Women* 69 (November 1975): 49.

43. Ruby Thompson to LSH, 11 July 1976, box 36, AAUW, Mississippi Division Papers; "Howorth Speaks at AAUW Spring Convention," *Cleveland (MS) Bolivar Commercial*, 4 April 1983.

44. Scott to LSH, 12 May 1978, LSHC, DSU; LSH, "United for Victory" (speech, May 1943), SHC, AES; LSH to Swain, 14 May 1984, in authors' possession.

45. Howorth's other subjects were Belle Kearney, Madge Quin Fugler, Mildred Spurrier Topp, Pauline Alston Clark, Ellen Woodward, and, of course, Nellie Nugent Somerville. Clark, one of the earliest Mississippi suffragists, was elected to the state legislature in 1928 and served one term. *Greenville (MS) Weekly Democrat,* 15 February 1928.

46. Dorothy Shawhan, "Three Lawyers from Mississippi," in *From Behind the Magnolia Curtain: Voices of Mississippi,* ed. Clyde V. Williams (Jackson: Mississippi Press Association, 1988), 71. On Carloss, see Virginia G. Drachman, *Sisters in Law: Women Lawyers in Modern American History* (Cambridge, MA: Harvard University Press, 1998), 199–200.

47. Speech, 28 October 1977, LSHC, DSU.

48. Karen Berger Morello to LSH, 13 October 1977, ibid.; Karen Berger Morello, *The Invisible Bar: The Woman Lawyer in America, 1638 to the Present* (New York: Random House, 1986), 96.

49. Scott to LSH, 19 June 1968, and LSH to Scott, 16 November 1970, both in LSHC, DSU.

50. Scott to LSH, 27 May 1987, ibid.

51. William M. Cash and LSH, eds., *My Dear Nellie: The Civil War Letters of William L. Nugent and Eleanor Smith Nugent* (Jackson: University Press of Mississippi, 1977).

52. Rheta Grimsley Johnson, "She led way so others could lead themselves," *Memphis Commercial Appeal,* 4 March 1984.

53. Anne Firor Scott, "Nellie Nugent Somerville," in *Notable American Women: The Modern Period,* ed. Barbara Sicherman and Carol Hurd Green (Cambridge, MA: Harvard University Press, 1980), 654–56.

54. Anne Firor Scott, *Making the Invisible Woman Visible* (Urbana: University of Illinois Press, 1984), 332. For Nellie's opposition to women jurors, see Somerville to Susie Powell, 14 February [1940s?], box 1, Susie V. Powell Papers, Mississippi Department of Archives and History, Jackson.

55. LePoint Smith, interview by Shawhan, 18 February 1997, Cleveland, MS.

56. Couprey Shands, interview by Shawhan, 26 October 1996, Jackson, MS.

57. Frank C. Waldrop, ed., *Mountain Voices: A Centennial History of the Monteagle Sunday School Assembly* (Nashville, TN: Parthenon, 1987), 208; Nell Savage Mahoney to LSH, 18 September 1998, LSHC, DSU.

58. Smith, interview by Shawhan, 18 February 1997.

59. Keith Frazier Somerville, "Thinking Back," unpaginated, in Capps Archives, DSU.

60. LSH, interview by Shawhan, 10 January 1993.

61. Nellie Nugent Somerville autobiography, box 2, SHC, AES.

62. Scott, "Nellie Nugent Somerville," 656; Federal Bureau of Investigation, Lucy Somerville Howorth file, 11 July 1933.

63. *Christian Science Monitor,* 14 February 1983. The previous three women named to the Mississippi Hall of Fame were Modena Lowrey Berry, longtime educator at Blue Mountain College; Annie Coleman Peyton, a fighter for the establishment in 1884 of Mississippi's Industrial Institute and College; and Ellen Woodward, New Deal administrator of women's work relief and member of the Social Security Board.

64. LSH to Swain, 8 May 1987, in authors' possession. See Susan Ware, *Beyond Suf-*

frage: Women in the New Deal (Cambridge, MA: Harvard University Press, 1981); and Leila J. Rupp and Verta Taylor, *Survival in the Doldrums: The American Women's Rights Movement, 1945 to the 1960s* (New York: Oxford University Press, 1987).

65. LSH, interview by Myers, 166.

66. LSH to Swain, 4 May 1987, 7 August 1989, in authors' possession. New books based upon extensive interviews with Howorth were Marjorie Spruill Wheeler, *New Women of the New South: The Leaders of the Woman Suffrage Movement in the Southern States* (New York: Oxford University Press, 1993); and Martha H. Swain, *Ellen S. Woodward: New Deal Advocate for Women* (Jackson: University Press of Mississippi, 1995). Dorothy Shawhan's *Lizzie* (Atlanta: Longstreet, 1995), a novel inspired by the life of Minnie Brewer, was influenced by extensive interviews with Howorth about her friend.

67. LSH to Mary Stokes, 20 November 1929, box 12, SHC, AES; "Lucy Somerville Library Fund," *Randolph-Macon Alumnae Bulletin* 65 (Winter 1972): 39.

68. See Mary Louise Merideth, "The Mississippi Women's Rights Movement, 1889–1923: The Leadership of Nellie Nugent Somerville and Greenville in Suffrage Reform" (master's thesis, DSU, 1974); and Jane Whiteside Elliott, "Lucy Somerville Howorth: Legislative Career, 1932–1935" (master's thesis, DSU, 1975).

69. LSH, interview by Hawks.

70. Jack Winton Gunn and Gladys C. Castle, *A Pictorial History of Delta State University* (Jackson: University Press of Mississippi, 1980), 154.

71. LSH, quoted in Dorothy Shawhan, "Lucy Somerville Howorth: A Remarkable Woman," *Bar Examiner* 65 (August 1996), 7; LSH to Hansen, 27 August 1987, in Hansen's possession.

72. Rea to LSH, 20 December 1958, and LSH to Norman, 28 November 1982, both in box 35, AAUW, Mississippi Division Papers; LSH to Swain, 16 October 1983, 20 October 1985, in authors' possession.

73. "Campus Brief," *University of Mississippi Alumni Review* 40 (Fall 1991): 16–17; *Randolph-Macon Alumnae Bulletin* 34 (November 1940): 7; *Phi Kappa Phi Newsletter* 83 (April 1985): 1.

74. *Jackson (MS) Clarion-Ledger*, 3 August 1975.

75. Phyllis Ten Elshof, in ibid., 28 December 1986.

76. *Jackson (MS) Clarion-Ledger*, 27 October 1983. The other honorees were Jean Fairfax, National Association for the Advancement of Colored People official; Mary Calderone, physician; Helen Taussig, pediatric cardiologist; Chien-Shiung Wu, physicist; Esther Peterson, former Women's Bureau chief; Barbara Tuchman, historian; and Georgia O'Keefe, painter.

77. Ibid.

78. LSH, speech, unprocessed, SHC, AES; Scott to LSH, 14 February 1984, LSHC, DSU.

79. LSH, interview by Wheeler.

Chapter 9

1. LSH, interview by Marjorie Spruill Wheeler, 15 March 1983, Cleveland, MS, transcript in Mississippi Oral History Collection, University of Southern Mississippi, Hattiesburg.

2. Joseph Blotner, *Faulkner: A Biography* (New York: Random House, 1974), 517.

3. LSH to Martha Swain, 18 May 1986, in authors' possession; LSH, "The Bill Faulkner I Knew," *Delta Review* 2 (July–August 1965): 38–39, 73; Carvel Collins, introduction to Ben Wasson, *Count No 'Count: Flashbacks to Faulkner* (Jackson: University Press of Mississippi, 1983), 7.

4. Polly Babcock Feustal to LSH, 3 March 1968, 26 July 1983, both in LSHC, DSU.

5. Augusta Stacy Marshall to LSH, 6 November 1956, 5 July 1965, 5 August 1973, all in unprocessed, SHC, AES.

6. Stella Perry, quoted in *Alpha Omicron Pi Alumnae Directory* (White Plains, NY: Harris, 1993), v.

7. Rheta Grimsley Johnson, "Paragon of daring turns 90," *Memphis Commercial Appeal*, 21 June 1985; LSH to Swain, 23 July 1985, in authors' possession.

8. LSH to Elizabeth Shenton, 15 May 1979, carton 3, SHC, AES.

9. Margaret Hickey to LSH, 7 January 1965, 8 June 1971; and clipping from *Tucson Globe-Democrat,* 19 May 1975, all in ibid.

10. Hickey to LSH, 1 December 1976, and LSH to James D. Leake, 28 October 1968, both in LSHC, DSU; LSH on Nixon, quoted in *Greenville (MS) Delta Democrat-Times,* 25 October 1976.

11. On Reagan, LSH, quoted in *Oxford Eagle,* 6 April 1984; on Helms, LSH to Marleen Hansen, 16 October 1985, in Hansen's possession, Columbus, MS.

12. Hickey to LSH, 23 April 1979, series 3, box 8, Margaret A. Hickey Papers, Western History Manuscript Collection, University of Missouri–St. Louis; Hickey to LSH, 2 December 1981, 1 June, 21 July 1987, and LSH to Boyer, 22 April 1987, all in LSHC, DSU.

13. LSH to Eleanor Harkiss, 14 September 1960, and LSH to Katherine Vickery, 6 March, 9 October 1964, all in box 35, AAUW, Mississippi Division Papers, Special Collections, Williams Library, University of Mississippi, Oxford.

14. Douglas W. Ferris Jr., to LSH, 26 June 1984, LSHC, DSU; LSH, interview by Edith Provost, 1975, Monteagle, TN, carton 2, SHC, AES; William Thomas, "A Very Special Place," *Memphis Commercial Appeal, Mid-South Magazine,* 13 September 1970.

15. LSH to Swain, 6 February 1985, in authors' possession; Arch Dalrymple, interview by authors, 19 February 2000, Amory, MS.

16. LSH to Margaret Mahoney, 4 August 1987, LSHC, DSU. Mahoney, with whom Howorth corresponded frequently, was an executive with the Carnegie Corporation and later vice president of the Robert Woods Johnson Foundation.

17. LSH, quoted in Thomas, "A Very Special Place"; LSH to Leake, 23 July 1968, LSHC, DSU. Leake was Eleanor's grandson.

18. Marshall to LSH, 17 November 1979, unprocessed, SHC, AES; LSH to Hickey, 27 May 1980, series 3, box 8, Hickey Papers. Obituaries for Joe appeared in both the *Cleveland (MS) Bolivar Commercial* and the *Greenville (MS) Delta Democrat-Times* on 18 May 1980.

19. LSH, interview by Constance Myers, 20, 23, 25 June 1975, Monteagle, TN, transcript in Southern Oral History Collection, University of North Carolina, Chapel Hill, 109; Mahoney to LSH, 13 May 1980, LSHC, DSU.

20. Anne Firor Scott to LSH, 14 March 1958, box 4, SHC, AES.

21. Frank C. Waldrop, ed., *Mountain Voices: The Centennial History of the Monteagle Sunday School Assembly* (Nashville, TN: Parthenon, 1982), 346–48.

22. "Mountain Voices" (Monteagle weekly bulletin), 29 June, 6 July 1986.

23. LSH to Swain, 25 July 1988, in authors' possession.

24. Rebecca Hood-Adams, "Eleanor Shands was homemaker extraordinaire," *Jackson (MS) Clarion-Ledger,* 4 November 1968.

25. Peter Taylor to LSH, 20 December 1993, and Mary Ellen Haley to LSH, undated card, [1993 or 1994], both in LSHC, DSU. The DSU collection contains numerous greetings from Monteagle friends.

26. LSH, interview by Myers, 106; Marshall to LSH, 26 May 1977, unprocessed, SHC, AES.

27. LSH to Leake, 19 November 1969, LSHC, DSU; LSH to Hickey, [April 1978], series 3, box 8, Hickey Papers.

28. *Cleveland (MS) Bolivar Commercial,* 20 November 1985; *Jackson (MS) Clarion-Ledger,* 28 December 1986.

29. Cora Norman, interview by Dorothy Shawhan, 13 June 1986, Cleveland, MS; Mahoney to LSH, 27 January 1987, LSHC, DSU.

30. LSH to Hansen, 16 February 1987, in authors' possession; LSH, speech at inauguration of Linda Koch Latimer, quoted in *Randolph-Macon Alumnae Bulletin* 81 (June 1988): 16–19.

31. LSH to Swain, 20 June 1990, 9 April 1988, in authors' possession; Gertrude Cleary to LSH, 31 December 1992, LSHC, DSU; David L. Cohn, *The Mississippi Delta and the World: The Memoirs of David L. Cohn,* ed. James C. Cobb (Baton Rouge: Louisiana State University Press, 1995), 93.

32. Rheta Grimsley Johnson, "Judge Lucy to Mark Her Centennial July 1," *Columbus (MS) Commercial Dispatch,* 29 June 1995. A folder of greetings is in the LSHC, DSU.

33. "Struggle for equality called slow," *Dallas Morning News,* 28 May 1995; the article carried Howorth's picture.

34. Scott's "Old Wives Tales" is included in her book *Making the Invisible Woman Visible* (Urbana: University of Illinois Press, 1984), 332; it appeared originally in *Perspectives on Aging: Exploding the Myths,* ed. Priscilla W. Johnson (Cambridge, MA: Ballinger, 1981), 71–84. For Bronte on Howorth, see Bronte, *The Longevity Factor: The New Reality of Long Careers and How It Can Lead to Richer Lives* (New York: HarperCollins, 1993), 92, 157, 265–69.

35. Bernard Edelman, *Centenarians: The Story of the 20th Century by the Americans Who Lived It* (New York: Farrar, Strauss & Giroux, 1999), 381.

36. Arch Dalrymple, interview by authors, 19 February 2000; LePoint Smith, interview by Shawhan, 1 September 1993, Cleveland, MS.

37. LSH, interview by Shawhan, 14 February 1995; all interviews of LSH by Shawhan were conducted in Cleveland, MS, and notes for all are in the authors' possession.

38. Ibid., 12 November 1994.

39. James Eaton, interview by authors, 12 August 2001, Cleveland, MS.

40. Dollie Forrest to Shawhan, 25 September 2001, in authors' possession.

41. LePoint Smith, interview by Shawhan, 24 August 1997, Cleveland, MS. Obituaries appeared in the *Memphis Commercial Appeal,* 24 August 1997, the *Washington Post,* 26 August 1997, and the *New York Times,* 2 September 1997; the death certificate is in LSHC, DSU.

42. Susan Ware, *Beyond Suffrage: Women in the New Deal* (Cambridge, MA: Harvard University Press, 1981), 143–57.

43. While Howorth returned to a federal assignment under President Kennedy in 1962, Beyer, who retired in 1958 from the Department of Labor, returned to serve as a consultant for the U.S. International Cooperation Administration before a second retirement in 1972. She died in 1990. Kristie Miller, "Clara Mortenson Beyer," in *Notable American Women: A Biographical Dictionary Completing the Twentieth Century,* ed. Susan Ware (Cambridge, MA: Harvard University Press, 1990), 55–56.

44. Nancy F. Cott, *The Grounding of Modern Feminism* (New Haven, CT: Yale University Press, 1987), 238.

45. LSH, interview by Myers, 82.

Select Bibliography

PRIMARY SOURCES

Archival and Manuscript Collections

Arthur and Elizabeth Schlesinger Library, Radcliffe Institute for Advanced Study, Cambridge, MA.
Somerville, Nellie Nugent—Lucy Somerville Howorth. Collection.
White, Sue Shelton. Papers.
Woodward, Ellen Sullivan. Papers.

Capps Archives, Delta State University, Cleveland, MS.
Howorth, Lucy Somerville. Collection.

Franklin D. Roosevelt Library, Hyde Park, NY.
Dewson, Mary W. Papers.
Papers of Women's Division, Democratic National Committee.
Roosevelt, Eleanor. Papers.

Harry S. Truman Library, Independence, MO.
Clark, Tom C. Papers.
Edwards, India. Papers.
Truman, Harry S. Papers.

Library of Congress, Washington, DC.
Williams, Charl O. Papers.

Mississippi Department of Archives and History, Jackson.
Howorth, Lucy Somerville File.
Powell, Susie V. Papers.
Woodward, Ellen S. Papers.

North Carolina State Archives, Raleigh.
Evans, May Thompson. Papers.

Sophia Smith Collection, Smith College, Northampton, MA.
Kenyon, Dorothy. Papers.
van Kleeck, Mary. Papers.

Southern Historical Collection, University of North Carolina, Chapel Hill.
Tillett, Gladys. Papers.

Special Collections, Mitchell Memorial Library, Mississippi State University, Starkville.
Stennis, John C. Papers.

Special Collections, Williams Library, University of Mississippi, Oxford.
American Association of University Women, Mississippi Division Papers.

Texas Woman's University, Denton.
American Association of University Women Papers. Microfilm edition.
National Woman's Party Papers. Microfilm edition.

Walter Clinton Jackson Library, University of North Carolina, Greensboro.
Elliott, Harriet. Papers.

Western History Manuscript Collection, University of Missouri–St. Louis.
Hickey, Margaret A. Papers.

Willis Library, University of North Texas, Denton.
Hughes, Sarah T. Papers.

Public Documents

Federal Bureau of Investigation. Lucy Somerville Howorth file. 77-HQ-7131.
Mississippi House of Representatives. *Journal of the House of Representatives of the State of Mississippi . . . 1932.* Jackson: Hederman Brothers, 1932.
———. *Journal of the House of Representatives of the State of Mississippi . . . 1934.* Jackson: Hederman Brothers, 1934.
Official and Statistical Register of the State of Mississippi, 1924–1928. Edited by Dunbar Rowland. New York: J. J. Little, 1928.

Report of the Commission on Government Security. Washington, DC: Government Printing Office, 1957.

Report of the Committee on Federal Employment to the President's Commission on the Status of Women. Washington, DC: Government Printing Office, 1963.

Interviews

Block, Margaret. Interview by Dorothy Shawhan. 3 July 2001. Cleveland, MS.

Dalrymple, Arch. Interview by authors. 19 February 2000. Amory, MS.

Eaton, James. Interview by authors. 12 August 2001. Cleveland, MS.

Howorth, Joseph. Interview by Jane Whiteside Elliott. 2 February 1975. Cleveland, MS. Transcript in Capps Archives, Delta State University, Cleveland, MS.

Howorth, Lucy Somerville. Interview by Ruth Campbell. *Faces.* Mississippi ETV, 2 January 1986.

———. Interview by Allen Dennis. 16 January 1973. Cleveland, MS. Transcript in Lucy Somerville Howorth Collection, Capps Archives, Delta State University, Cleveland, MS.

———. Interviews by Jane Whiteside Elliott. 20, 28, 30 January 1975. Cleveland, MS. Transcript in Lucy Somerville Howorth Collection, Capps Archives, Delta State University, Cleveland, MS.

———. Interview by Joe Hairston. 20 November 1991. Cleveland, MS. Transcript in American Association of University Women, Mississippi Division Papers, Special Collections, Williams Library, University of Mississippi, Oxford.

———. Interview by Joanne Varner Hawks. 11 April 1979. Oxford, MS. Videotape in American Association of University Women, Mississippi Division Papers, Special Collections, Williams Library, University of Mississippi, Oxford.

———. Interview by Chester Morgan. 30 May 1984. Cleveland, MS. Transcript in Mississippi Oral History Collection, University of Southern Mississippi, Hattiesburg.

———. Interview by Constance Myers. 20, 23, 25 June 1975. Monteagle, TN. Transcript in Southern Oral History Collection, University of North Carolina, Chapel Hill.

———. Interview by Edith Provost. 1975. Monteagle, TN. Transcript of tape in carton 2, Nellie Nugent Somerville—Lucy Somerville Howorth Collection, Arthur and Elizabeth Schlesinger Library, Radcliffe Institute for Advanced Study, Cambridge, MA.

———. Interviews by Dorothy Shawhan. 1983–97. Cleveland, MS. Notes in authors' possession.

———. "The Flood." Interview by Dorothy Shawhan. 21 June 1986. Cleveland,

MS. Tape in Lucy Somerville Howorth Collection, Capps Archives, Delta State University, Cleveland, MS.

———. Interview by Martha Swain. 19 June 1984. Tape in Lucy Somerville Howorth Collection, Capps Archives, Delta State University, Cleveland, MS.

———. Interview by Marjorie Spruill Wheeler. 15 March 1983. Cleveland, MS. Transcript in Mississippi Oral History Collection, University of Southern Mississippi, Hattiesburg.

McLean, Keith Somerville Dockery. Interview by Dorothy Shawhan. 30 July 1986. Cleveland, MS.

Norman, Cora. Interview by Dorothy Shawhan. 13 June 1986. Cleveland, MS.

Rawalt, Marguerite. Interview by Martha Swain. 5 July 1987. Washington, DC.

Shands, Couprey. Interview by Dorothy Shawhan. 26 October 1996. Jackson, MS.

Shands, Eleanor Somerville. Interview by Dorothy Shawhan. 5 July 1985. Cleveland, MS.

Smith, LePoint. Interviews by Dorothy Shawhan. 1989–2001. Cleveland, MS.

Correspondence

Lucy Somerville Howorth to Marleen Hansen. 1982–88. In possession of Hansen, Columbus, MS.

Lucy Somerville Howorth to Martha Swain. 1977–95. In authors' possession.

Works by Lucy Somerville Howorth

Edited with Ruth Chivvis. *A Handbook for Delegates: National Industrial Conference.* New York: National Board of the Young Women's Christian Association of the USA, 1919.

"The Mississippi Flood of 1927." *Woman's Press,* June 1927.

"The National Democratic Convention." *Mississippi Business Woman* 1 (1932).

"A Representative of the People." *Randolph-Macon Alumnae Bulletin* 28 (April 1935).

"Program Coordinator." *Independent Woman* 18 (August 1939).

"We Remember Class Parties." *Randolph-Macon Alumnae Bulletin* 36 (September 1943).

"Women's Responsibility in World Affairs." *Journal of the American Association of University Women* 37 (Summer 1944).

"The Wheel Spins Faster." *Journal of the American Association of University Women* 38 (Spring 1945).

"Women Jurors." *Journal of the American Association of University Women* 41 (February 1947).

"From a One-Horse Surrey into the Atomic Age." *Randolph-Macon Alumnae Bulletin* 41 (June 1948).

"Task Force '49." *Phi Delta Kappan* 27 (March 1949).

"Committee on Status of Women." *Journal of the American Association of University Women* 43 (Fall 1949).

"The War Claims Commission." *United Nations League of Lawyers Review* 1 (November 1950).

"Progress in Cooperation." *American Soroptimist* 25 (January 1952).

"Madrid and the Spanish University Women." *Journal of the American Association of University Women* 47 (May 1954).

"The Bill Faulkner I Knew." *Delta Review* 2 (July–August 1965).

"Library Trustees: A Maxi or Mini Officer." *Mississippi Library News* 34 (March 1986).

Edited with William M. Cash. *My Dear Nellie: The Civil War Letters of William L. Nugent to Eleanor Smith Nugent.* Jackson: University Press of Mississippi, 1977.

SECONDARY SOURCES

Barnwell, Marion. *A Place Called Mississippi: Collected Narratives.* Jackson: University Press of Mississippi, 1997.

Blair, Emily Newell. "Why New Deal Washington Fascinates Women." *Liberty*, 8 December 1934.

Blotner, Joseph. *Faulkner: A Biography.* New York: Random House, 1974.

Bowman, Geline. *A History of the National Federation of Business and Professional Women's Clubs, 1919–1944.* New York: NFBPW, 1944.

Bronte, Lydia. *The Longevity Factor: The New Reality of Long Careers and How It Can Lead to Richer Lives.* New York: HarperCollins, 1993.

Brown, Mary Agnes. "New Dealer Feted." *Women Lawyers Journal* 21 (November 1934).

Buck, Pearl. *My Several Worlds: A Personal Record.* New York: Day, 1954.

Cabaniss, James. *A History of the University of Mississippi.* University: University of Mississippi, 1949.

Chester, Ronald. *Unequal Access: Women Lawyers in a Changing America.* South Hadley, MA: Bergin & Garvey, 1945.

Clarke, Ida Clyde. *American Women and the World War.* New York: Appleton, 1918.

Cobb, James C. *The Most Southern Place on Earth: The Mississippi Delta and the Roots of Regional Identity.* New York: Oxford University Press, 1992.

Cohn, David L. *The Mississippi Delta and the World: The Memoirs of David L.*

Cohn. Edited by James C. Cobb. Baton Rouge: Louisiana State University Press, 1995.

Cornelius, Roberta D. *The History of Randolph-Macon Woman's College.* Chapel Hill: University of North Carolina Press, 1951.

Cott, Nancy F. *The Grounding of Modern Feminism.* New Haven, CT: Yale University Press, 1987.

Daniel, Pete. *Deep'n As It Comes: The 1927 Mississippi Flood.* New York: Oxford University Press, 1977.

Deakin, Phyllis A. *In Pride and With Pleasure.* London: International Federation of Business and Professional Women, 1970.

Drachman, Virginia G. *Sisters in Law: Women Lawyers in Modern American History.* Cambridge, MA: Harvard University Press, 1998.

Edelman, Barnard. *Centenarians: The Story of the 20th Century by the Americans Who Lived It.* New York: Farrar, Strauss & Giroux, 1999.

Edwards, India. *Pulling No Punches: Memoirs of a Woman in Politics.* New York: G. P. Putnam's Sons, 1977.

Elliott, Jane Whiteside. "Lucy Somerville Howorth: Legislative Career, 1932–1935." Master's thesis, Delta State University, 1975.

———. "Profile: Lucy Somerville, One of Mississippi's Finest." *Delta Scene* 1 (Winter 1973).

Epstein, Cynthia Fuchs. *Women in Law.* New York: Basic Books, 1981.

Finerty, Nancy. "Lucy Howorth: 'The Little Lady from Mississippi.'" *Ole Miss Magazine,* January 1983.

Goode, James M. *Best Addresses.* Washington, DC: Smithsonian Institution Press, 1988.

Griffin, Isabel K. "Women You Hear About." *Democratic Digest* 8 (August 1934).

Gunn, Jack Winton, and Gladys C. Castle. *A Pictorial History of Delta State University.* Jackson: University Press of Mississippi, 1980.

Hairston, Joe E. "Practicing Law: Lucy Somerville Howorth, in Court and Elsewhere, 1922–1934." Seminar paper, Department of Anthropology, University of Mississippi, 1992.

Harrison, Cynthia. *On Account of Sex: The Politics of Women's Issues, 1945–1968.* Berkeley and Los Angeles: University of California Press, 1988.

Harrison, Evelyn. "Women in the Federal Service." *Civil Service Journal* 4 (October–December 1963).

Hartmann, Susan M. *The Home Front and Beyond: American Women in the 1940s.* Boston: Twayne, 1982.

———. "Women's Employment and the Domestic Ideal in the Early Cold War Years." In *Not June Cleaver: Women and Gender in Postwar America,*

1945–1960, edited by Joanne Meyerowitz. Philadelphia: Temple University Press, 1994.

Hawks, Joanne V., M. Carolyn Ellis, and J. Bryan Morris. "Women in the Mississippi Legislature (1924–1981)." *Journal of Mississippi History* 43 (November 1981).

"Here Are Your 1939–40 Committee Chairmen." *Independent Woman* 18 (October 1939).

James, Edward T., ed. *Notable American Women, 1607–1950.* Cambridge, MA: Harvard University Press, 1971.

"Judge Lucy Somerville Howorth." *Randolph-Macon Alumnae Bulletin* 45 (April 1952).

Kimball, Mary Alice. "Your Delegate Looks at Norway." *Independent Woman* 18 (September 1939).

Landon, Michael De L. *For the Honor and Dignity of the Profession: A History of the Mississippi State Bar, 1906–1976.* Jackson: University Press of Mississippi, 1979.

———. "The Origins of the Mississippi Law Journal." *Mississippi Law Journal* 50 (March 1979).

Laville, Helen. *Cold War Women: The International Activities of American Women's Organisations.* Manchester: Manchester University Press, 2002.

Leone, Janice. "Integrating the American Association of University Women, 1946–1949." *Historian* 51 (May 1989).

Levine, Susan. *Degrees of Equality: The American Association of University Women and the Challenge of Twentieth-Century Feminism.* Philadelphia: Temple University Press, 1995.

Litoff, Judy Barrett, and David C. Smith, eds. *American Women in a World at War: Contemporary Accounts from World War II.* Wilmington, DE: Scholarly Resources, 1997.

———. *What Kind of World Do We Want? American Women Plan for Peace.* Wilmington, DE: Scholarly Resources, 2000.

Lynn, Susan. *Progressive Women in Conservative Times: Racial Justice, Peace, and Feminism, 1945 to the 1960s.* New Brunswick, NJ: Rutgers University Press, 1991.

McCain, William D., and Charlotte Capers, eds. *Papers of the Washington County Historical Society.* Jackson: Mississippi Historical Society, 1954.

McCandless, Amy Thompson. *The Past in the Present: Women's Higher Education in the Twentieth Century American South.* Tuscaloosa: University of Alabama Press, 1999.

McDowell, John Patrick. *The Social Gospel in the South: The Woman's Home*

Mission Movement in the Methodist Episcopal Church, South, 1886–1939. Baton Rouge: Louisiana State University Press, 1982.

McElnaney, Laura. *Civil Defense Begins at Home: Militarization Meets Everyday Life in the Fifties.* Princeton, NJ: Princeton University Press, 2000.

McLemore, Richard A., ed. *A History of Mississippi.* Vol. 2. Jackson: University & College Press of Mississippi, 1973.

"Meet Three New Committee Chairmen." *Independent Woman* 16 (October 1937).

Merideth, Mary Louise, "The Mississippi Woman's Rights Movement, 1889–1923: The Leadership of Nellie Nugent Somerville and Greenville in Suffrage Reform. Master's thesis, Delta State University, 1974.

Meyerowitz, Joanne, ed. *Not June Cleaver: Women and Gender in Postwar America, 1945–1960.* Philadelphia: Temple University Press, 1994.

Minor, Bill. *Eyes on Mississippi: A Fifty-Year Chronicle of Change.* Jackson, MS: Prichard Morris Books, 2001.

Morello, Karen Berger. *The Invisible Bar: The Woman Lawyer in America, 1638 to the Present.* New York: Random House, 1986.

"Mrs. Howorth in Germany." *Journal of the American Association of University Women* 47 (March 1954).

Patterson, Judith. *Be Somebody: A Biography of Marguerite Rawalt.* Austin, TX: Eakin, 1986.

Percy, William Alexander. *Lanterns on the Levee: Recollections of a Planter's Son.* New York: Knopf, 1941.

Power, Anabel. "The Lady from Hinds." *To Dragma* (Alpha Omicron Pi) 27 (May 1932).

Price, Vinton. "Women, Politics, and the Press: The Mississippi *Woman Voter.*" *Southern Studies* 19 (Winter 1980).

Rawalt, Marguerite, comp. *History of the National Federation of Business and Professional Women's Clubs, Inc.* Vol. 2, *1944–1960.* Washington, DC: NFBPWC, 1960.

Rice, Anna V. *A History of the World's Young Women's Christian Association.* New York: Woman's Press, 1947.

Riley, Elizabeth L. "Women and the Law: Beginnings." *Mississippi Lawyer* 31 (January–February 1985).

Roberts, Richard. *Florence Simms: A Biography.* New York: Woman's Press, 1926.

Robinson, Marion O. *Eight Women of the YWCA.* New York: National Board of the Young Women's Christian Association of the USA, 1966.

Roosevelt, Eleanor. "Women at the Peace Conference." *Reader's Digest* 14 (April 1944).

Rossiter, Margaret. *Women Scientists in America: Before Affirmative Action, 1940–1972.* Baltimore: Johns Hopkins University Press, 1995.

Rupp, Leila J., and Verta Taylor. *Survival in the Doldrums: The American Women's Rights Movement, 1945 to the 1960s.* New York: Oxford University Press, 1987.

Sansing, David. G. *The University of Mississippi: A Sesquicentennial History.* Jackson: University Press of Mississippi, 1999.

Scott, Anne Firor. *Making the Invisible Woman Visible.* Urbana: University of Illinois Press, 1984.

———. "Nellie Nugent Somerville." In *Notable American Women: The Modern Period,* edited by Barbara Sicherman and Carol Hurd Green. Cambridge, MA: Harvard University Press, 1980.

———. *The Southern Lady: From Pedestal to Politics, 1830–1930.* Twenty-fifth Anniversary Edition. Charlottesville: University Press of Virginia, 1995.

Sergio, Lisa. *A Measure Fulfilled: The Life of Lena Madesin Phillips.* New York: Breese, 1972.

Shawhan, Dorothy. "Lucy Somerville Howorth: A Remarkable Woman." *Bar Examiner* 65 (August 1996).

———. "Three Lawyers from Mississippi." In *From Behind the Magnolia Curtain: Voices of Mississippi,* edited by Clyde V. Williams. Jackson: Mississippi Press Association, 1988.

———. "Women behind the *Woman Voter.*" *Journal of Mississippi History* 49 (May 1987).

Sherman, JanAnn. *No Place for a Woman: A Life of Senator Margaret Chase Smith.* New Brunswick, NJ: Rutgers University Press, 2000.

Sicherman, Barbara, and Carol Hurd Green, eds. *Notable American Women: The Modern Period.* Cambridge, MA: Harvard University Press, 1980.

Sillers, Florence Warfield, comp. *History of Bolivar County, Mississippi.* Jackson, MS: Hederman Brothers, 1948. Reprint, Spartanburg, SC: Reprint Publishers, 1976.

Somerville, Keith Frazier. "Random Thoughts." Typescript. Capps Archives, Delta State University, Cleveland, MS.

———. "Thinking Back." Typescript. Capps Archives, Delta State University, Cleveland, MS.

Storrs, Landon R. Y. "Red Scare Politics and the Suppression of Popular Front Feminism: The Loyalty Investigation of Mary Dublin Keyserling." *Journal of American History* 90 (September 2003).

Swain, Martha H. *Ellen S. Woodward: New Deal Advocate for Women.* Jackson: University Press of Mississippi, 1995.

———. "Organized Women in Mississippi: The Clash over Legal Disabilities in the 1920s." *Southern Studies* 23 (Spring 1984).

"Three Lawyers Visit Germany." *Journal of the American Bar Association*, September 1954.

Waldrop, Frank C., ed. *Mountain Voices: The Centennial History of the Monteagle Sunday School Assembly*. Nashville, TN: Parthenon, 1987.

Wallace, Frank. "A History of the Conner Administration." Master's thesis, Mississippi State University, 1959.

Wallis, Patricia Carol. "Defining Their Liberties: Women's Organizations during the McCarthy Era." PhD diss., University of Maryland, College Park, 1994.

Ware, Susan. *Beyond Suffrage: Women in the New Deal*. Cambridge, MA: Harvard University Press, 1981.

———. *Partner and I: Molly Dewson, Feminism, and New Deal Politics*. New Haven, CT: Yale University Press, 1987.

———, ed. *Notable American Women: A Biographical Dictionary Completing the Twentieth Century*. Cambridge, MA: Harvard University Press, 2004.

Wasson, Ben. *Count No 'Count: Flashbacks to Faulkner*. Jackson: University Press of Mississippi, 1983.

Wells, Dean Faulkner, and Hunter Cole, eds. *Mississippi Heroes*. Jackson: University Press of Mississippi, 1980.

Wheeler, Marjorie Spruill. *New Women of the New South: The Leaders of the Woman Suffrage Movement in the Southern States*. New York: Oxford University Press, 1993.

———, ed. *One Woman, One Vote: Rediscovering the Woman Suffrage Movement*. Troutdale, OR: New Sage, 1995.

Wilson, Elizabeth. *Fifty Years of Association Work among Young Women*. New York: YWCA, 1916.

Winter, William. "Governor Mike Conner and the Sales Tax, 1932." in *Mississippi Heroes*, edited by Dean Faulkner Wells and Hunter Cole. Jackson: University Press of Mississippi, 1980.

Wyatt-Brown, Bertram. *The House of Percy: Honor, Melancholy, and Imagination in a Southern Family*. New York: Oxford University Press, 1994.

Index

AAUW. *See* American Association of University Women (AAUW)
AAUW Journal, 112, 113, 144
Abzug, Bella, 157
Acheson, Dean, 160
Adkins, Bertha, 128
African Americans. *See* Racial issues
Allen, Florence, 32
Allen, George E., 106
Allen, Virginia, 17
Allied Bureau of Aircraft Production, 20–21
Alpha Omicron Pi, 14, 90, 152, 155
American Association of University Women (AAUW): and Assembly of Women's Organizations for National Security, 124–25; and class issues, 117–18; and Cleveland Public Library, 139; Committee on the Economic and Legal Status of Women, 95, 98, 101, 102, 108, 112, 118–19; Committee on the Status of Women, 108, 112–13, 118–22, 126–27, 128; and Communist threat, 120–21; and Equal Rights Amendment, 118–19, 142–43; fellowships of, 131, 146; and House Un-American Activities Committee, 125; Howorth as second vice president of, 118, 130; and Howorth on Survey Committee, 131–32; and Howorth's advancement of women, 108, 165; Howorth's continued involvement in, 143–46, 159, 161–62; Howorth's joining of, 25, 59; Howorth's leadership role in, 94, 112; and Howorth's race for state representative, 65; and Howorth's symposium on women in policymaking, 101; and Howorth's visits to branches, 127, 130–31; and Hughes, 95; and New Deal women, 88; and peace movements, 125; and racial issues, 116–17, 130–31, 144–45; and Woman's Centennial Congress, 90; and women in military, 96, 120, 127; and women in office, 98, 128; and women's contributions to defense, 119–20; and women's education, 102–3, 113–14, 115, 131, 144, 145, 152; and women's employment, 102
American Association of University Women (AAUW) Building Commission, 131
American Association of University Women (AAUW) Papers, 100
American Bar Association, 45, 47
American Farm Bureau, 127
American Legion, 59
American Legion Auxiliary, 127
American Newspaper Women's Club, 90
Anderson, Reuben, 138
Armstrong, Florence, 88–89
Arthur and Elizabeth Schlesinger Library at Radcliffe College, 89, 126, 148, 150, 153, 163
Assembly of Women's Organizations for National Security, 122–26

Babcock, Will, 155
Bache, Louise Franklin, 92

Bailey, Thomas L., 67, 69, 70, 78, 80
Beard, Mary, 89
Benedict, Ruth, 101
Beyer, Clara, 164, 209n43
Bilbo, Theodore G., 40, 42–43, 60, 62, 68, 72
Blacks. *See* Racial issues
Blackstone Club, 31
Blair, Emily Newell, 137
Blair, Harry, 82
B'nai B'rith, 127
Bobo, Henry, 60
Boeth, Dick, 185–86n6
Boeth, Margaret "Sissy," 161
Bollman, Mary, 110
Bond, Willard F., 45
Booze, Eugene, 38
Booze, Mary, 38
Boyd, Rosamonde, 112, 126
Boyer, Elizabeth, 157
BPW. *See* National Federation of Business and Professional Women's Clubs (BPW)
Bradley, Omar, 97
Bragdon, Helen, 101, 117–18, 121
Brewer, Claudia, 46
Brewer, Earl, 39, 40, 42–45, 46, 47
Brewer, Minnie, 14, 39–40, 41, 42, 43, 44–47, 56
Brinkley, David, 88
Bronte, Lydia, 162–63
Brookings Institution, 72–73
Brown, Kate, 60
Brown, Linda Reeves, 29
Brown, Mary Agnes: photograph of, following p. 66; as reference for Howorth, 115; and Veterans Administration, 84, 97, 110; and Women's Army Corps, 96–97
Brown, Mrs. Thorton Lee (Laura), 81, 85, 95
Brunauer, Esther Caukin, 121, 126
Bryan, William Jennings, 136
Buck, Pearl Sydenstricker, 13–14, 17
Burn, Harry, 27

Burns, Lucy, 15
Business and Professional Women's Clubs. *See* National Federation of Business and Professional Women's Clubs (BPW)
Butler, Eliza, 21
Butler, Nicholas Murray, 21

Capers, Walter, 62, 65–66
Caraway, Hattie, 110
Carloss, Helen R., 99, 147
Carter, Jimmy, 156
Cash, William M., 3, 148
Catfish industry, 70
Catt, Carrie Chapman, 15, 59, 60, 89
Chadwick, Carl, 62
Chadwick, Mrs. Wyman, 123
Chambers, Whittaker, 136
Child Labor Amendment, 79–80
Children's Bureau, 86
Chivvis, Ruth, 24
Civic Improvement Club, 5–6, 11, 73
Civil rights movement, 138–40, 145. *See also* Racial issues
Civil Service Commission, 95–96, 101, 141
Civil War, 4, 10, 137
Civilian Conservation Corps, 77
Civilian Defense Organization, 125
Clark, Pauline Alston, 205n45
Clark, Tom C., 105–6, 109
Clarksdale, Mississippi, 38–39
Clearing House of Women's Organizations for National Defense, 121–22
Cleary, Daniel F., 109, 129, 162
Cleary, Gertrude, 162
Cleveland Business and Professional Women's Club, 137
Cleveland Public Library Commission, 139
Cleveland Woman's Club, 37, 137
Clinton, Bill, 162
Clinton, Hillary, 151, 162
Cobb, James C., 6
Coen, Hooker, 71
Cohn, David L., 6, 10, 29, 162

Cohn, Herman, 10
Coleman, Linda, 138
Collins, Carvel, 154
Columbia University, 19–20, 27, 28
Commission on Government Security, 134–36
Committee for Participation of Women in Postwar Planning (CWPP), 126
Committee of Ten, 103–4, 105
Committee on International Understanding and Goodwill, 90
Committee on the Economic and Legal Status of Women (CELSW), 95, 98, 101, 102, 108, 112, 118–19
Committee on the Status of Women, 108, 112–13, 118–22, 126–27, 128
Committee on Women in World Affairs (CWWA), 103, 105, 125, 126
Communism, 23, 120–21, 125, 135, 136
Concordia, Frances, 145
Conference of Allied Ministers of Education, 99
Congressional Union, 15
Conkey, Elizabeth A., 99
Conn, Mollie Heath, 38
Conner, Martin Sennett "Mike," 42, 43, 61, 68, 70–72, 77–78, 80
Conservation Committee, 70
Continuation Committee, 100
Cook, Vivian, 29
Corbett, Mildred, 27
Cott, Nancy, 165
Council of Women for World Missions, 59
Counterculture movements, 143–44
Crooks, Ezra B., 16–17
Cummings, Homer, 76

Dalrymple, Arch, 163
Daniel, Jonathan W., 98
Daniel, Pete, 49
Darwin, Charles, 33
Daughters of the American Colonists, 137
Daughters of the American Revolution, 137

Defense organizations, 119–26. *See also* Military
Delta Kappa Gamma, 137
Delta Preparatory College, 10–11
Delta State Teachers College, 45, 62
Delta State University, 136, 151–52, 161
Democratic National Convention of 1933, 73
Democratic Party: and May T. Evans, 111; and Joe Howorth, 64, 65, 74; Lucy Howorth's work in, 25, 73–75, 105; and Nellie Somerville, 47, 149; Women's National Democratic Club (WNDC), 86–89; Young Democrats in Mississippi, 66, 73
Democratic Women's Division, 108, 109, 111
Dewson, Mary W. "Molly": and appointments for women, 74–75; and Child Labor Amendment, 79, 80; on Howorth's achievements, 133; and Howorth's job at Veterans Administration, 81–82, 84–85; Howorth's meeting of, 23; on living in Washington, 136; and Washington BPW, 92; and Woodward, 76, 80, 87
District Bar Association, 106
Dolan, Eleanor, 122
Domesticity, 114, 124
Drachman, Virginia, 56–57, 58
Dulles, John Foster, 136
Durr, Virginia Foster, 20, 138, 178n40
Dyer, Edward, 18

Eastern Star, 37, 59
Eastland, James O., 60, 135, 138–39
Eaton, James, 163–64
Education of women. *See* Women's education
Edwards, India, 109, 128, 129
Eisenhower, Dwight D., 128, 129, 134, 135, 141, 164
Elizabeth Female Academy, 2
Elysian Club, 6
Employment of women. *See* Women's employment and labor issues

Enochs, Martha Catching, 59, 79
Equal Rights Amendment (ERA): and American Association of University Women, 118–19, 142–43; and Committee on the Status of Women, 112; and Hickey, 157; Howorth on, 41–42, 143; and National Federation of Business and Professional Women's Clubs, 91, 119; and PCSW report, 142; and protective legislation for women, 24, 40–41
Equal Suffrage League, 14–15
ERA. See Equal Rights Amendment (ERA)
Espy, Mike, 138
Evans, May Thompson, 87, 104, 111

Fair Employment Hearing Board, 95
Farley, James F., 74
Farmer, Hallie, 114, 116, 131–32
Faulkner, William, 6, 30, 32, 55, 154, 180n75
FBI. See Federal Bureau of Investigation (FBI)
Federal Bar Association, 94, 134
Federal Bureau of Investigation (FBI): queries on Howorth, 126, 135, 150, 200n67, 202n3; and Roosevelt appointees, 75
Federal Civil Defense Administration (FCDA), 122, 123, 124
Federal Emergency Relief Administration, 76, 85, 89
Federal Employment Policies and Practices Committee, 140, 141
Federal Home Loan Bank, 81
Federal Security Agency, 105
Federal Women's Award, 140
Feminism, 113, 124, 143, 146, 150, 157, 165. See also Women's movement
Feustal, Henry, 155
Feustal, Polly Graham Babcock, 37–38, 155
Fleeson, Doris, 103, 108, 109
Flexner, Eleanor, 114

Forbes, Ligon, 40
Forrest, Dollie, 164
Forrestal, James, 119
Fortune, Porter, 152
France, Anatole, 31
Franklin, Esther Cole, 102
Franklin Literary Society, 16, 17
Frantz, F. F., 8
Frayser, Mary E., 101
Frazier, James B., 75–76
Freud, Sigmund, 31
Fugler, Madge Quin, 67, 70–71, 73, 77, 187–88n4, 188n13
Furman, Bess, 74

Gallagher, Nadine, 106
Gas and oil industry, 77
General Federation of Women's Clubs, 122
German Association of University Women, 130
German Federation of Business and Professional Women, 129–30
GI Bill of 1944, 95
Gildersleeve, Virginia, 108
Gillespie, Emy Lou, 43, 183n30
Gold, P. D., 85
Goodykoontz, Bess, 104
Gray, Laura Anna, 2
Great Depression, 61, 77, 78, 80
Green, Edith, 151
Guyton, Kate Smallwood, 31

Hannegan, Robert, 105
Hardeman, Nancy, 2
Harriman, Florence, 91
Harrison, Evelyn, 141
Harrison, Pat, 47, 73–76, 81, 88
Harvard Law School, 113
Hatfield, Mark, 151
Hawks, Joanne Varner, 151
Helms, Jesse, 156
Herron, Marion J., 106
Hickey, Margaret: and Clearing House of

Women's Organizations for National Defense, 122; correspondence with Howorth, 156–57, 159; and federal employment practices, 140, 141–42; and Howorth's prospective judgeship appointment, 106; and National Federation of Business and Professional Women's Clubs, 92, 93, 98; as reference for Howorth, 115; and Truman, 107; and War Manpower Commission, 93, 102, 120; and women in office, 100; and women's education, 132; and working women, 101–2
Hickman, Emily, 103, 104, 105
Hill, Mrs. Ivy, 45
Hines, Frank, 76, 81–82, 95
Hiss, Alger, 100, 136
History. *See* Women's history
Hobby, Oveta Culp, 96
Holmes, Edwin R., 49
Home Owners' Loan Corporation, 82
Hood, Frances, 163
Hoover, Herbert, 49, 74
Hopkins, Harry L., 76, 87–88
Horner, Eva, 32, 37
Hottel, Althea, 116, 124–25
Houghton, Mrs. Hiram Cole, 122
House Un-American Activities Committee, 125
House-Senate Joint Committee on the Reorganization of State Government, 71
Howard, Katherine, 124
Howlett, Virginia, 17
Howorth, Carl, 64–65
Howorth, Emma Beauchamp, 31
Howorth, Joseph Marion: death of, 154, 158–59, 160; and Democratic Party, 64, 65, 74; legal practice of, 55, 56, 57, 58–59, 61, 136, 138; legal studies of, 31, 88; and Lucy as state representative, 67; Lucy's advocacy for position in Roosevelt administration, 75; Lucy's friendship with, 31, 32, 46, 55, 56; and Lucy's race for state representative, 63–65; marriage of, 55, 56–59, 61, 133, 154, 159; painting of, 88, 192*n*11; Pentagon duty of, 136; photograph of, following p. 66; and racial issues, 138; and retirement, 157; and State Board of Law Examiners, 48, 55, 56, 60, 61; and Washington, DC move, 87–88

Howorth, Joseph Robert, 31
Howorth, Lucy Somerville:
—education of: in childhood, 7, 8, 10–11, 12; and Columbia University, 19–20, 27; and legal studies, 18, 20, 27, 28–34; as psychology department assistant, 18; and Randolph-Macon Woman's College, 12, 13, 16–18; and student employment, 20–26, 27
—government work of: and Commission on Government Security, 134–36; and Veterans Administration, 19–20, 76, 81–85, 92–93, 95, 97, 107, 109–10, 132; and War Claims Commission, 109, 120, 128–29
—legal practice of: and civil rights movement, 138; and family influence, 4; and James Somerville Associates, 134; and marriage, 55, 56–59, 61; and Mississippi River flood of 1927, 35, 49, 53–54; and Shands's firm, 35, 36–40, 42, 44–45, 47–48; solo practice in Greenville, 35, 36, 48–49; and Abram Somerville's practice, 136, 160; as state law examiner, 48, 55, 56, 60, 61; and state representative duties, 73
—personal life of: on aging, 163; childhood and youth of, 5–11; and correspondence, 155–57, 159, 160; death of, 164; family background of, 1–5; and friendships with authors, 147–48; health of, 6, 7, 161; and honors, 152, 158; and horse races, 10; marriage of, 55, 56–59, 61, 133, 154, 159; one-hundredth birthday celebration, 162; and retirement from government, 133, 134, 136; and theater, 9, 14, 26, 160; and travel, 129–30, 154, 160–61, 162

Howorth, Lucy Somerville (*continued*)
—photographs of, following p. 66;
—political career of: and Democratic Party, 25, 73–75, 105; and Roosevelt administration, 75–76; and state legislature race of 1931, 61–65; as state representative, 56, 65, 67–73, 76–83
—political strategy of: Howorth as state representative, 67–68, 77–78, 81; and Howorth's state representative race, 62–65; Howorth's writings on, 44; and leftist organizations, 125; and National Federation of Business and Professional Women's Clubs, 90–91; and New Deal network, 86–87; and Nellie Somerville's campaign for state representative, 42, 43–44; and Whitfield race, 42–43; and women in office, 75, 89, 91, 96–107, 108, 109–12, 119–21, 128, 140–42, 165; and women's advancement, 102–3, 108, 113–14, 127; and women's organizations for national defense, 121–26; and women's suffrage, 14–16, 39–41
—speeches of: at Alabama College, 114; and appointment of women in federal government, 1; at Business and Professional Women's Club of Jackson, 147; at Delta State University, 151; law school commencement address, 29, 33–34; at Mississippi Bar Association, 47; at Mississippi State College for Women, 141, 145; Randolph-Macon commencement address, 112–13; recorded speeches, 167–71; speaking and debating skills, 16; at White House Conference on Women in Post-War Policy Making, 98–100
—and women's organizations: and advancement of women, 91; and Howorth's government service, 86; importance of, 153, 165; in Jackson, 59; and McCarthy era, 124; for national defense, 121–26; and parliamentarian skills, 81, 116; and Randolph-Macon Woman's College, 13, 14; and World Center for Women's Archives, 89–90. *See also* American Association of University Women (AAUW); National Federation of Business and Professional Women's Clubs (BPW)
Howorth and Howorth, 58, 61, 73
Hughes, Sarah T., 92, 95–96, 98, 101, 115, 119, 141
Hull, Cordell, 76
Hypatia Club, 5

Industrial War Service Centers, 22
Ingram, Ashton Somerville, 159
International Congress of Working Women, 24
International Federation of Business and Professional Women's Clubs, 91, 130
International Federation of University Women (IFUW), 125, 126, 130
International Labor Conference, 99
Internationalism, 121, 126
Iselin, Cecile, 25

Jackson Business and Professional Women's Club, 40, 59, 65, 67–68, 72, 90, 147
James Somerville Associates, 134
Jarnigan, R. L., 95
Jefferson Literary Society, 16
Jiggets, Louis, 73
Jobs. *See* Women's employment
Johnson, Lady Bird, 88
Johnson, Louis, 119
Johnson, Lyndon B., 88, 142, 156
Johnson, Rheta Grimsley, 155, 162
Johnston, Mary, 15
Johnston, Oscar, 41
Joint Orientation Defense Conference, 119

Kassebaum, Nancy, 151
Kearney, Belle, 42, 44, 46, 148
Kelley, Florence, 23

Kennedy, John F., 140–41, 142, 164
Kennedy, Laurens, 67
Kennedy, Robert F., 141
Kennington, R. E., 68
Kenyon, Dorothy, 105, 121
Key, Samuel, 62
Keyserling, Mary Dublin, 200n66
Knox, Rush H., 45
Korean War, 120, 121, 123–24
Kretschmar, Kate, 9
Kretschmar, Wils, 9, 56
Kross, Anna K., 110–11
Ku Klux Klan, 33, 43

Labor interests, 65. *See also* Women's employment and labor issues
Larew, Gillie A., 94, 101, 116, 117
Latimer, Linda Koch, 161
Lawyers Guild, 125
League of Nations, 60
League of Women Voters: and endorsement of Howorth, 45; and Equal Rights Amendment, 41; and Fugler, 70–71; Howorth as chair of Committee on Women in Industry, 39, 182n15; Howorth's attitude toward, 86; and peace movements, 59
Lee, Muna, 154
Legal practice of Lucy Howorth. *See* Howorth, Lucy Somerville
LeHand, Missy, 81
Lehman, Herbert, 100
Lenroot, Katharine, 86, 100, 104
Levine, Susan, 117, 144
Lewenstein, Lili von, 11, 12, 16
Lewis, Seth, 2, 4
Lindsay, Malvina, 100, 103, 104, 106, 202n93
Lucy Somerville Howorth Fellowship Endowment, 146
Lusk, Georgia L., 109, 129
Lynn, Susan, 144
Lytle, Andrew, 146, 158

Macy, John, 140, 142
Maffett, Minnie, 92–93, 98, 101
Mahoney, Margaret, 159, 161
Mandigo, Pauline, 123
Marionettes, 30, 154; photograph of, following p. 66
Marlett, Frances, 27
Marshall, Augusta Stacy: and Columbia University, 19; death of, 159; as Howorth's childhood friend, 10; and Howorth's comments on husband, 158–59; and Howorth's involvement in AAUW, 144; on Howorth's leadership, 91; on Howorth's move to Washington, DC, 83, 87; on Howorth's retirement from government, 133, 137; and Howorth's speeches, 100, 112–13; Howorth's sustained contact with, 155, 160; and Randolph-Macon College, 14; and socialism, 25
Marshall, George, 122
Mason, Lucy Randolph, 23, 79–80
Matthews, Burnita Shelton, 111, 112, 147
Mayhall, Beth, 54
McAdoo, William Gibbs, 47
McCarran, Pat, 120–21
McCarthy, Joseph, 23, 121
McCarthy Committee, 126, 135
McCarthy era, 124, 125
McElnaney, Laura, 124
McGehee, Mrs. Edward, 19
McGrath, J. Howard, 112
McHale, Kathryn, 95–96, 98, 101, 116, 118, 120–21, 127
McLean, Keith Dockery, 159, 164
Meyerowitz, Joanne, 126
Military, women in, 96–97, 101, 120, 127, 140
Mims, Edwin, 8
Mineral Lease Commission, 69–70, 77–78
Mississippi Art Association, 71–72
Mississippi Bar Association, 47, 67, 69, 71
Mississippi Bar Commission on the Study of State Government, 78

Mississippi Board of Girl Reserves, 37–38, 45
Mississippi Board of Levee Commissioners, 5, 6, 7
Mississippi Business and Professional Women's Clubs, 74, 93
Mississippi Club, 14
Mississippi Democratic convention, 73
Mississippi Federation of Women's Clubs: and Dewson, 75; Howorth as legal advisor for, 59; and Howorth as state representative, 71–72; and political strategy, 43; Nellie Somerville's speech for, 39
Mississippi Historical Society, 147
Mississippi Law Review, 31
Mississippi River flood of 1927: effects of, 49–50, 52; Howorth's account of, 50–55; and Howorth's legal practice, 35, 49, 53–54; and William Percy's evacuation plan, 52–53
Mississippi Society, 88, 90
Mississippi Sovereignty Commission, 203*n*16
Mississippi State College for Women, 116, 141, 145. *See also* Mississippi University for Women
Mississippi State Hall of Fame, 147, 150, 205*n*63
Mississippi State University, 152
Mississippi University for Women, 152. *See also* Mississippi State College for Women
Mississippi Woman of the Year, 152
Mississippi Woman Suffrage Association, 5, 11
Mississippian, 30, 31, 154
Mitchell, Henrietta, 66
Monteagle Sunday School Assembly, Tennessee, 8–9, 27, 36, 149, 150, 156–59, 161
Montgomery, Goode, 48
Montgomery, Isaiah, 38
Moore, Amzie, 138
Morello, Karen, 147–48

Multi-Party Committee of Women, Inc., 110–11
My Dear Nellie (Howorth and Cash), 3, 148
Myers, Constance, 23, 58, 125, 139, 150, 157, 159, 160
Myrdal, Alva, 91

NAACP, 138
Natchez Trace Military Highway Association, 79
Natchez Trace Parkway, 79
National American Woman Suffrage Association (NAWSA), 15–16, 41
National Association for the Advancement of Colored People, 138
National Association of Deans of Women, 115
National Association of Women Lawyers (NAWL), 45
National Child Labor Committee, 79
National Committee on the Cause and Cure of War (NCCCW), 59–60
National Consumers' League, 23, 41
National Council of Negro Women, 127
National Federation of Business and Professional Women's Clubs (BPW): and Clearing House of Women's Organizations for National Defense, 122; Cleveland BPW, 137; and Equal Rights Amendment, 91, 119; Howorth's interest in, 26, 90, 95; Howorth's work for, 92–94, 102; Jackson BPW, 40, 59, 65, 67–68, 72, 90, 147; Mississippi BPW, 74, 93; and New Deal women, 88; and Richardson, 89; Washington BPW, 89, 90, 91–92, 94; and Woman's Centennial Congress, 90
National Industrial Conference, 24
National Manpower Council (NMC), 132
National Organization of Women, 143
National Recovery Administration, 82
National Security Resources Board, 122

National Woman's Party (NWP), 15–16, 40–41, 111
NAWL. *See* National Association of Women Lawyers (NAWL)
NAWSA. *See* National American Woman Suffrage Association (NAWSA)
NCCCW. *See* National Committee on the Cause and Cure of War (NCCCW)
Nellie Nugent Somerville Lectures in Government and Public Affairs, 151
New Deal, 83, 85–88, 97, 150, 164
Nietzsche, Friedrich, 46
Nineteenth Amendment, 27, 41, 162
Nixon, Richard, 156
NMC. *See* National Manpower Council (NMC)
Norman, Cora, 146
Nugent, Anne Lewis, 2–3
Nugent, Eleanor Smith, 3, 148
Nugent, John Pratt, 2–3
Nugent, William Lewis, 2–3, 4, 58, 61, 64, 148
NWP. *See* National Woman's Party (NWP)

Office of Defense Planning, 119

Paul, Alice, 15–16
PCSW. *See* President's Commission on the Status of Women (PCSW)
Peace movements, 59, 98–99, 125
Pennybacker, Anna, 60
Percy, LeRoy, 7, 35–36, 43–44, 50, 53, 63
Percy, William Alexander, 6, 50, 51–54
Perkins, Frances, 23, 99, 104, 113
Perry, Stella, 155
Peterson, Esther, 142
Phi Beta Kappa, 152
Phillips, Lena Madesin, 26, 90, 91
Pohl, Emma Ody, 12
Political officeholders: American Association of University Women (AAUW) and women as, 98, 128; Howorth's political strategy for women in, 75, 89, 91, 96–107, 108, 109–12, 119–21, 128, 140–42, 165; Woodward and women as, 76, 99, 100, 104–5. *See also* specific persons
Pollard, John G., 85
Posey, L. L., 62, 65
Powers, Joseph Neely, 33
President's Commission on the Status of Women (PCSW), 140–42, 156
Prohibition, 46, 63, 76–77, 78
Prostitution, 43
Public Lands Committee, 69–70, 77–78
Public Lands Office, 69

Quakenbos, Mary Grace, 35

Racial issues: and American Association of University Women, 116–17, 130–31, 144–45; and child labor amendment, 80; and civil rights movement, 138–39; and Howorth's Columbia University experience, 20; and Howorth's YWCA work, 25; and Mississippi River flood of 1927, 52, 53; and Randolph-Macon Woman's College, 13; and Nellie Somerville, 149
Radcliffe College honorees, 153; photograph of, following p. 66
Ralston, Blanche Montgomery, 43, 72
Randolph, Bessie, 116
Randolph-Macon Alumnae Bulletin, 113
Randolph-Macon Woman's College (RMWC): academic reputation of, 12, 19; alumnae chapter of, 25; curriculum of, 116; educational philosophy of, 13–14; and Howorth's Alumnae Achievement Award, 152; Howorth's commencement address for, 112–13; and Howorth's education, 12, 13, 16–18; and women's education, 161; and women's studies collection, 151
Ravens, 31
Rawalt, Marguerite, 94, 123
Rea, Katherine, 151, 152
Reagan, Ronald, 156

Red Cross, 25, 49, 51–54, 97
Reform. *See* Social reform; Women's suffrage
Religion: Howorth's views on, 31, 139; and Somerville, 5, 149
Republican National Committee Women's Division, 128
Research Commission, 72–73
Rice, Greek, 82–83
Rice, Jessie Pearl, 112
Richardson, Eudora Ramsey, 89
Riley, Susan: death of, 156; and Howorth's Commission on Government Security work, 136; on Howorth's contributions, 133; and leadership in AAUW, 127; and McCarthy era, 124; and political spectrum in AAUW, 121; and racial issues, 116; recommendation of Howorth, 135; and Survey Committee of AAUW, 131, 132
RMWC. *See* Randolph-Macon Woman's College (RMWC)
Robins, Margaret Drier, 23
Robins, Raymond, 23
Robinson, Lucy, 7
Roebuck, Sidney, 80
Rohde, Ruth Bryan, 100
Roosevelt, Eleanor, 1, 85–87, 98, 100, 140, 142, 147
Roosevelt, Franklin D.: appointments of, 75–76, 81–83, 86, 100, 104, 109, 164; death of, 103; Howorth's support for candidacy of, 73–74
Rosborough, Melanie, 112, 127
Rosenman, Samuel I., 98
Ross, Nellie Tayloe, 75, 86
Rossiter, Margaret, 131
Rupp, Leila, 150
Russell, Lee, 29–30
Russia, and YWCA, 26–27

Saunders, Mrs. Ben F., 37, 41, 45
Schain, Josephine, 99

Schlesinger Library at Radcliffe College, 89, 126, 148, 150, 153, 163
Schumann-Heink, Ernestine, 20
Scott, Anne Firor, 143, 146–50, 153, 159, 162
Scott, Frank, 48
Sexton, Kathleen, 88
Shands, Audley, 18, 35–40, 44–45, 47–48, 56, 82, 160
Shands, Bessie Nugent, 58, 61, 65
Shands, Couprey, 58
Shands, Dorothy, 97
Shands, Eleanor Somerville: and American Bar Association meeting, 45; death of, 158, 159–60; education of, 11, 12, 14; and Howorth's law school commencement address, 34; marriage of, 18; and Monteagle reunion, 159; and patriotic societies, 137; photograph of, following p. 66; as sister, 2; and Abram Somerville, 9; as witness for Howorth's marriage, 56
Shands, Harley, 58, 61, 64–65
Shands, Elmore, and Causey, 36
Shaw, Anna Howard, 11–12, 14–15, 16
Shawhan, Dorothy, 149, 160
Sherman, William T., 49
Sillers, Walter L., 67, 78, 80
Simms, Florence, 21–23, 32, 34; photograph of, following p. 66
Simpson, O. J., 163
Smith, Abram Fulkerson, 3, 4, 49–50
Smith, Alfred E., 25
Smith, Ergie Lee, 163–64
Smith, Hilda Worthington, 86
Smith, LePoint, 139, 160, 161, 162, 163, 164
Smith, Margaret Chase, 99–100, 110
Smith, Myra Cox, 3–4, 8, 9, 49, 159
Social reform: and Howorth as state representative, 79; Howorth's commitment to, 4, 24, 28, 47; and National Woman's Party, 41; and power of organized women, 1; and prostitution, 43; and Simms, 21, 22; and women's suffrage, 38

Social Security, 101, 102
Social Security Board, 104
Socialism, 23, 25
Socialist Party, 25
Somerville, Abram: as brother, 2; education of, 11; Howorth's conflicts with, 9; legal practice of, 136, 160; marriage of, 18–19; photograph of, following p. 66; speeches of, 34
Somerville, Ella, 30
Somerville, Evelyn Estes, 18–19
Somerville, James, 26, 28, 134
Somerville, Keith Frazier, 18, 136, 137
Somerville, Nellie Nugent: and child labor, 79; childhood of, 3; and Delta State Teachers College, 45; as Democratic National Convention delegate, 47; education of, 4–5; health of, 128; and home atmosphere, 5; Howorth's defense of, 148–49; and Howorth's law school commencement address, 34; and Howorth's marriage, 56; and Howorth's race for state representative, 62; influence of, on Howorth's career plans, 18–19, 82, 150; and Mississippi River flood of 1927, 49, 51, 52, 53, 54–55; as mother, 2, 7, 8, 11, 12; and National Woman's Party, 41; and perceptions of Mississippians, 90; photograph of, following p. 66; political interests of, 42, 149–50; and prohibition, 46, 63, 76; and prostitution issue, 43; religious conviction of, 5, 149; and Scott, 148, 162; and Eleanor Somerville's wedding, 18; speeches of, 39; as state representative, 48, 67; and state representative races, 42, 43–44, 62–63; and women's rights, 5, 7, 39; and women's suffrage, 5–6, 9–12, 15, 16, 27
Somerville, Robert Briggs, 2
Somerville, Robert (brother): as brother, 2; childhood of, 5; death of, 94, 148; education of, 11, 29; legal practice of, 12, 18; Lucy's living with, 36; marriage of, 18;

photograph of, following p. 66; and Nellie Somerville's state representative race, 44
Somerville, Robert (father), 2, 5, 6–7, 42, 45, 48, 50
Somerville, Thomas H., 29
Somerville-Howorth Collection, Schlesinger Library, 148
Somerville-Howorth International Study Grant, 128
Soroptimist Club, 90, 137
Southern Conference on Human Welfare, 138
Southern District of Mississippi, Howorth as U.S. commissioner of, 49, 60–61
Southern Society of Washington, 90
Southern Summer School for Women Workers, 59
Southwick, Henry L., 8
Spanish Association for University Women, 130
Spencer, Elizabeth, 30
Spider Web chart, 125
Stacy, Augusta. See Marshall, Augusta Stacy
Stahlman, Mary, 17
State Board of Law Examiners, 48, 55, 56, 60, 61
States Rights Party, 149
Stein, Gertrude, 26
Stennis, John C., 135
Stephens, Hubert D., 73, 75
Stewart, Mrs. Carroll Lee, 81, 85, 86, 95
Stockholm Peace Appeal, 125
Stone, Harlan Fiske, 27, 147
Stone, Phil, 30
Storrs, Landon R. Y., 126
Subversive Activities Control Board, 120–21
Suffrage for women. See Women's suffrage
Sullens, Fred, 65
Surplus Property Board, 102
Swofford, Jewel, 104
Symington, Stuart, 122

Taussig, Helen Brooke, 153
Taylor, Peter, 158, 160
Temple Sisterhoods, 59
Terrell, Mary Church, 116
Texas State College for Women, 115–16
Thomas, S. Bun, 48–49
Thompson, C. Mildred, 99
Thurmond, J. Strom, 101
Tillett, Gladys, 105, 106, 107, 108–9
Tobin, Maurice, 111
Tompkins, Pauline, 139, 144, 145
Topp, Mildred Spurrier, 67, 71, 73, 77, 188nn4, 13
Trigg, Mrs. W. R., 9
Trigg, W. R., 9
Truman, Bess, 104
Truman, Harry S.: and appointment of women, 106–7, 108, 109, 111, 112, 119–21, 128, 141, 164; and reorganization of executive branch, 104; Nellie Somerville's opposition to, 149; and transition from Roosevelt administration, 103
Twain, Mark, 33

Underwood, Oscar W., 46
United Daughters of the Confederacy, 137
United Nations, 108–9
United Nations Commission on the Status of Women, 113
United Nations Conference on Food and Agriculture, 99
United Nations General Assembly, 108
United Nations Relief and Rehabilitation Administration (UNRRA), 99, 126
United States Employment Compensation Commission (USEC), 104
University Club, 116
University of Mississippi, 151, 152, 154, 156
University of Mississippi Law School, 27, 28–33, 56
UNRRA. *See* United Nations Relief and Rehabilitation Administration (UNRRA)

USEC. *See* United States Employment Compensation Commission (USEC)

VA. *See* Veterans Administration
Van Horn, Olive, 23, 28
Van Kleeck, Mary, 32
Vardaman, James K., 40, 106
Veterans Administration: and Mary Agnes Brown, 84, 97, 110; and Howorth as attorney in Office of Solicitor, 95, 107; Howorth's appointment to, 81–83; and Howorth's Board of Appeals work, 84–85, 132; and Howorth's credentials, 76, 81; and Howorth's examination of clinical records, 19–20; and Howorth's membership on BPW board, 92–93; Howorth's recommendations from colleagues in, 109–10; and Howorth's Red Cross work, 97
Voice of America, 123, 125
Von Hess, Elizabeth, 87

WAC. *See* Women's Army Corps (WAC)
Walls, Patricia Carol, 125
War Claims Act of 1948, 109
War Claims Commission, 109, 120, 128–29
War Manpower Commission, 102, 120
Ware, Susan, 150, 164, 204n34
Washington Business and Professional Women's Club, 89, 90, 91–92, 94
Washington County Council of National Defense, 19
Wasson, Ben, 10, 30, 50, 55, 154
WCTU. *See* Women's Christian Temperance Union (WCTU)
Weiner, Myron, 129
Welty, Eudora, 58, 152, 153, 164
White Citizens' Council, 139
White, Earlene, 40, 90–91
White, Lynn, 115
White, Sue Shelton, 87, 88–89, 138, 192n14

Index   233

White House Conference on Women in Post-War Policy Making, 1, 98–100, 101, 103
Whitfield, Henry L., 42, 43, 48, 56
Whittington, Will, 75
Williams, Charl O., 97–98, 100
Williams, Tennessee, 6, 49
Wilson, Woodrow, 16, 59
Winsor, Mary, 41
WJDX, 63, 74
Woman Voter, 39–40, 42, 43, 45, 46
Woman's Advisory Committee of the War Manpower Commission, 93, 102
Woman's Bar Association, 106
Woman's Centennial Congress, 89
Woman's Committee, Washington County Council of National Defense, 19
Woman's Press, 44, 51, 62
Women in military, 96–97, 101, 120, 127, 140
Women legislators, 67–68, 187*n*1
Women's Armed Services Integration Act of 1948, 120
Women's Army Corps (WAC), 96, 120
Women's Bureau, 41, 113, 142
Women's Christian Temperance Union (WCTU): and Howorth as state representative, 76; and peace movements, 59; Nellie Somerville's involvement in, 5, 6, 54–55
Women's City Club, 90
Women's education: and American Association of University Women, 102–3, 113–14, 115, 131, 144, 145, 152; and curriculum, 114–15, 116; and enrollment, 115; Howorth on future of, 132–33; Howorth's commitment to, 152, 161; and quota system, 113–14
Women's employment and labor issues: and conferences for working women, 24–25; and equal pay, 94, 101, 114; and federal employment policies, 140, 141, 142; Howorth's New York City experiences with, 164; and married women, 92, 102, 133; and National Federation of Business and Professional Women's Clubs, 91, 92, 94; post-World War II issues of, 93, 101–2, 114; and pregnancy, 132; and Young Women's Christian Association, 21, 22–24
Women's history, 31, 143, 147, 150, 151–52, 157
Women's movement, 143, 157, 165. *See also* Feminism; Women's rights; Women's suffrage
Women's National Democratic Club (WNDC), 86–89
Women's rights: and Howorth, 4, 112, 139–40; Nellie Somerville's advocacy of, 5, 7, 39. *See also* Feminism; Women's movement; Women's suffrage
Women's suffrage: anniversaries of, 103; and Clarksdale, 39; Howorth's work toward, 14–16, 39–41; and social reform, 38; Nellie Somerville's work toward, 5–6, 9–12, 15, 16, 27
Women's Trade Union League of America (WTUL), 24, 59
Wood, Margaret Wells, 23, 54
Woodward, Ellen S.: depression of, 137; and Dewson, 76, 80, 87; friendship with Howorth, 73, 75, 89, 93; Howorth's eulogy on, 147; as leader, 94; and Mason, 79–80; and Mississippi Federation of Women's Clubs conference, 59; and Mississippi State Hall of Fame, 147, 205*n*63; and New Deal, 85–86; and Nellie Somerville, 67, 73, 136; and UNRRA assemblies, 126; and Von Hess, 87; and women in office, 76, 99, 100, 104–5
Wooley, Mary, 103
Work. *See* Women's employment
Works Progress Administration, 85–86, 89, 104

World Center for Women's Archives, 89
World War I, 18, 19, 50
World War II, 91, 92, 93, 105, 115
Wright, Loyd, 134
WTUL. *See* Women's Trade Union League of America (WTUL)
Wyatt-Brown, Bertram, 6

Young, Bessie, 29, 147
Young Democrats in Mississippi, 66, 73
Young Women's Christian Association (YWCA): in Germany, 130; Howorth as chair of board in Mississippi, 32, 37; Howorth's continued involvement in, 59, 137; Howorth's employment at, 21–26, 27, 178n47; at Randolph-Macon Woman's College, 13; and Russia, 26–27; Simms leadership of, 21, 22; Nellie Somerville's fundraising for, 21; and Woman's Centennial Congress, 89, 90; and women in military, 127; and women's labor issues, 21, 22–24
YWCA. *See* Young Women's Christian Association (YWCA)

Zerfoss, Kate Savage, 8–9

www.ingramcontent.com/pod-product-compliance
Lightning Source LLC
Chambersburg PA
CBHW060947230426
43665CB00015B/2096